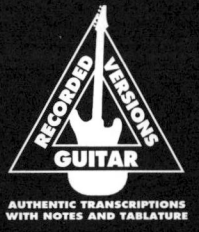

U218 SINGLES

I Will Follow 2

Beautiful Day 10

I Still Haven't Found What I'm Looking For 18

Pride (In The Name Of Love) 26

With Or Without You 34

Vertigo 41

New Year's Day 48

Mysterious Ways 55

Stuck In A Moment You Can't Get Out Of 62

Where The Streets Have No Name 70

Sweetest Thing 79

Sunday Bloody Sunday 86

One 93

Desire 102

Walk On 111

Elevation 118

Sometimes You Can't Make It On Your Own 123

The Saints Are Coming 132

Window In The Skies 138

Guitar Tablature Explained 144

ISBN-13: 978-1-4234-2755-1
ISBN-10: 1-4234-2755-6

7777 W. BLUEMOUND RD. P.O. BOX 13819 MILWAUKEE, WI 53213

For all works contained herein:
Unauthorized copying, arranging, adapting,
recording or public performance is an infringement of copyright.
Infringers are liable under the law.

Book design by Four5One°Creative, Dublin.
Printed in the EU.

Visit Hal Leonard Online at
www.halleonard.com

I Will Follow

Words & Music by U2

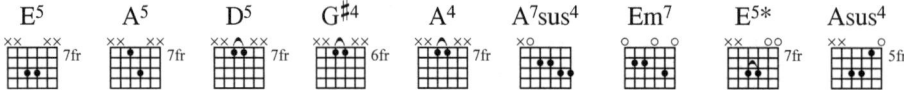

Tune guitars down a semitone

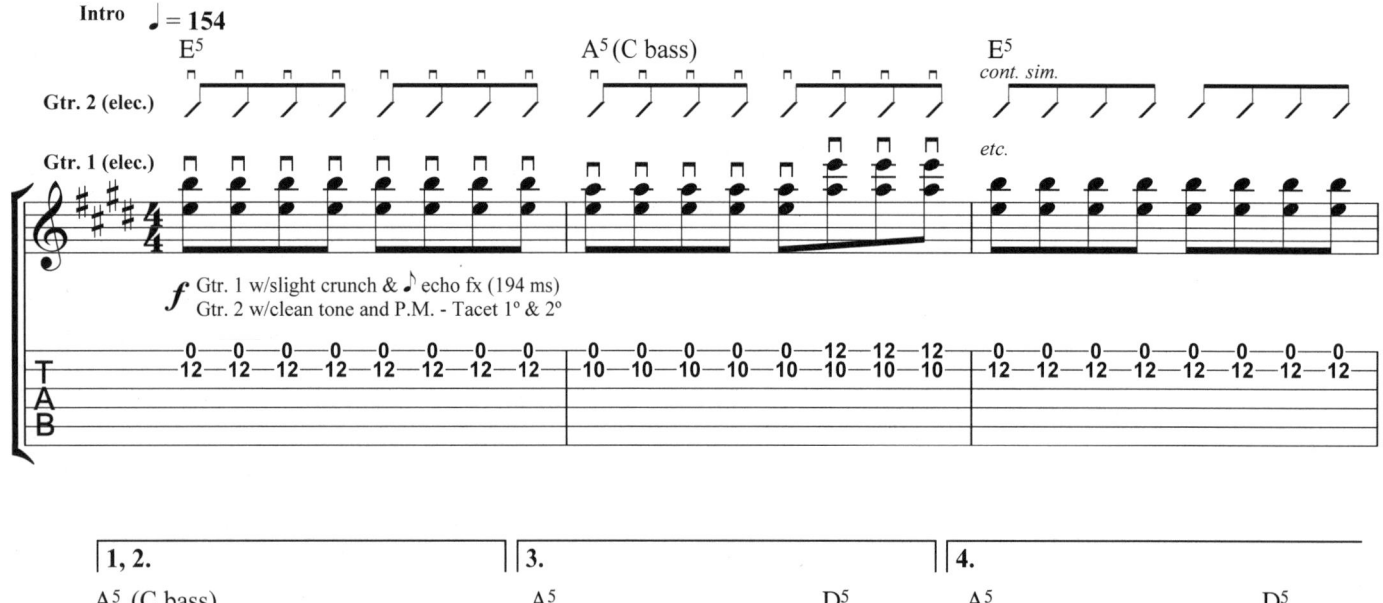

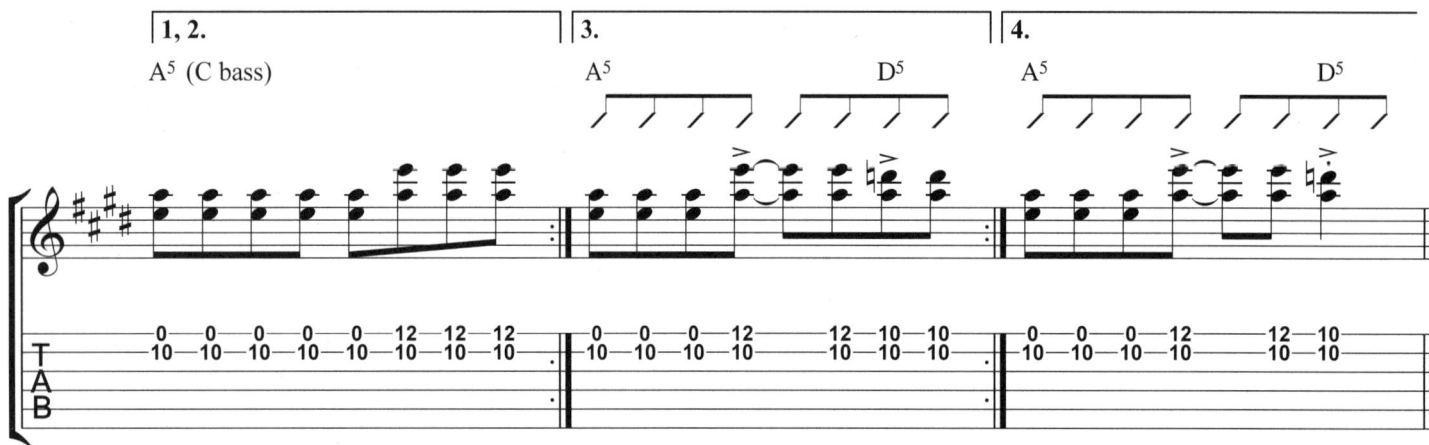

* combined part, Gtr. 2 plays same part at 9th position (see chord boxes)

© Copyright 1980 Blue Mountain Music Limited/Mother Music/
Taiyo Music Incorporated/PolyGram International Music Publishing Limited.
All Rights Reserved. International Copyright Secured.

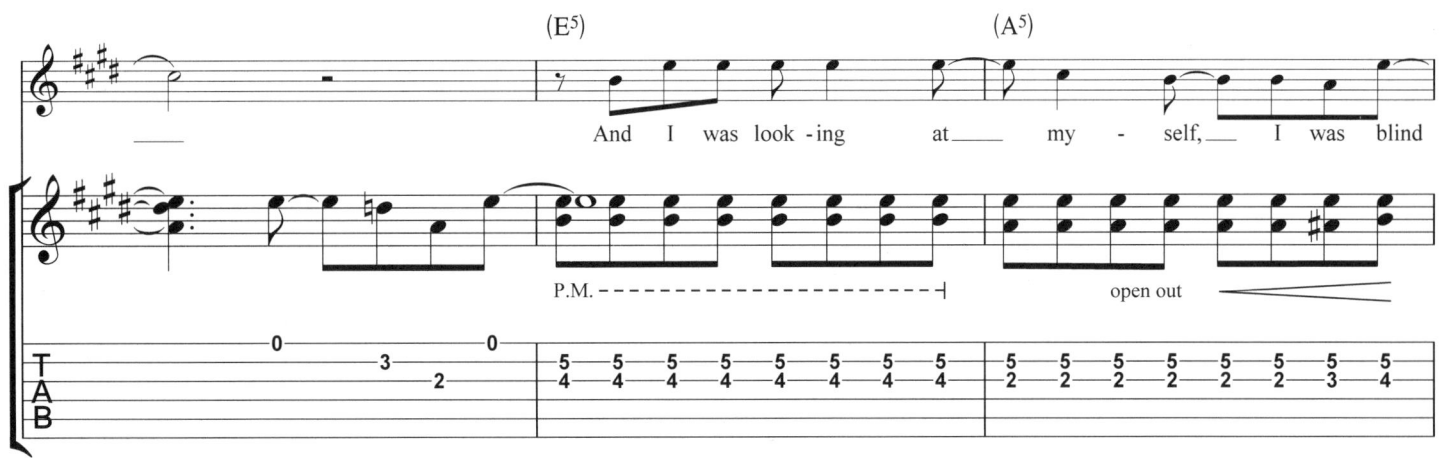
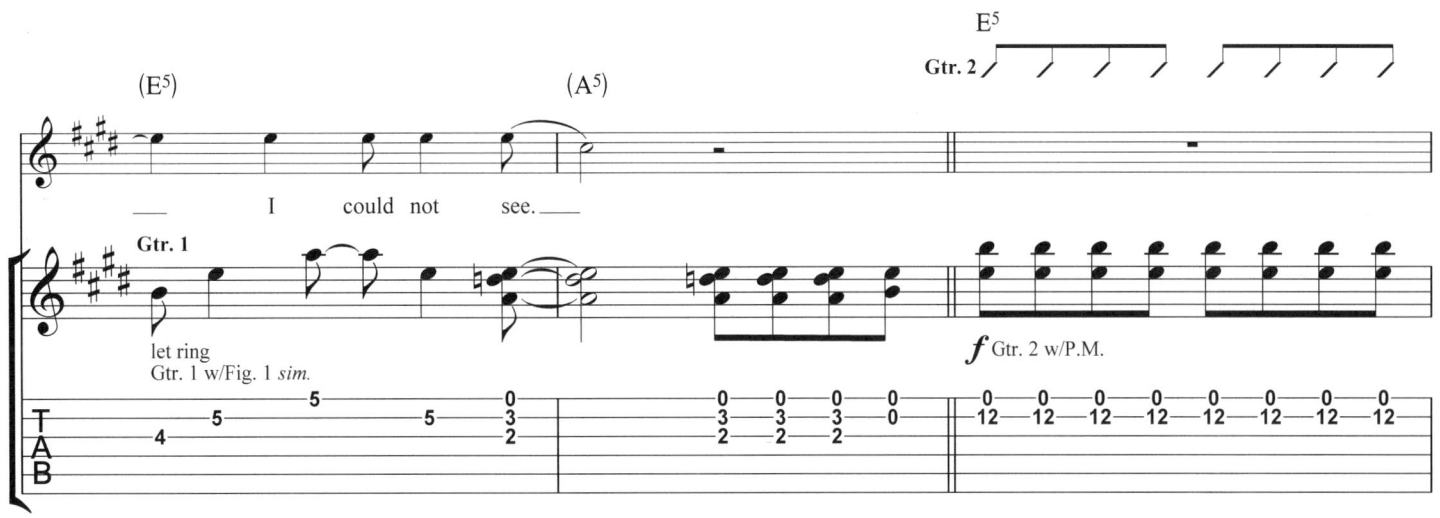
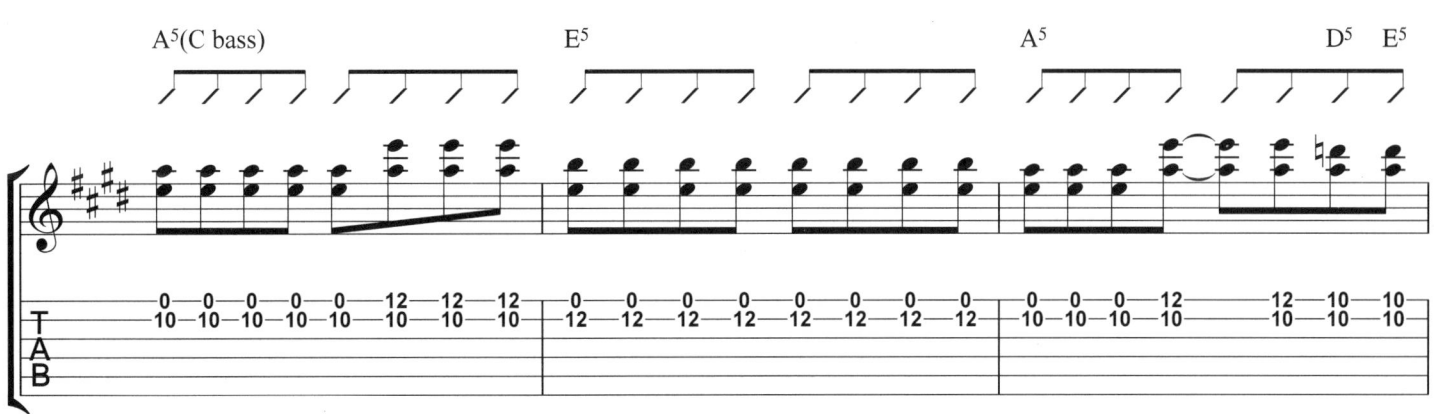
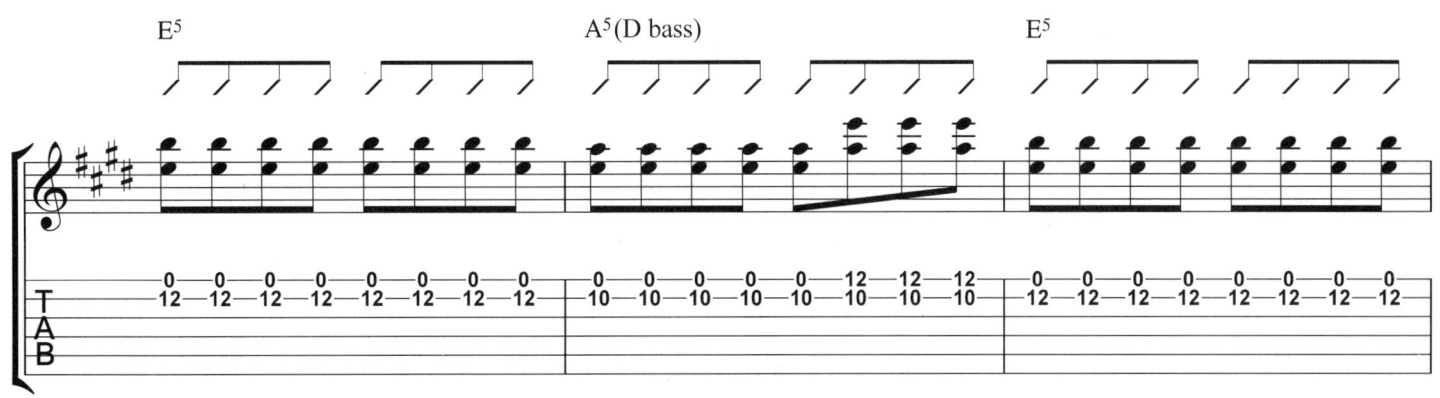

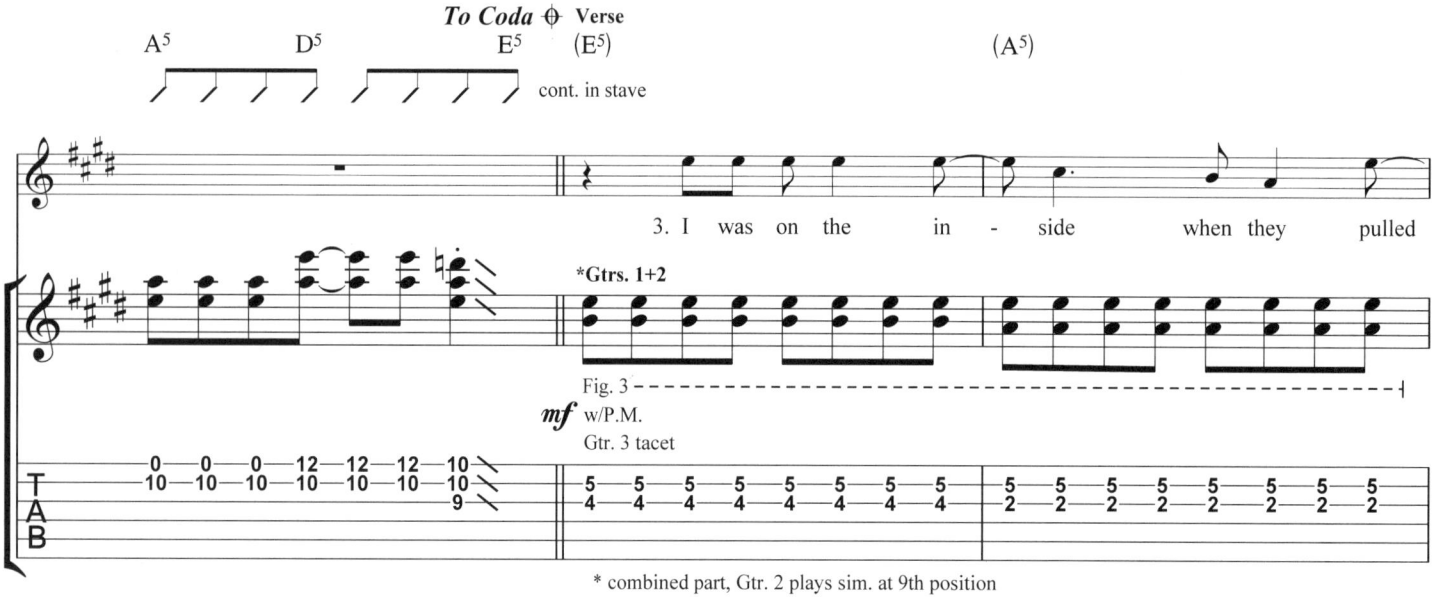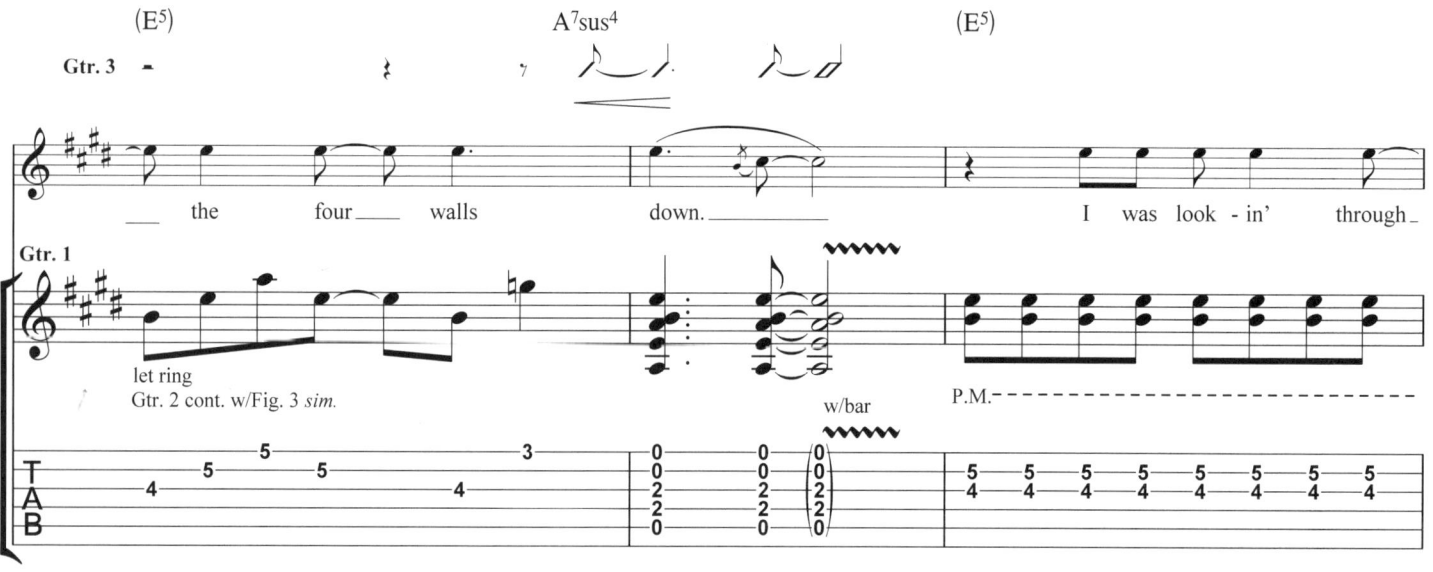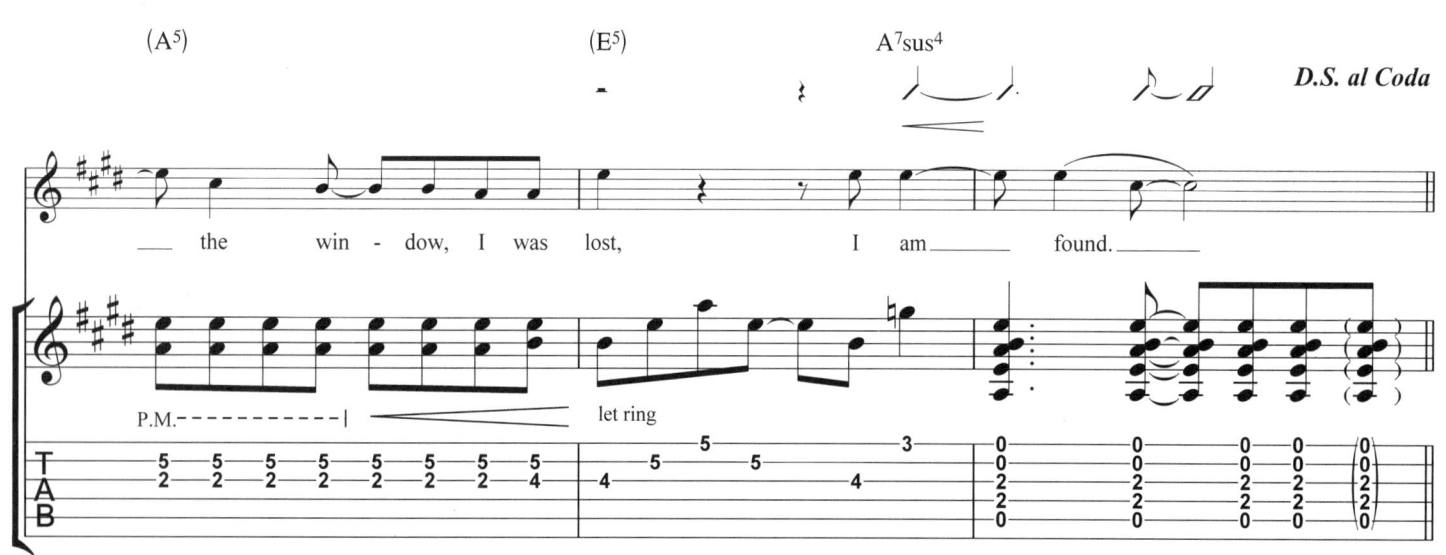

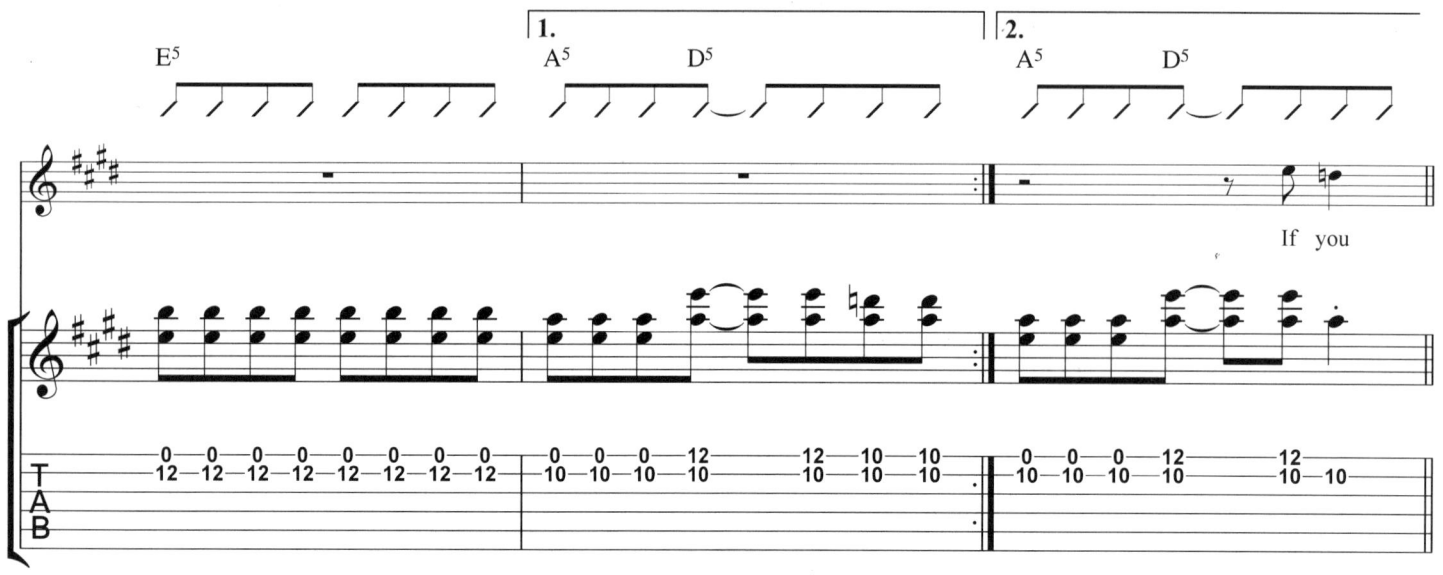

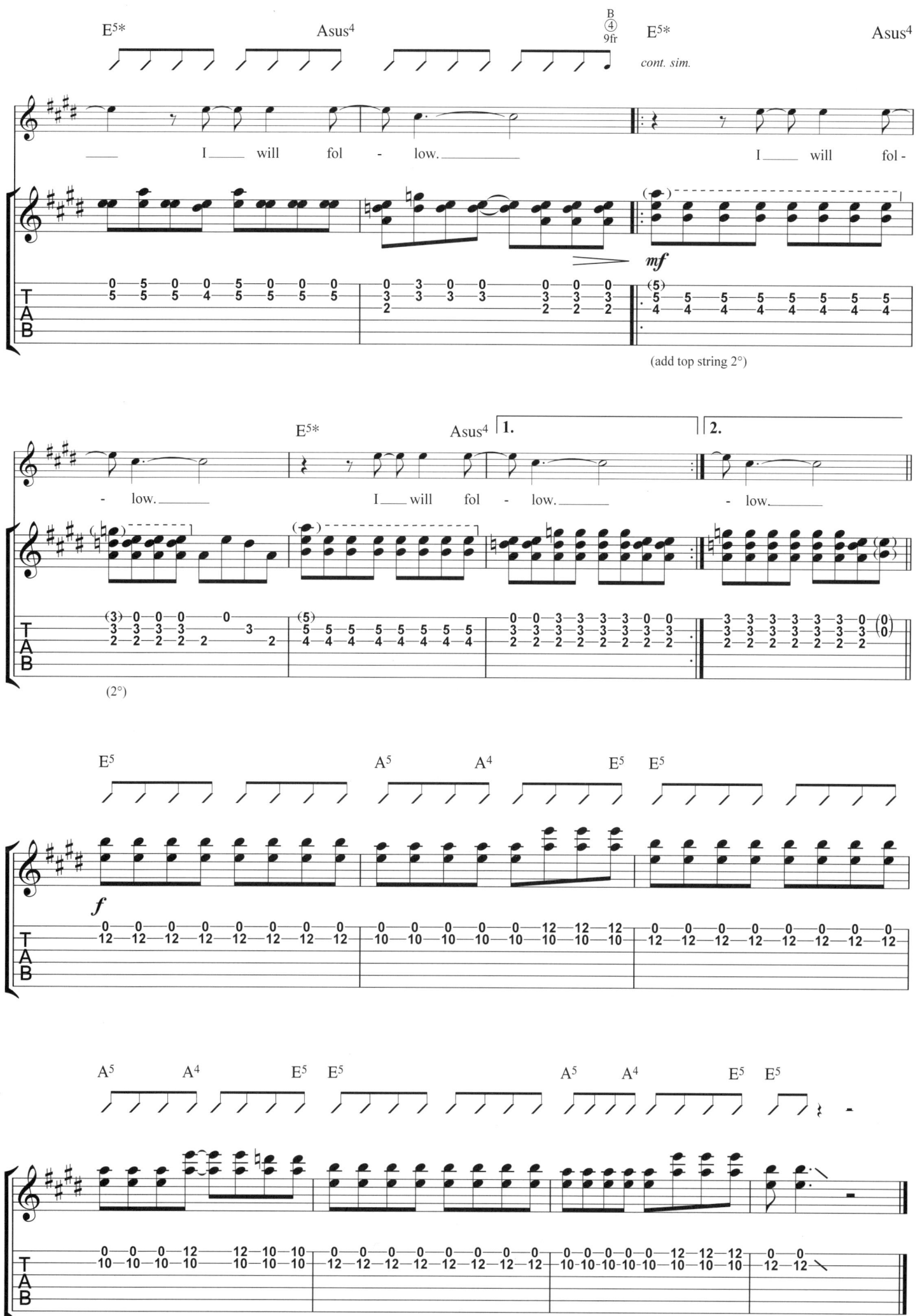

Beautiful Day

Words by Bono
Music by U2

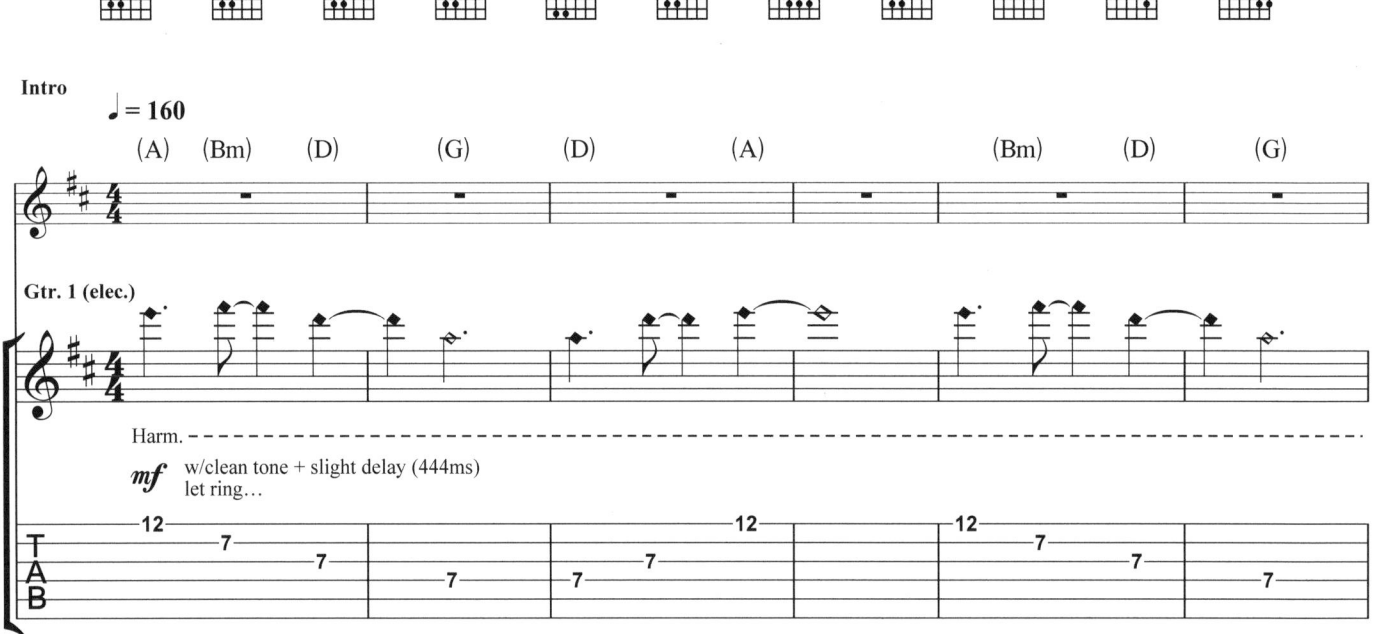

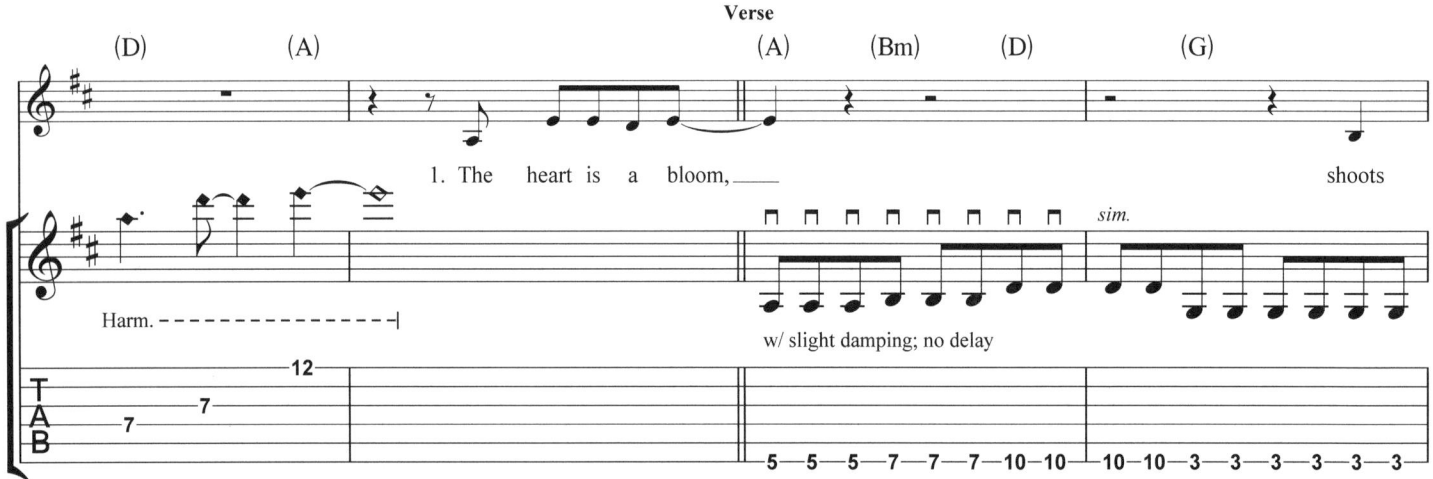

© Copyright 2000 Blue Mountain Music Limited/
Mother Music/PolyGram International Music Publishing Limited.
All Rights Reserved. International Copyright Secured.

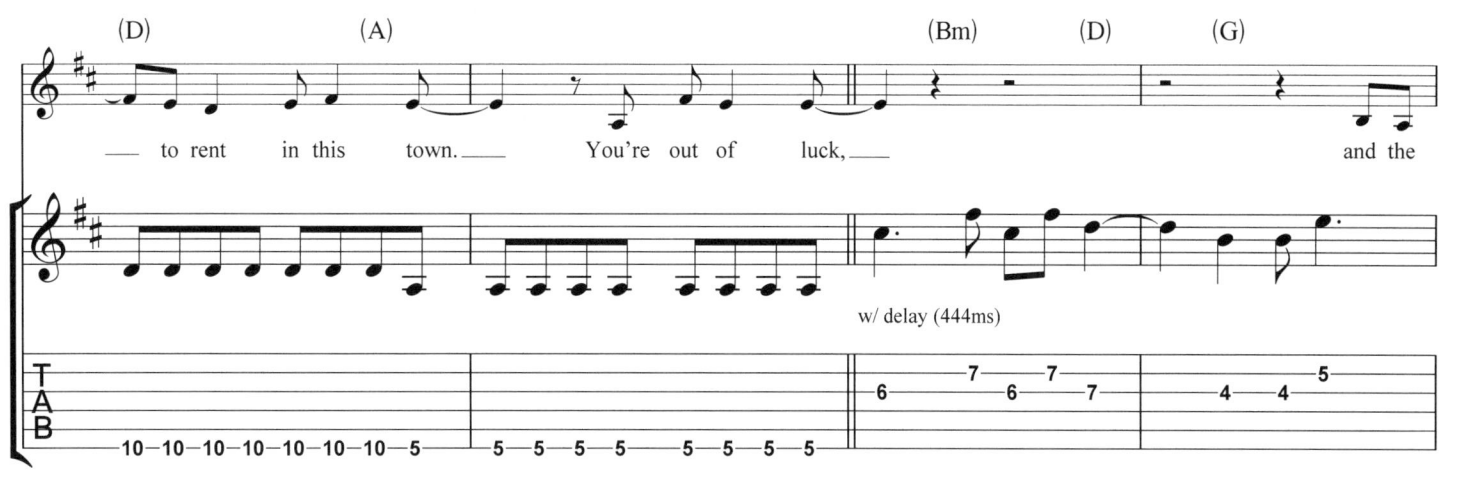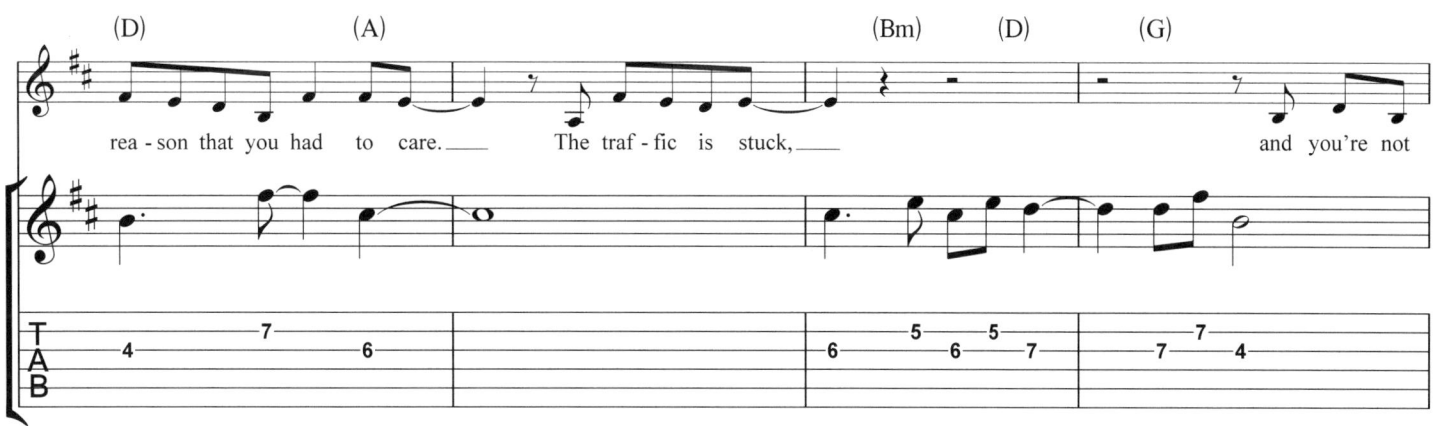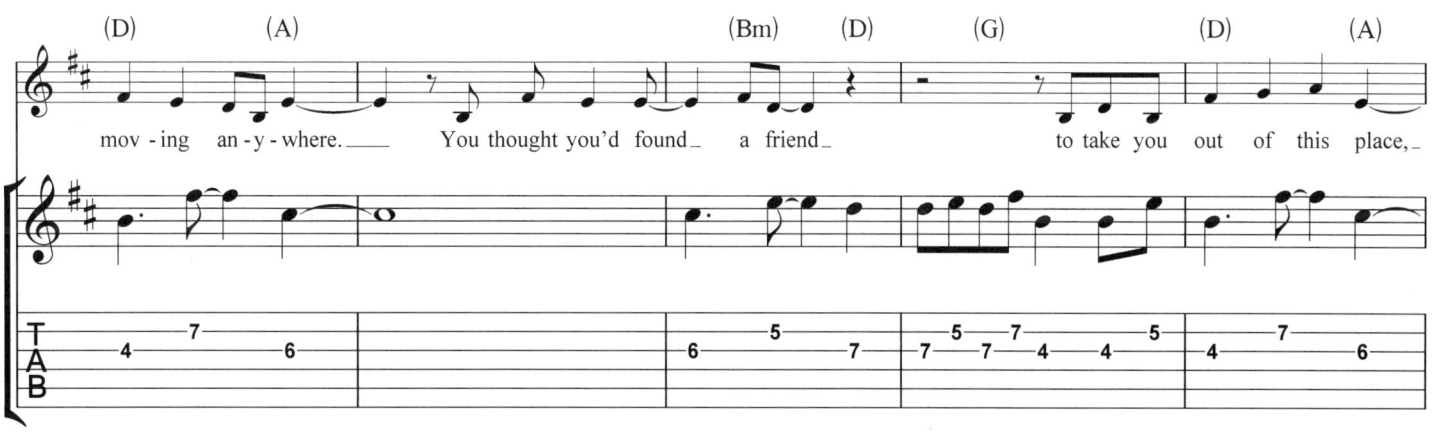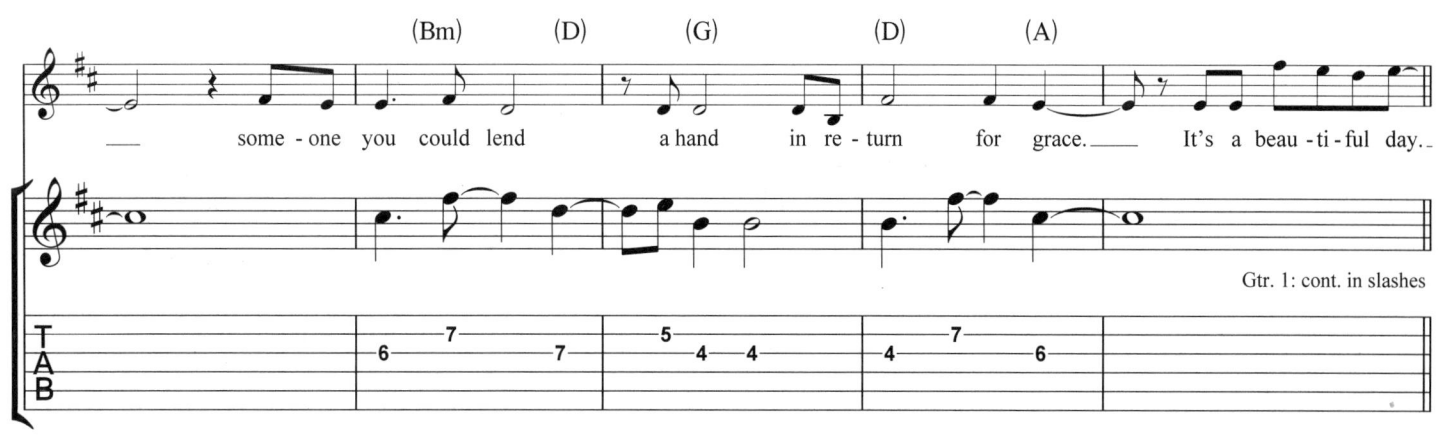

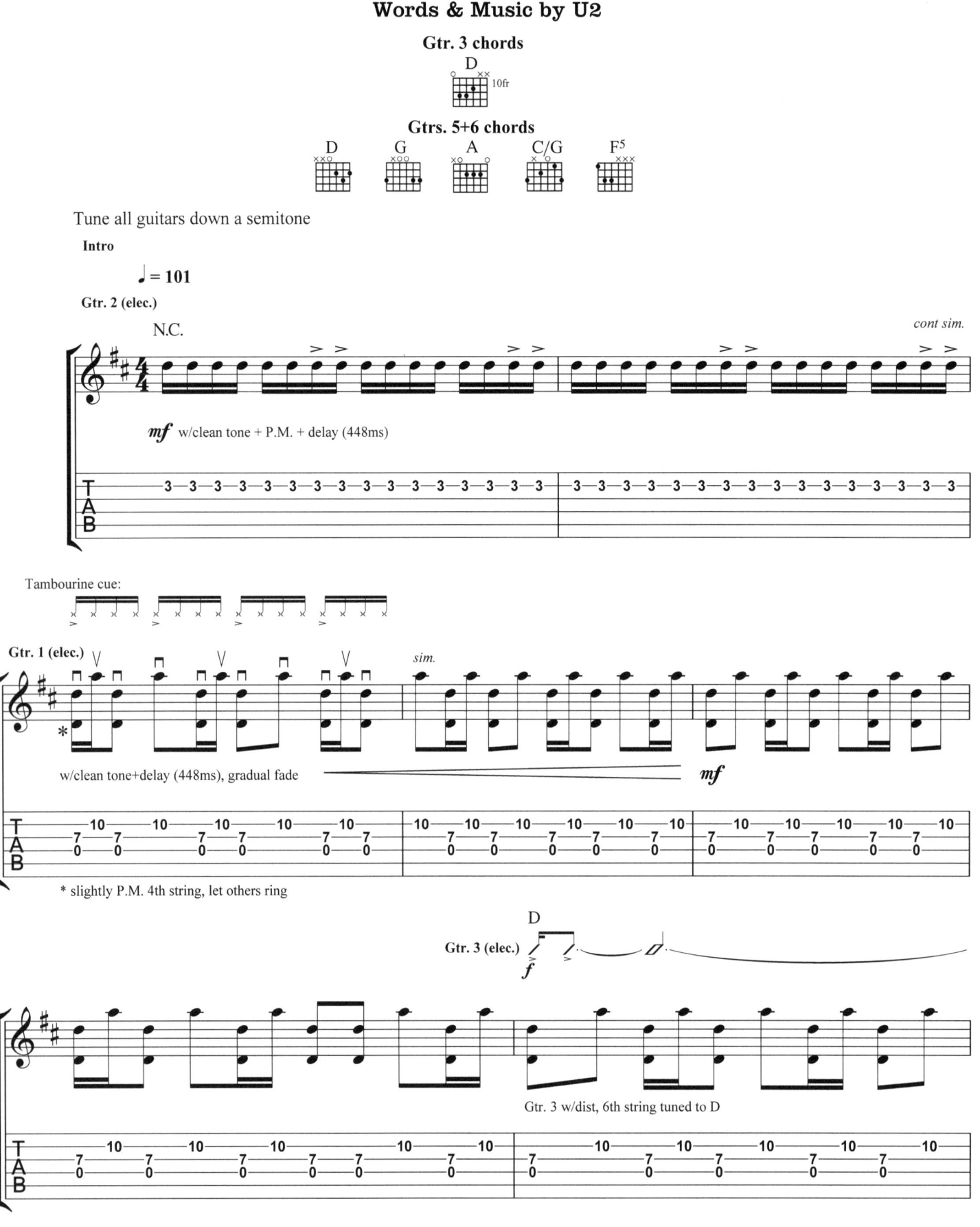

A ⑥ 7fr
G ⑥ 5fr
D
1.
have -n't found
what I'm look - ing for.
2. I have

Interlude
2.
Gtr. 6 (acous.)
C/G
D
Gtrs. 3+5 tacet
Gtr. 3 cue

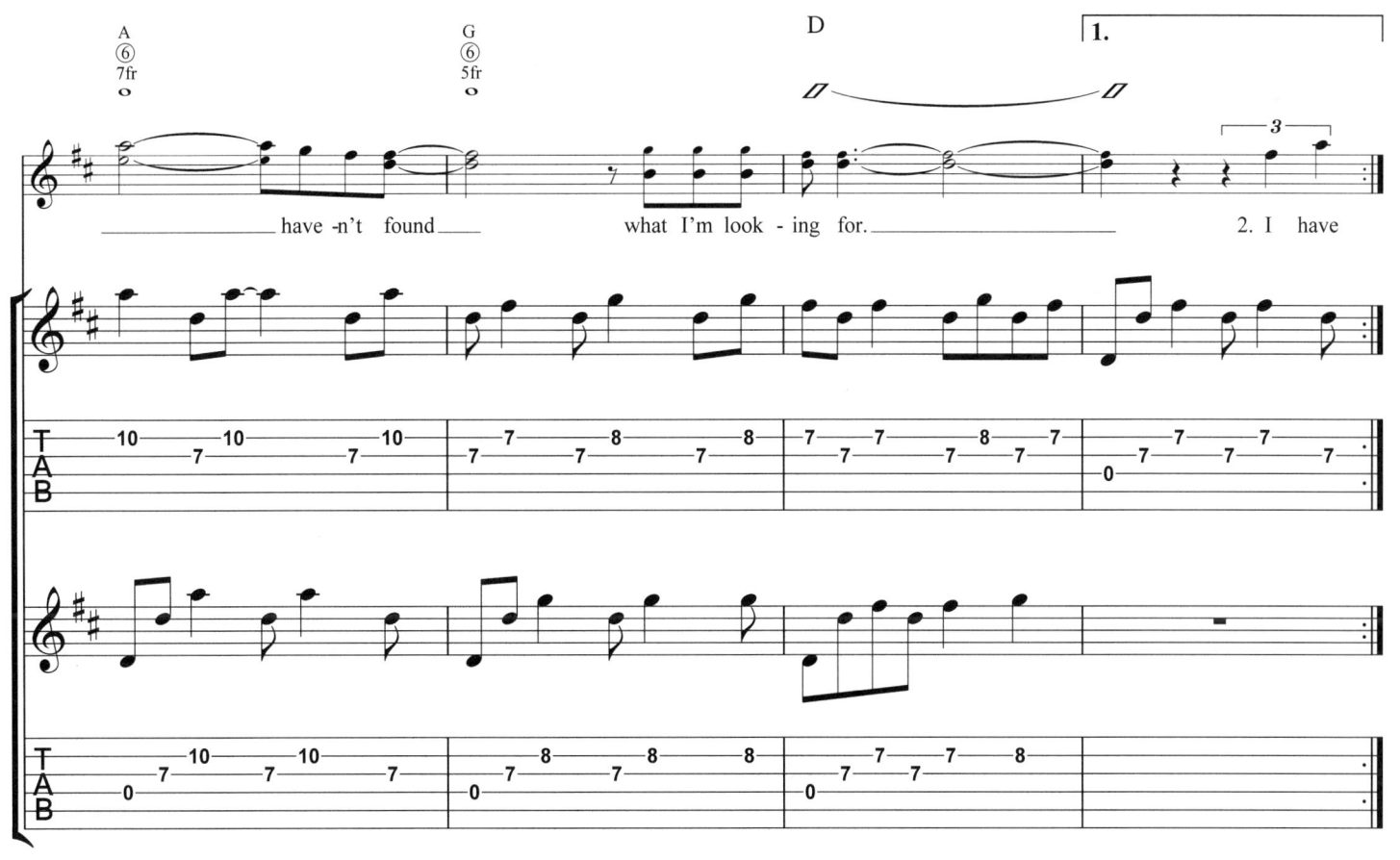

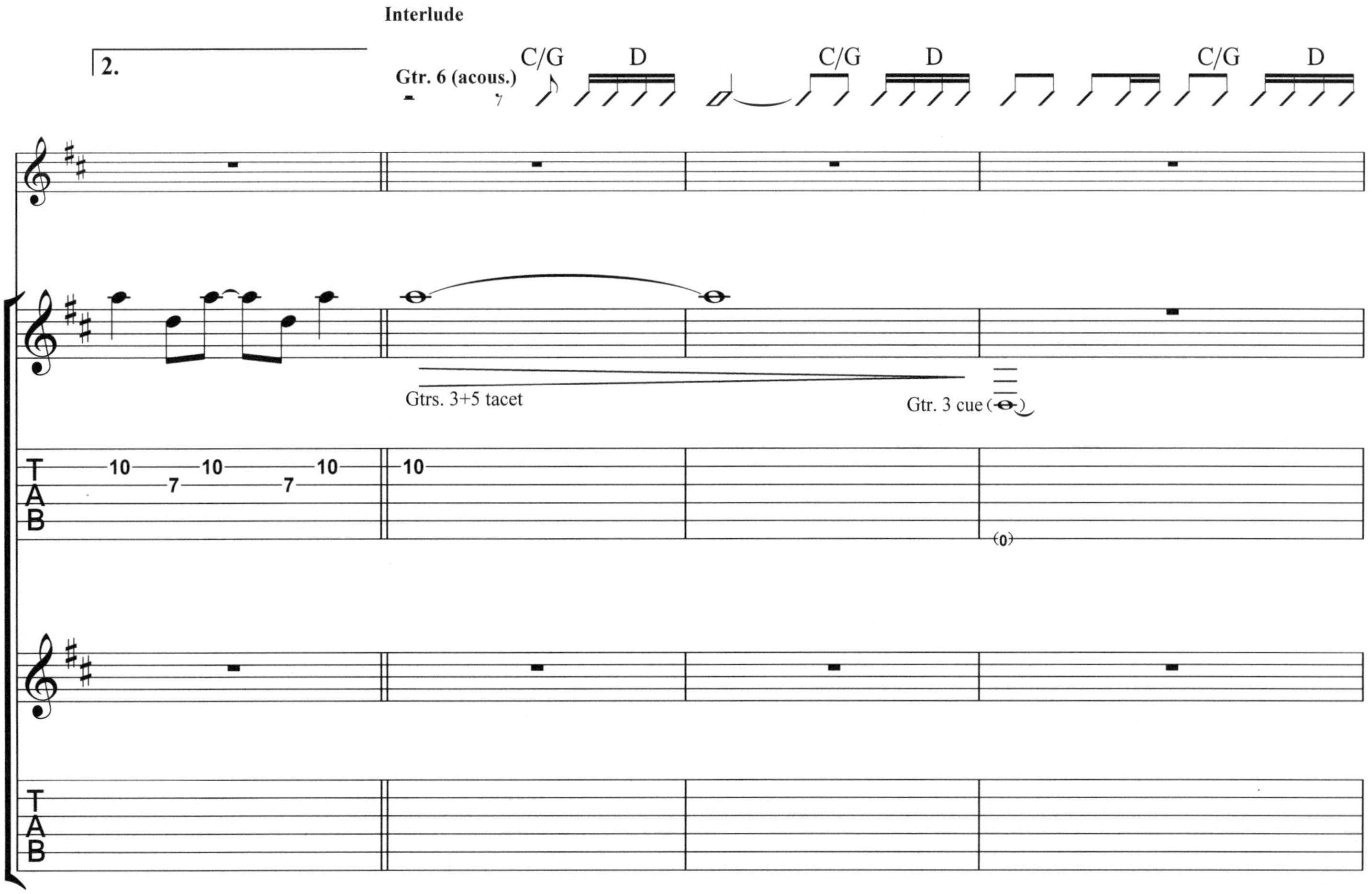

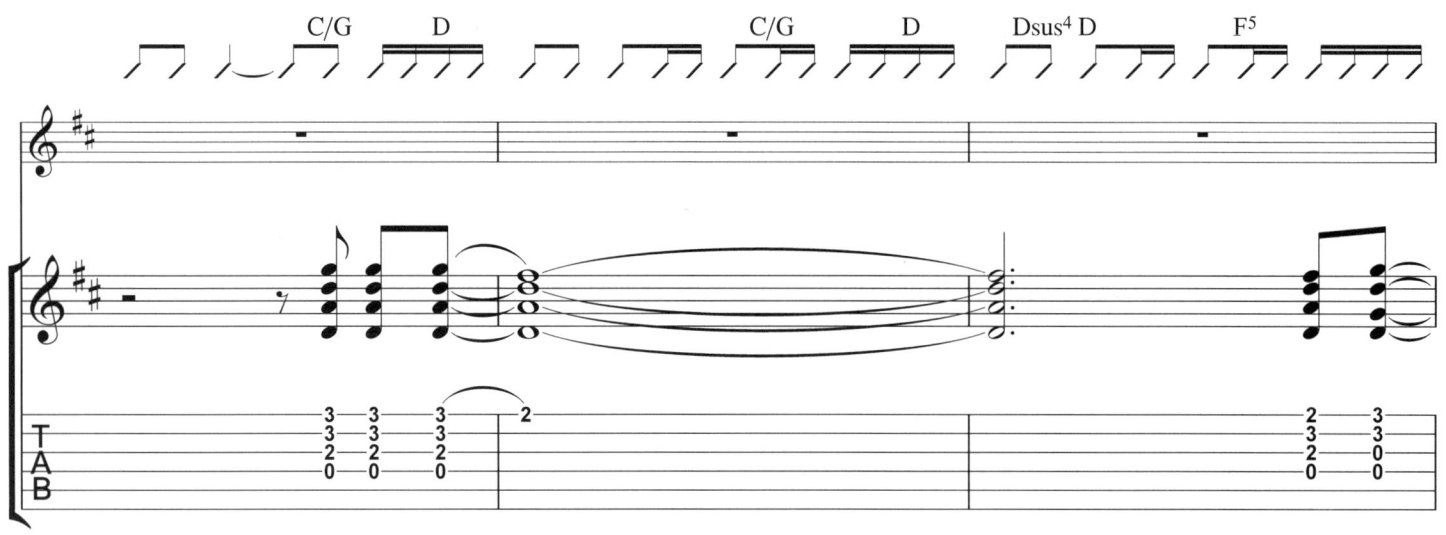
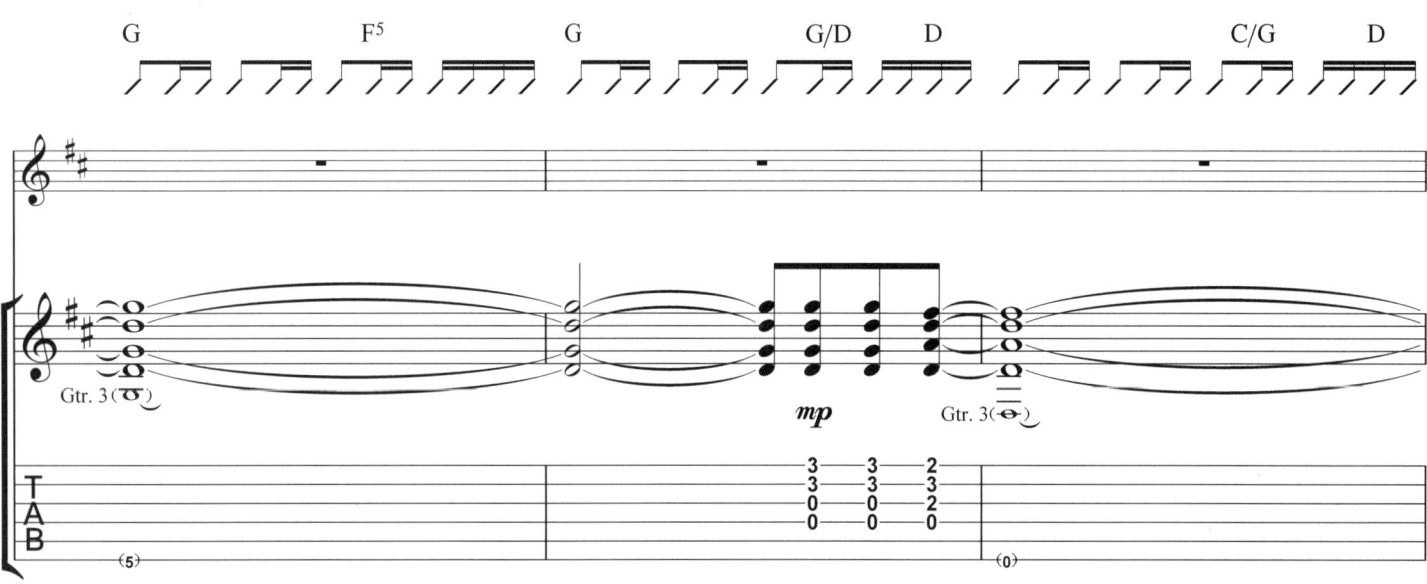
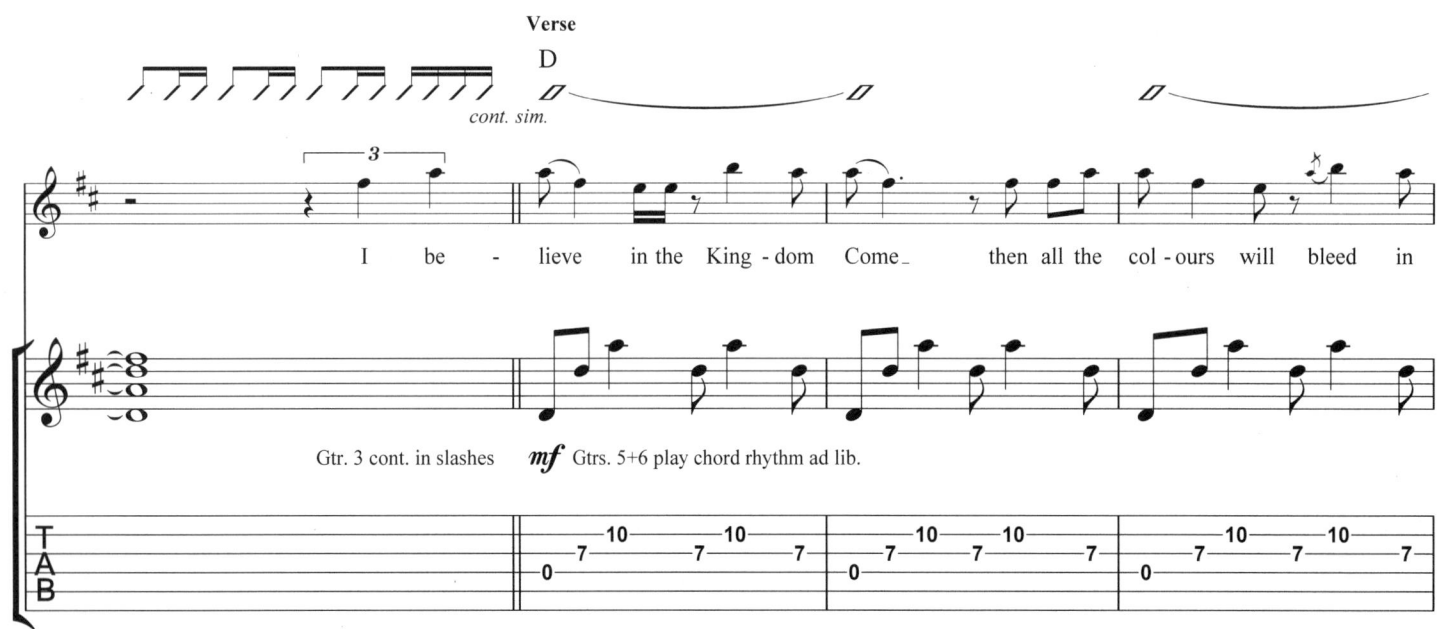

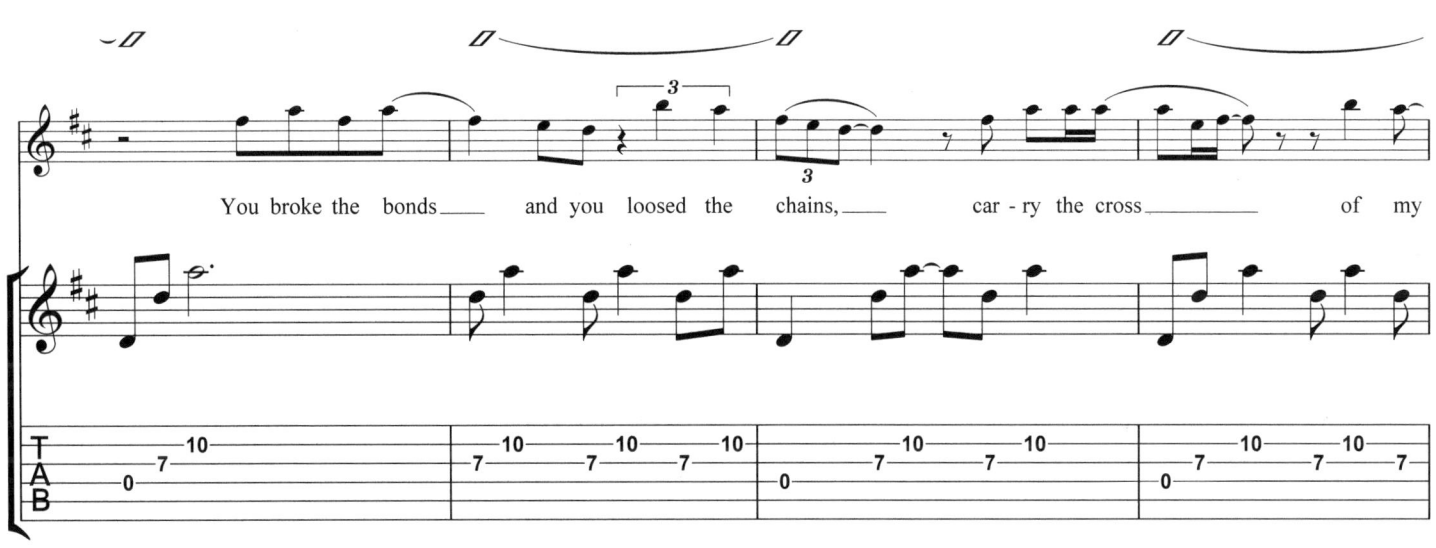
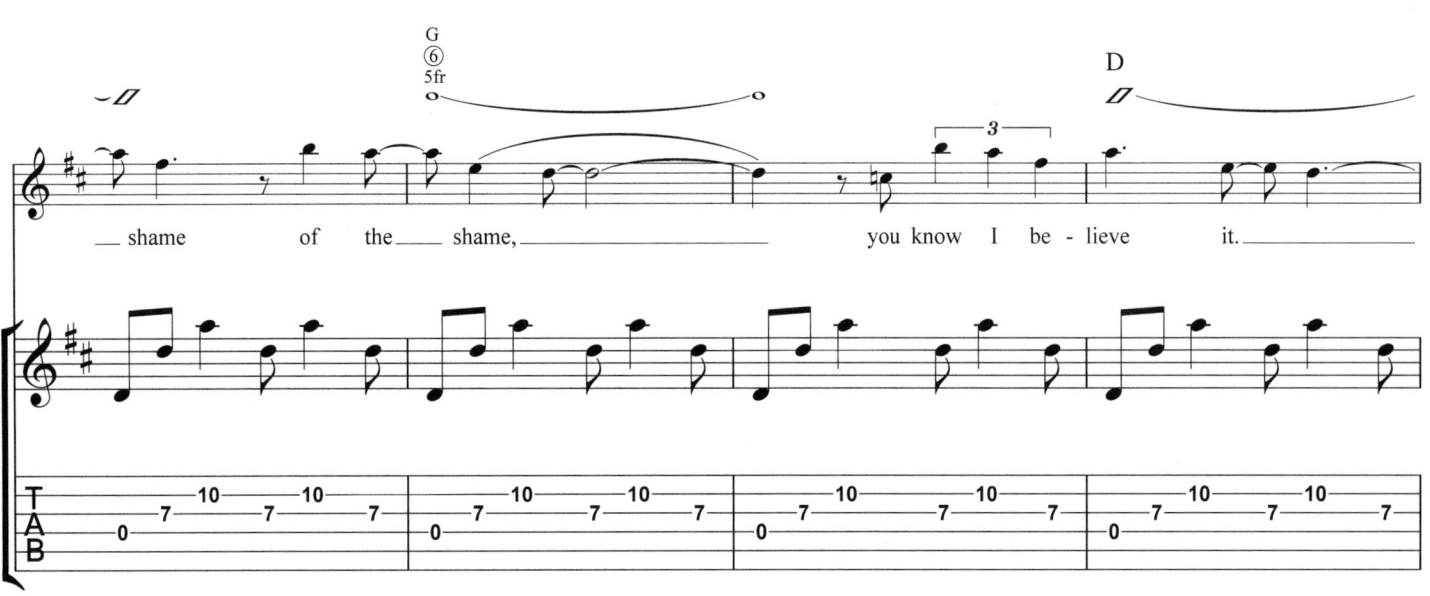

23

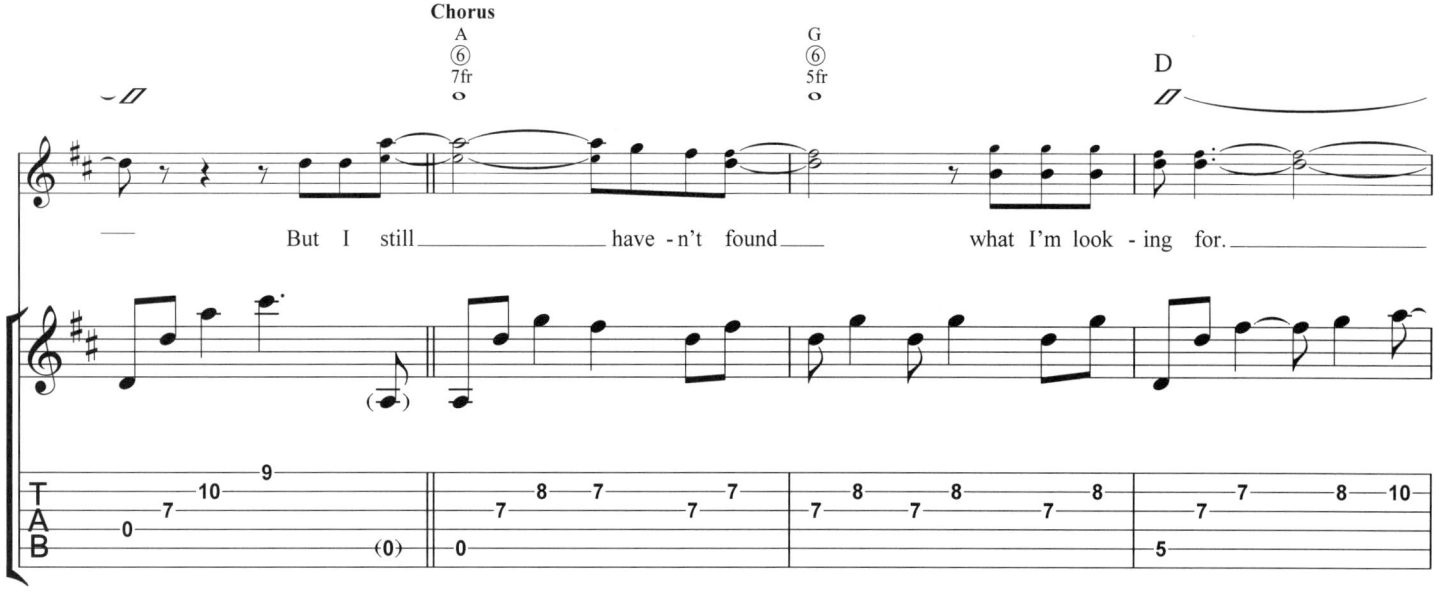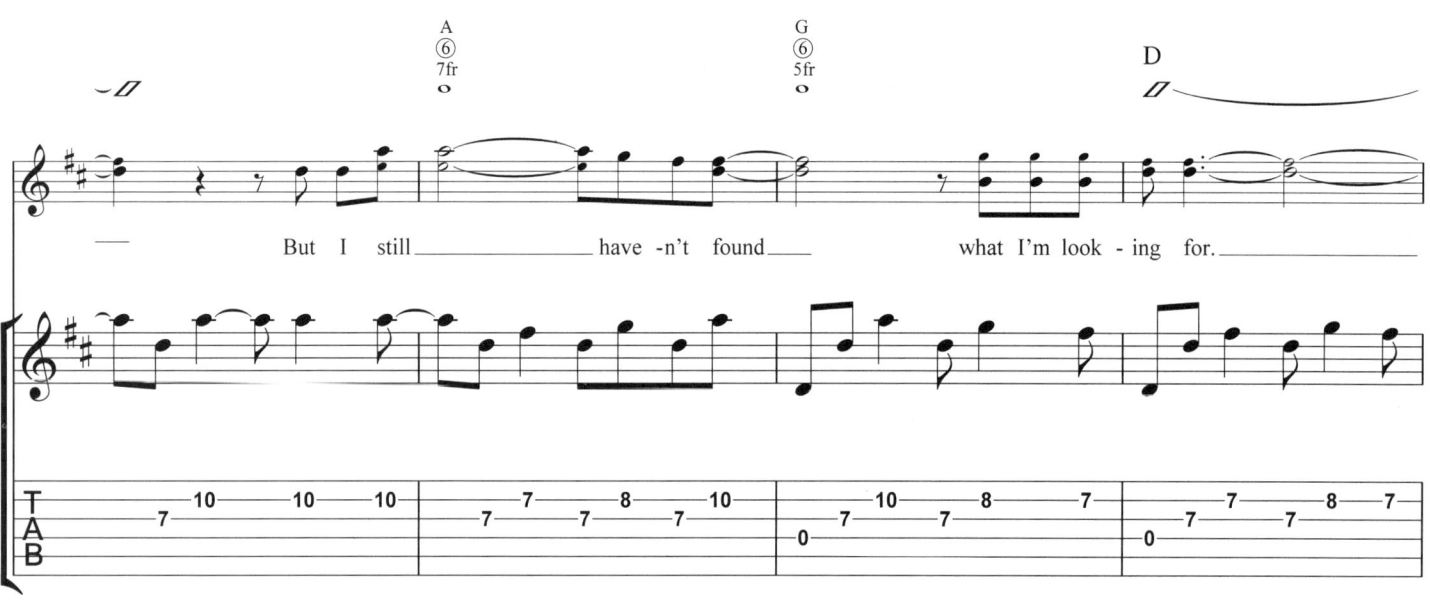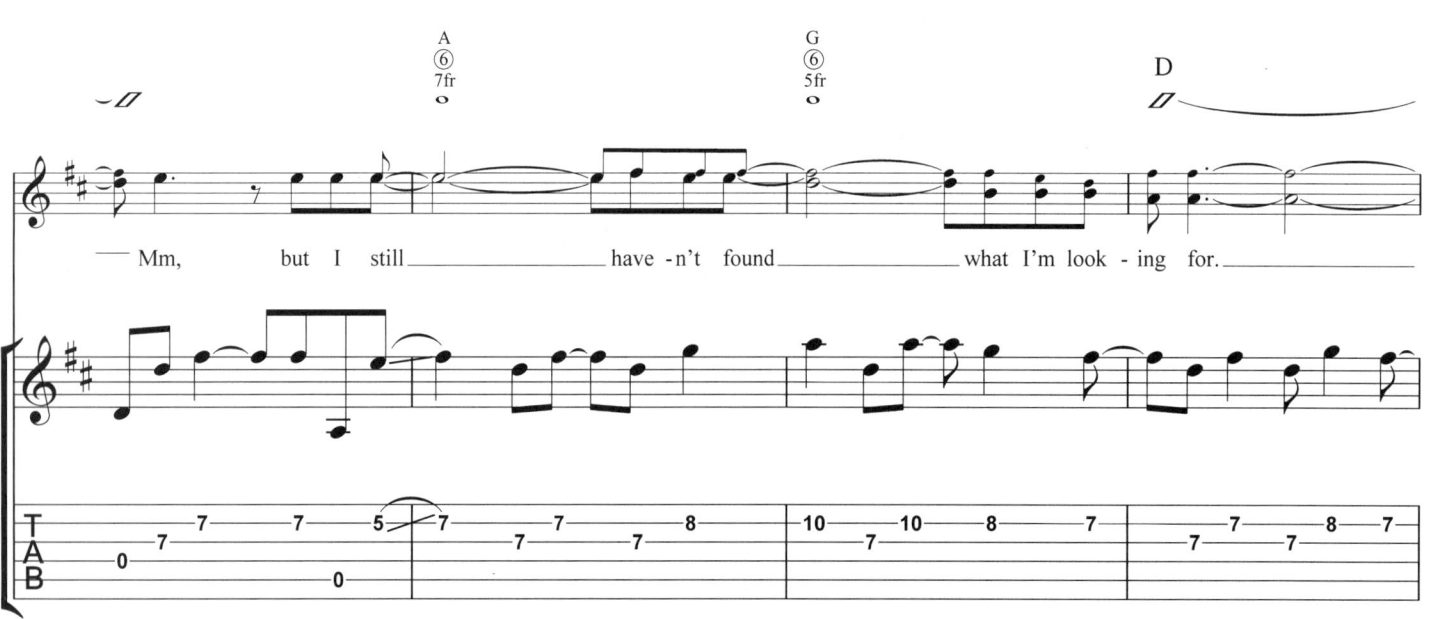

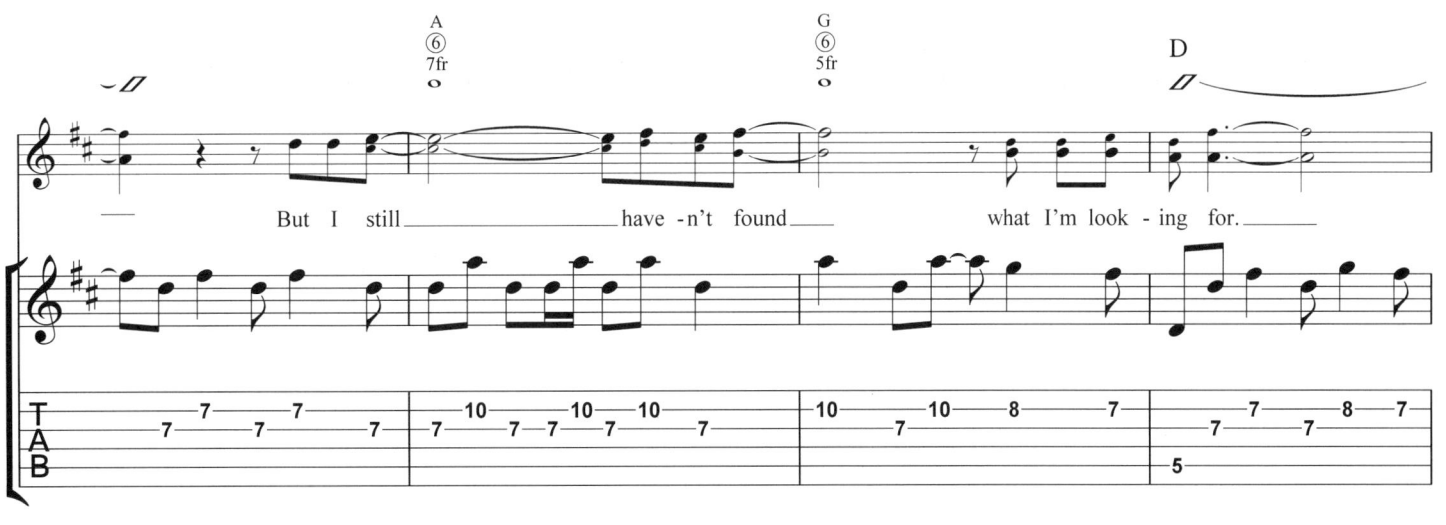

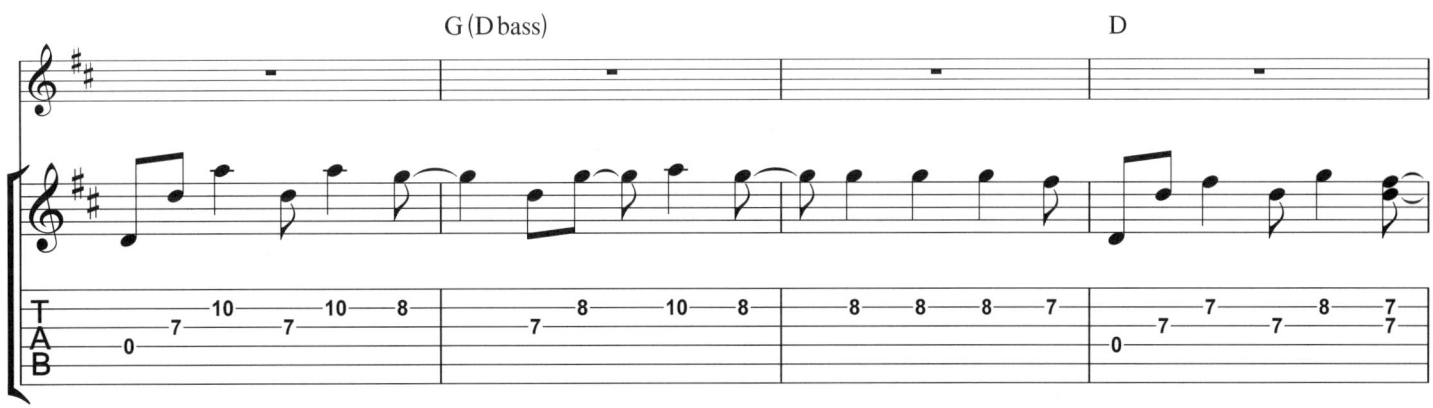
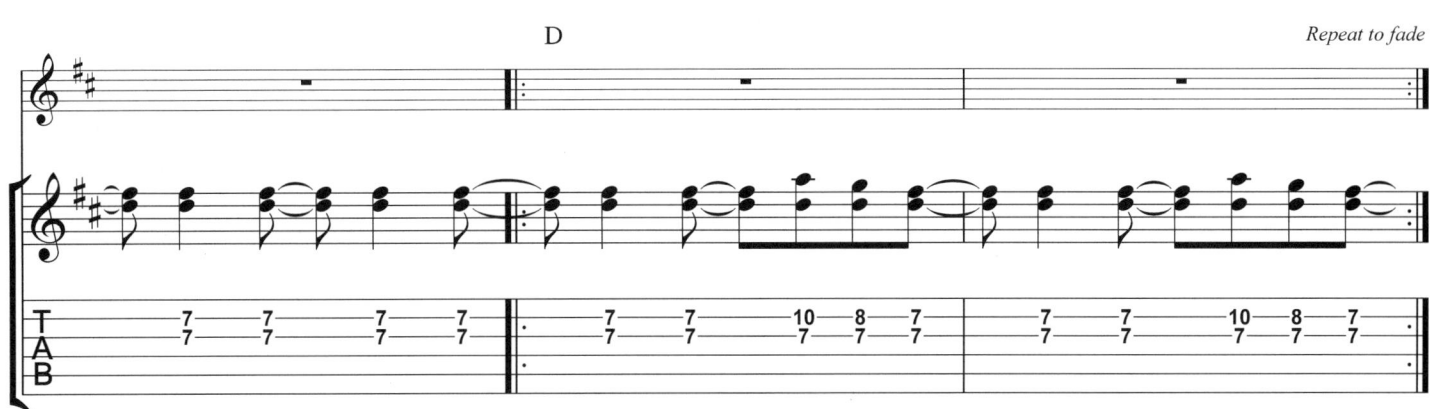

Pride (In The Name Of Love)
Words & Music by U2

26

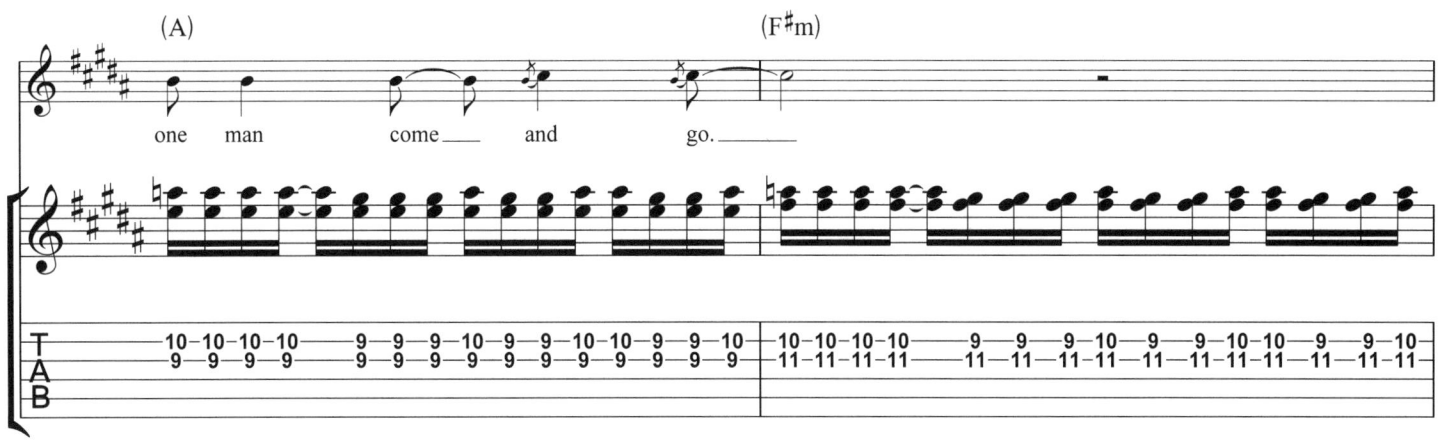
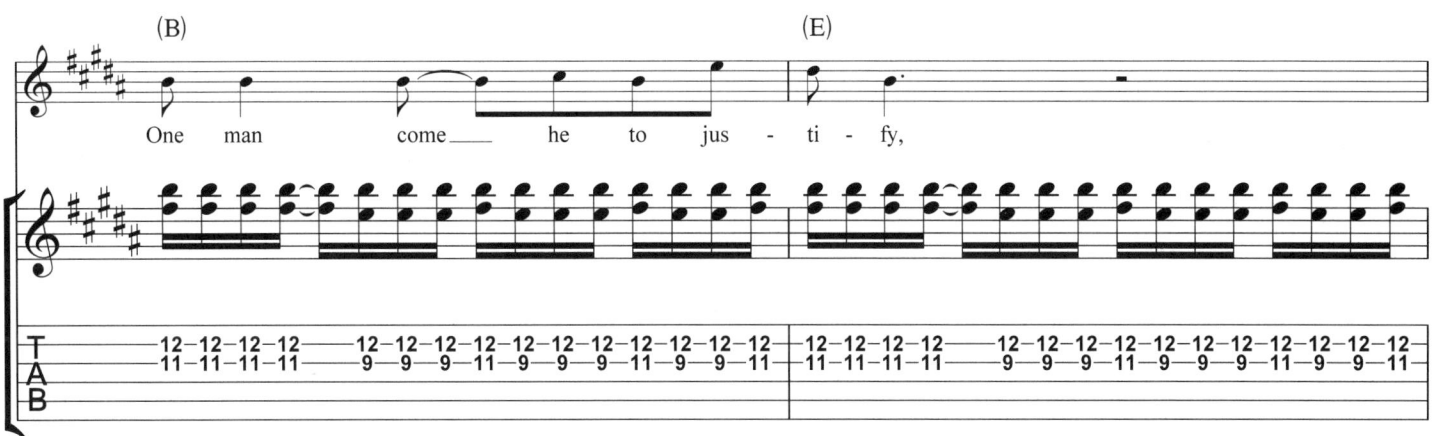
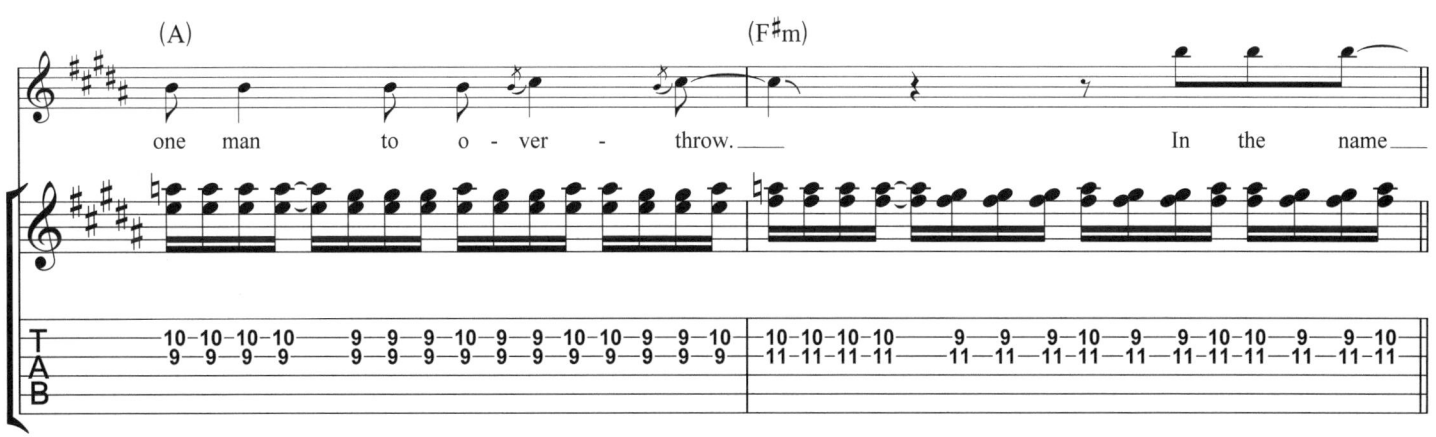
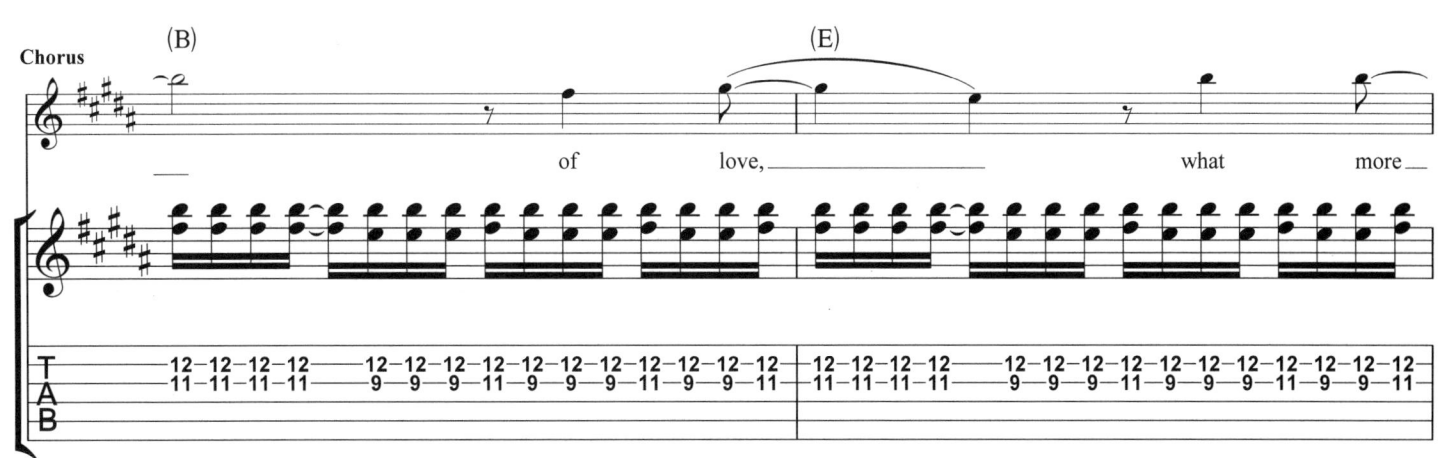

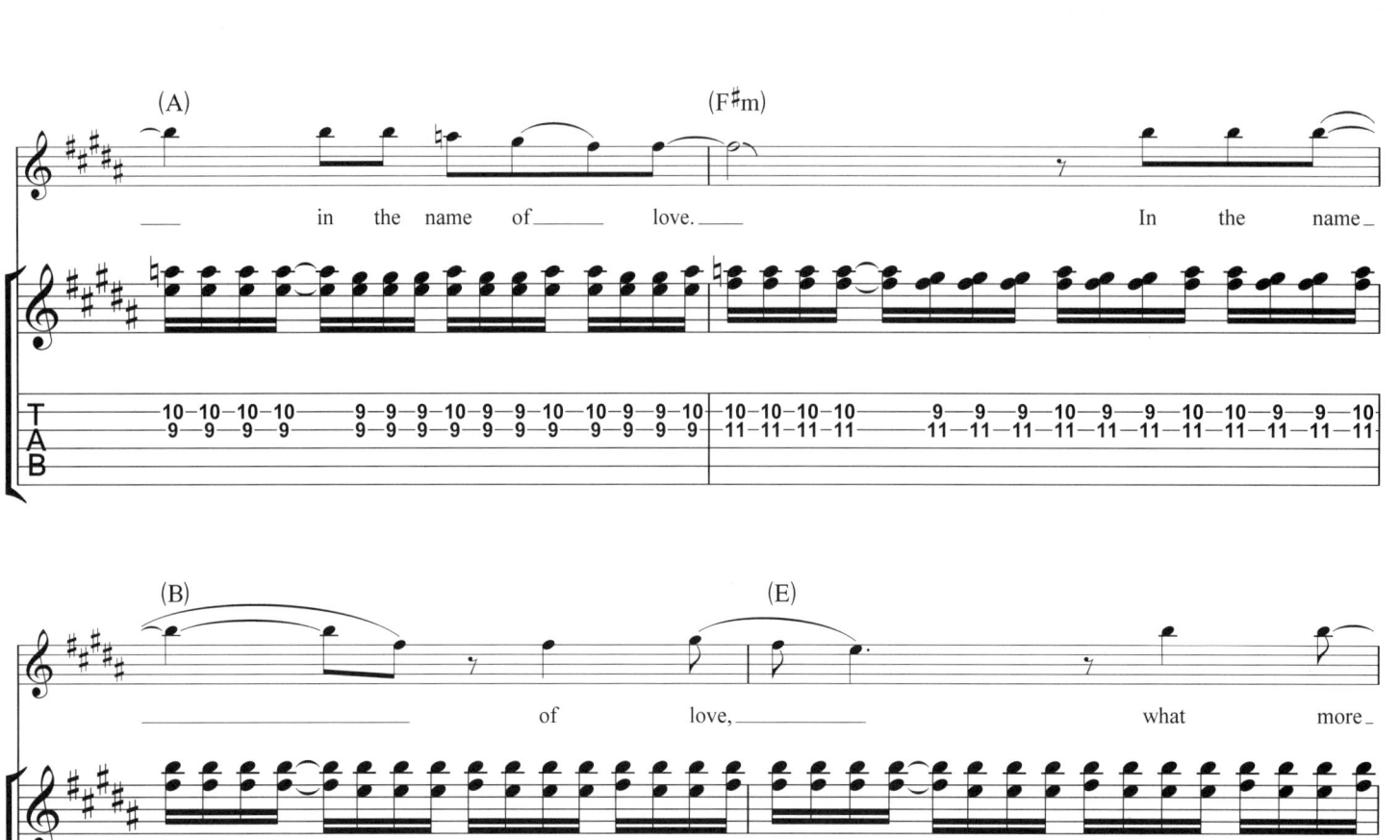
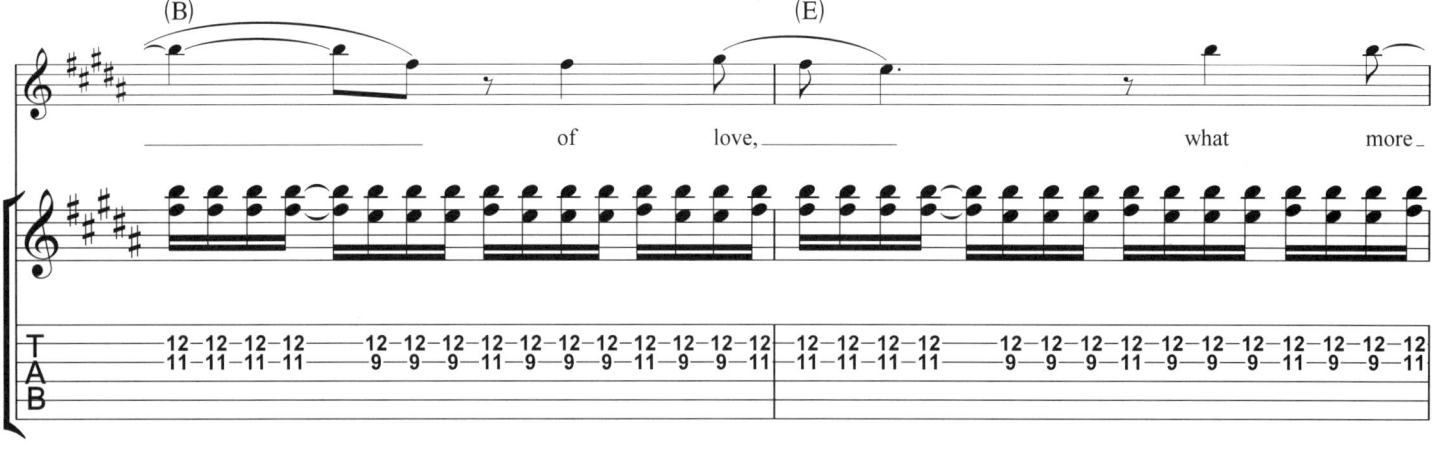
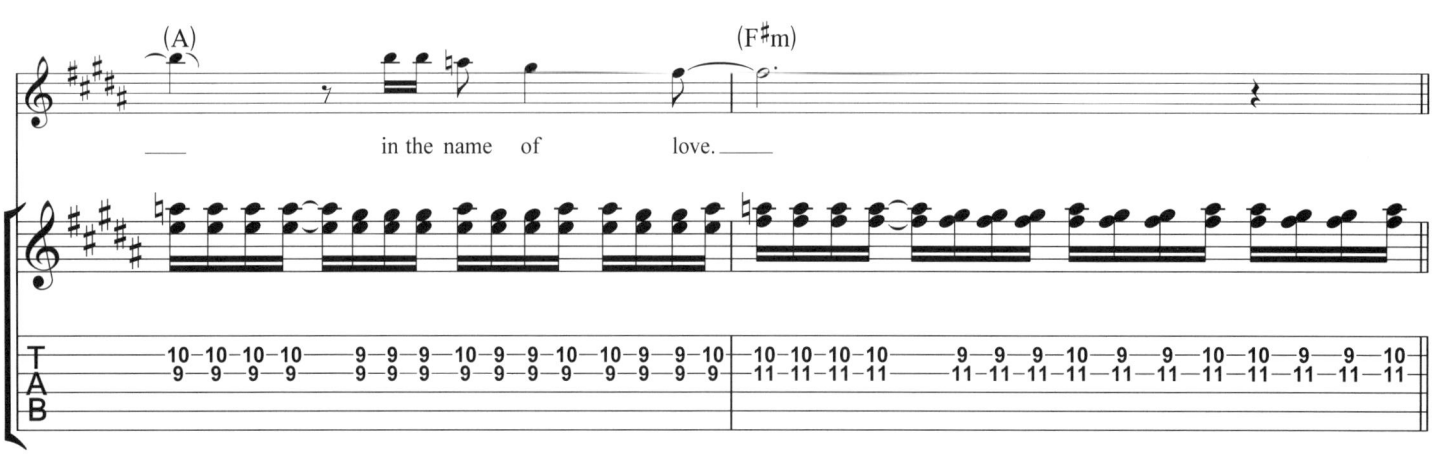

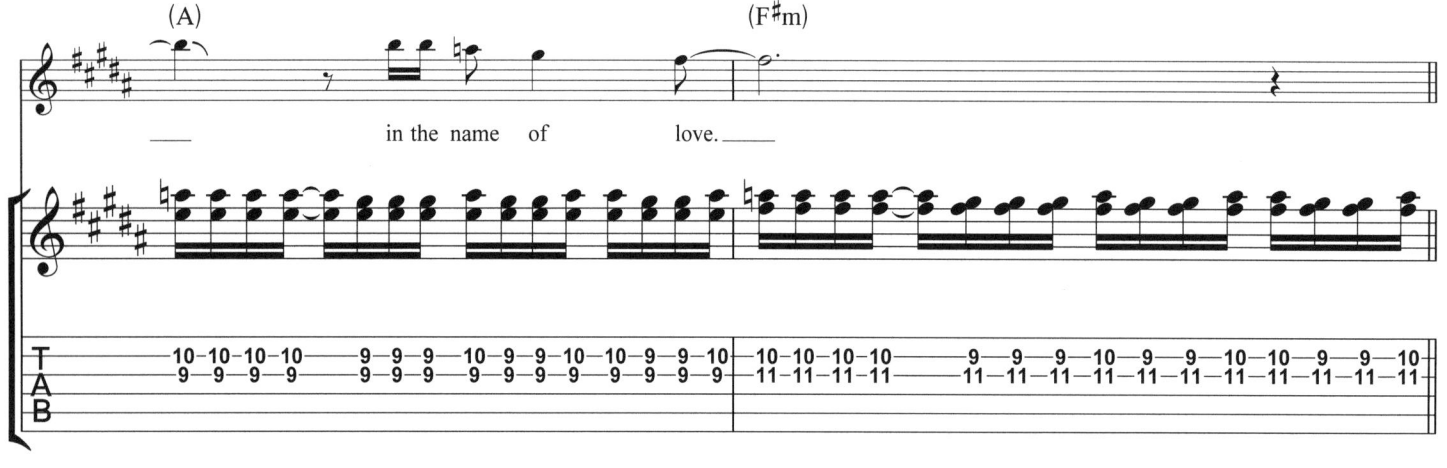

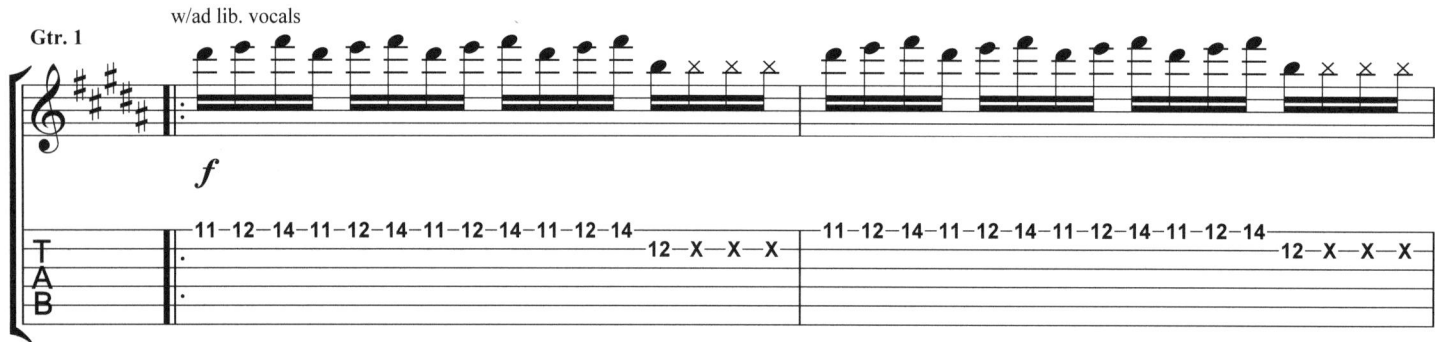
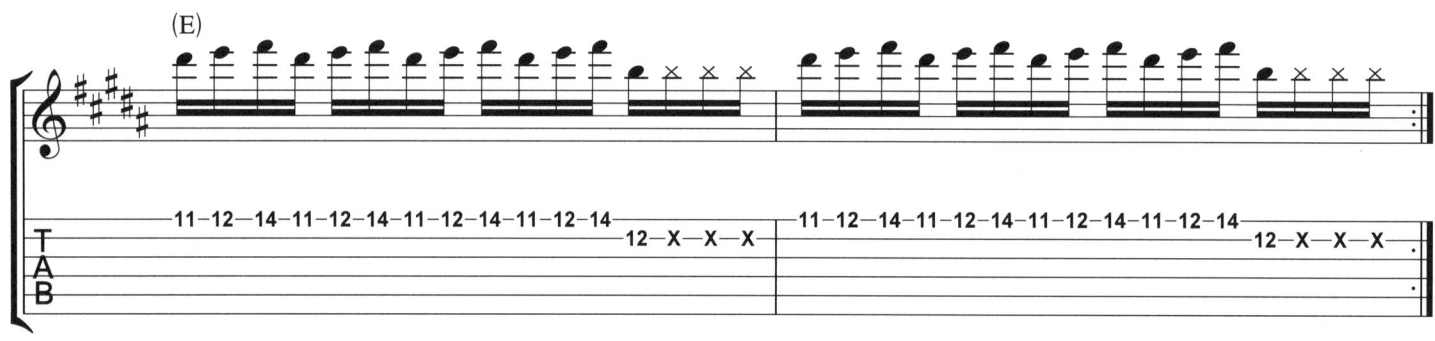
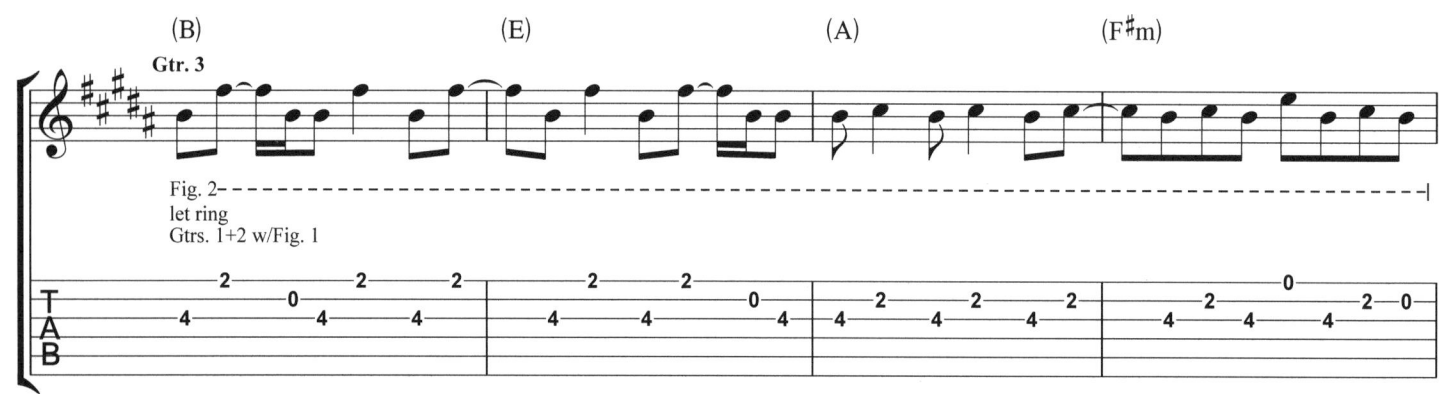

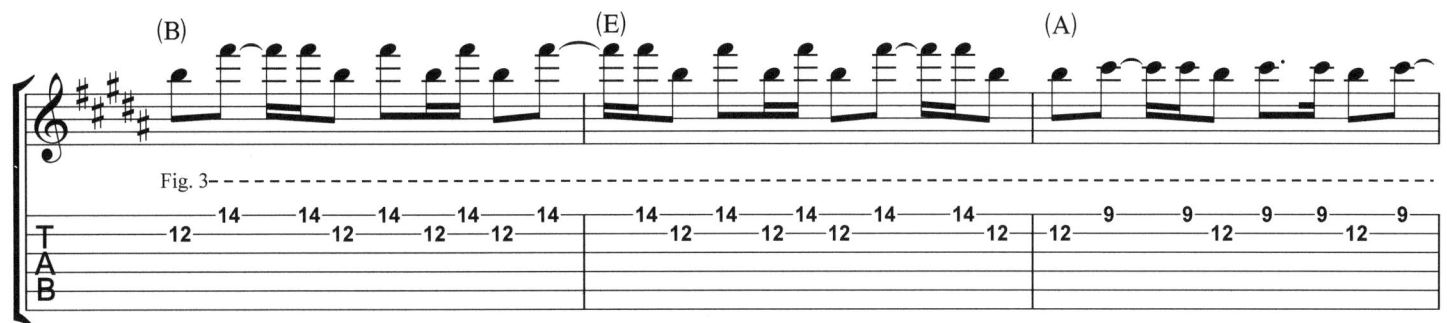
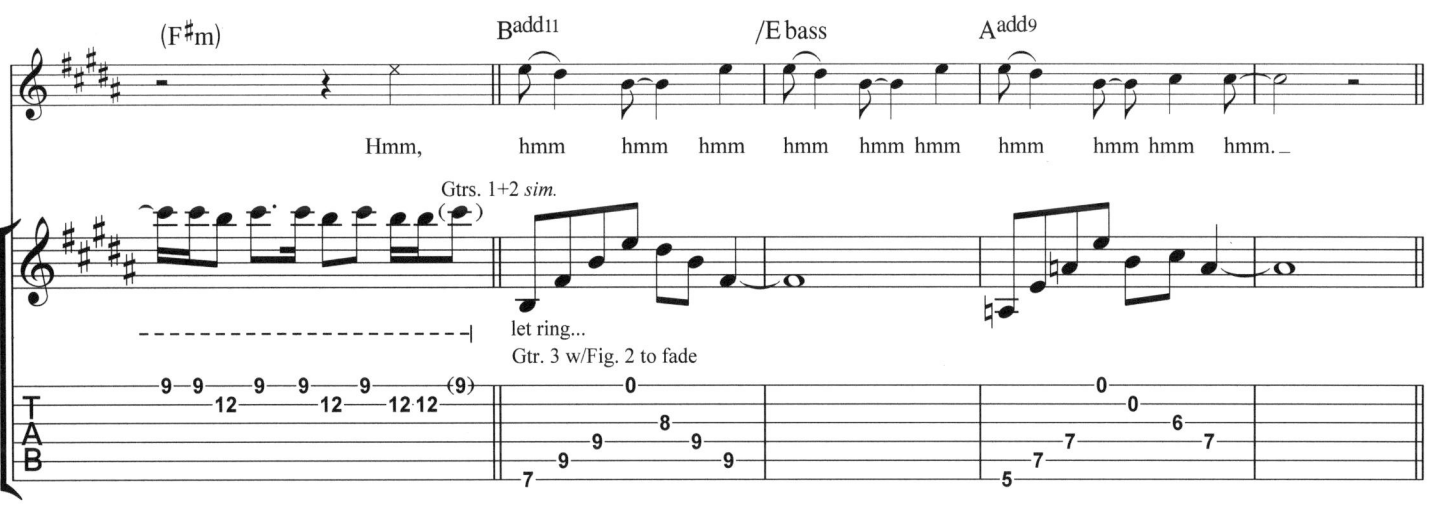
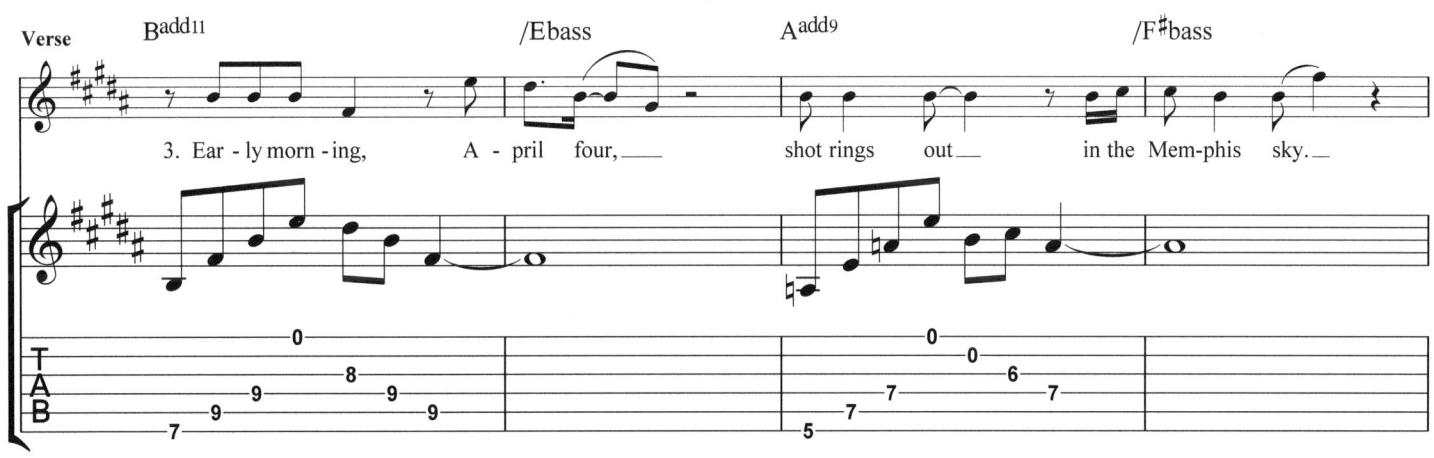
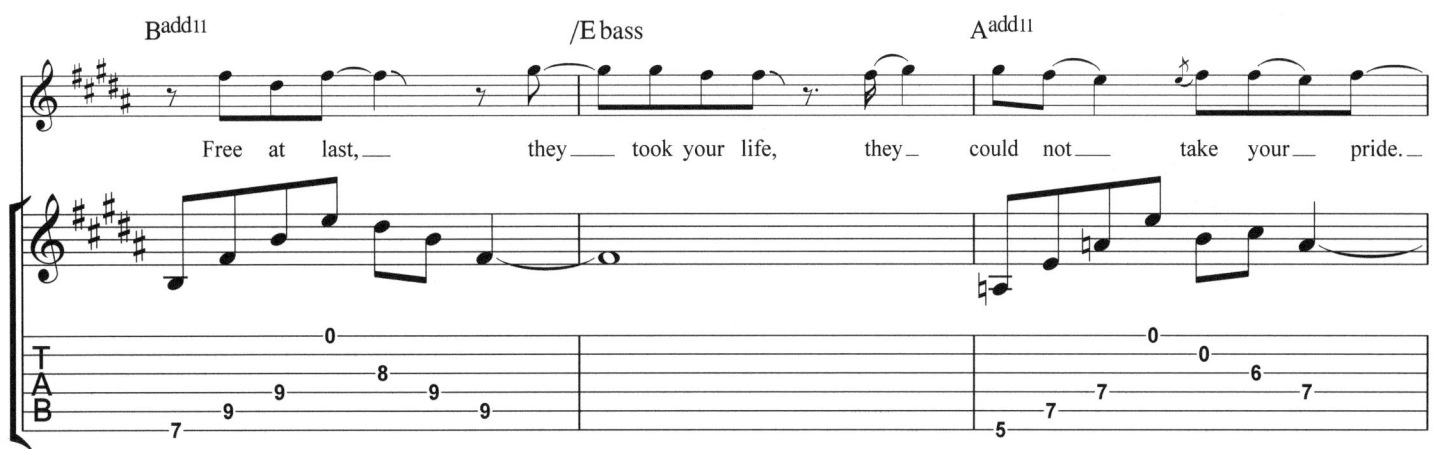

31

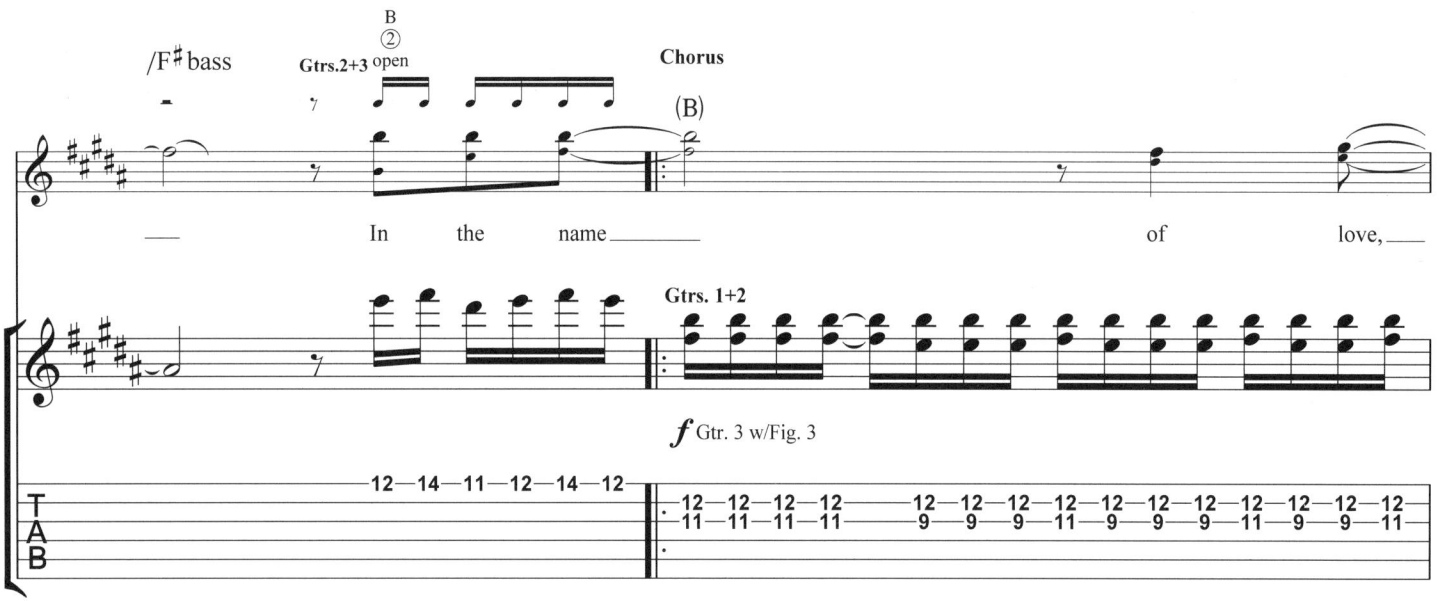
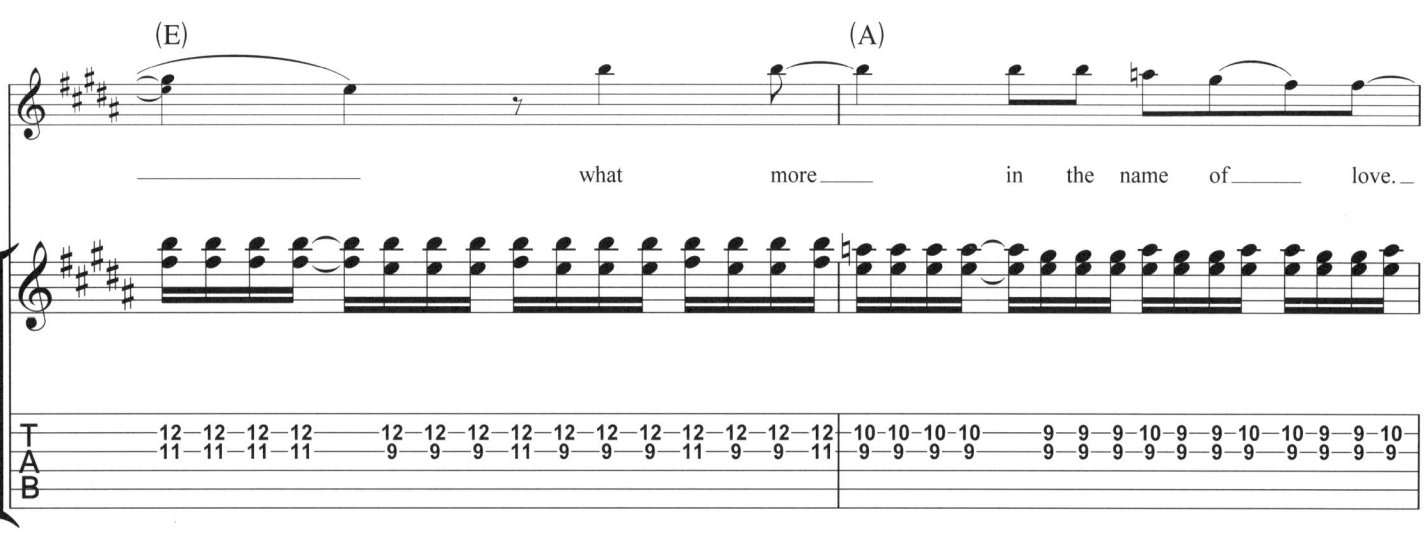
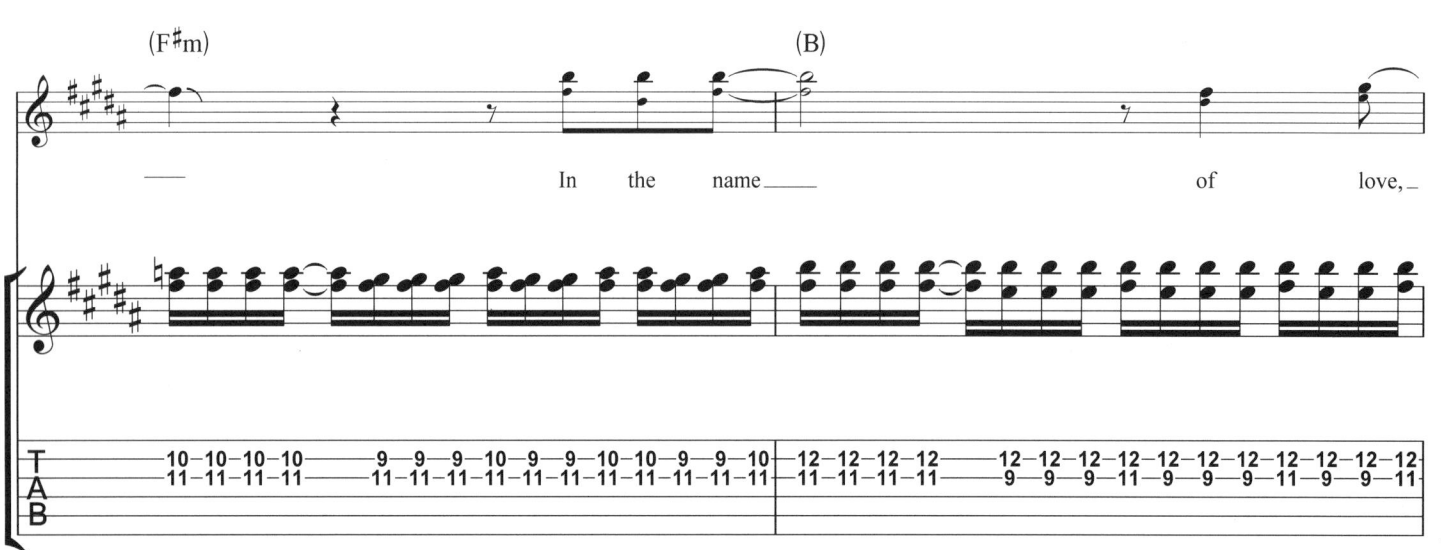

32

With Or Without You

Words & Music by U2

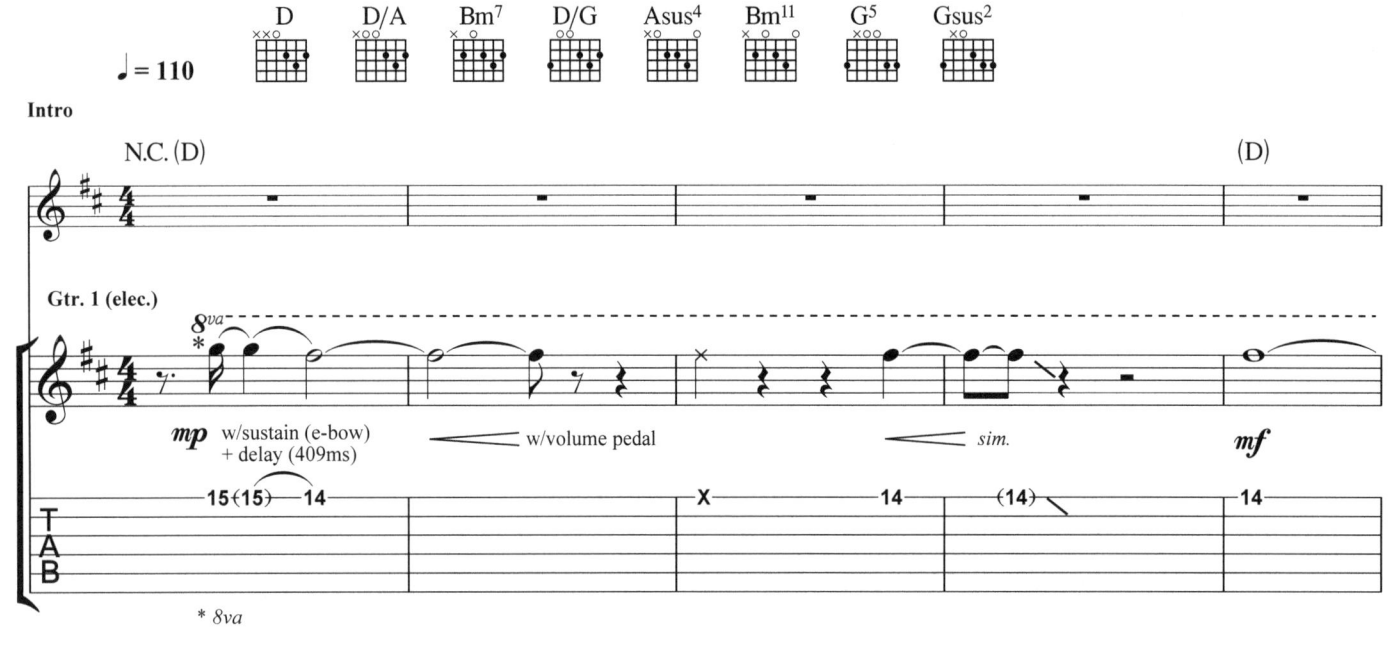
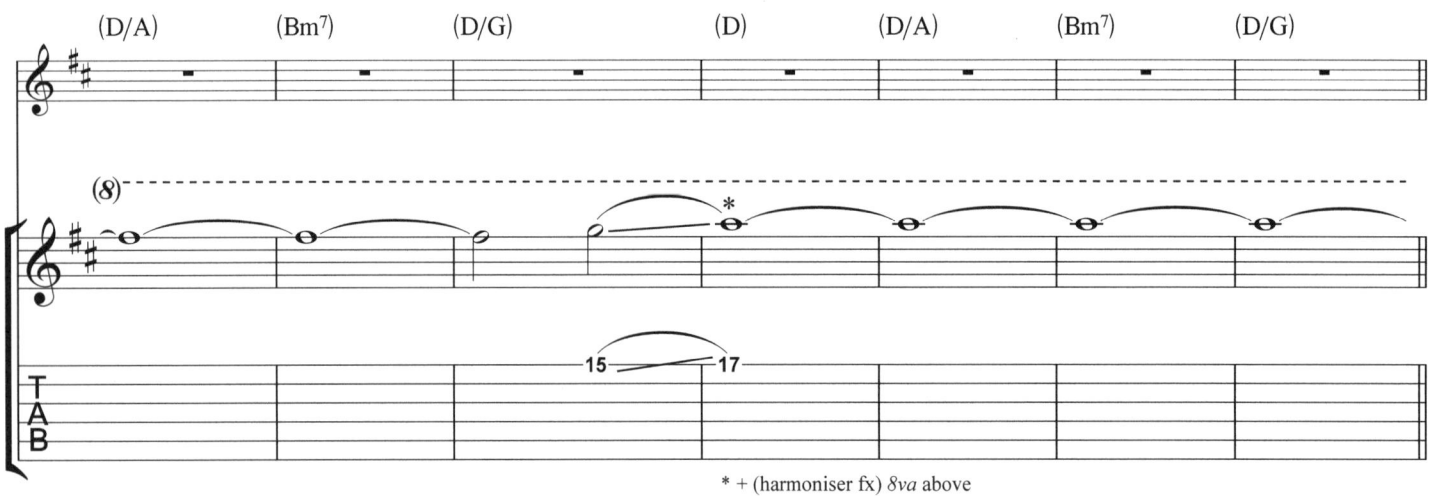
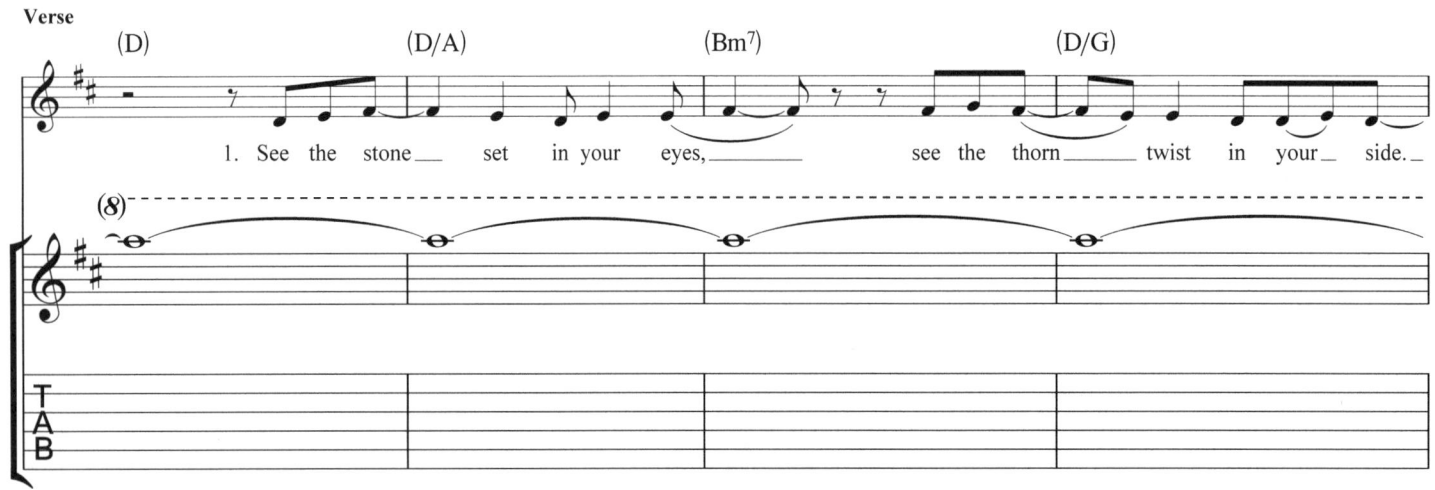

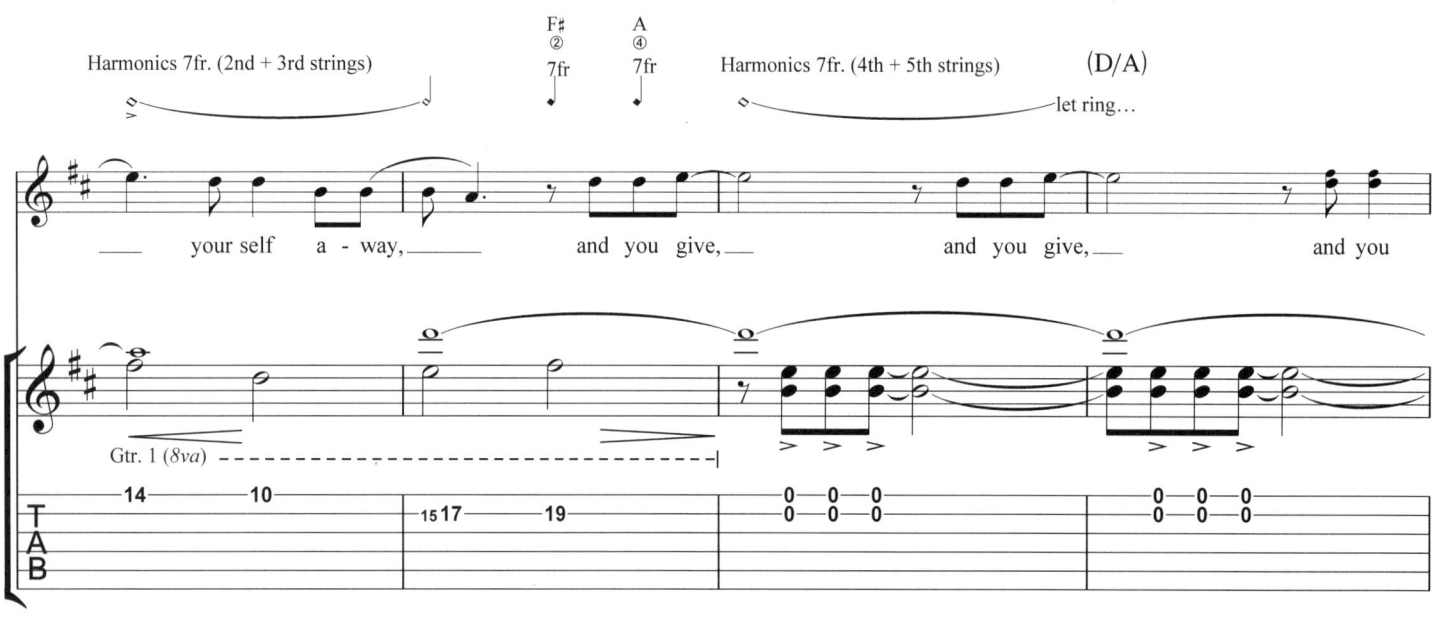
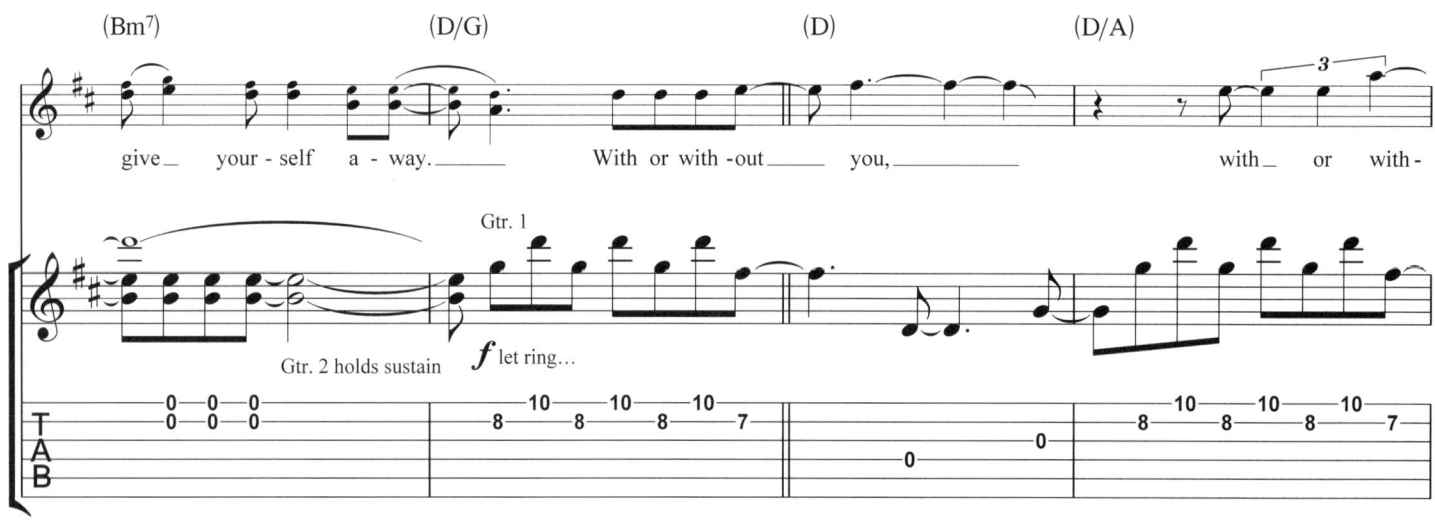
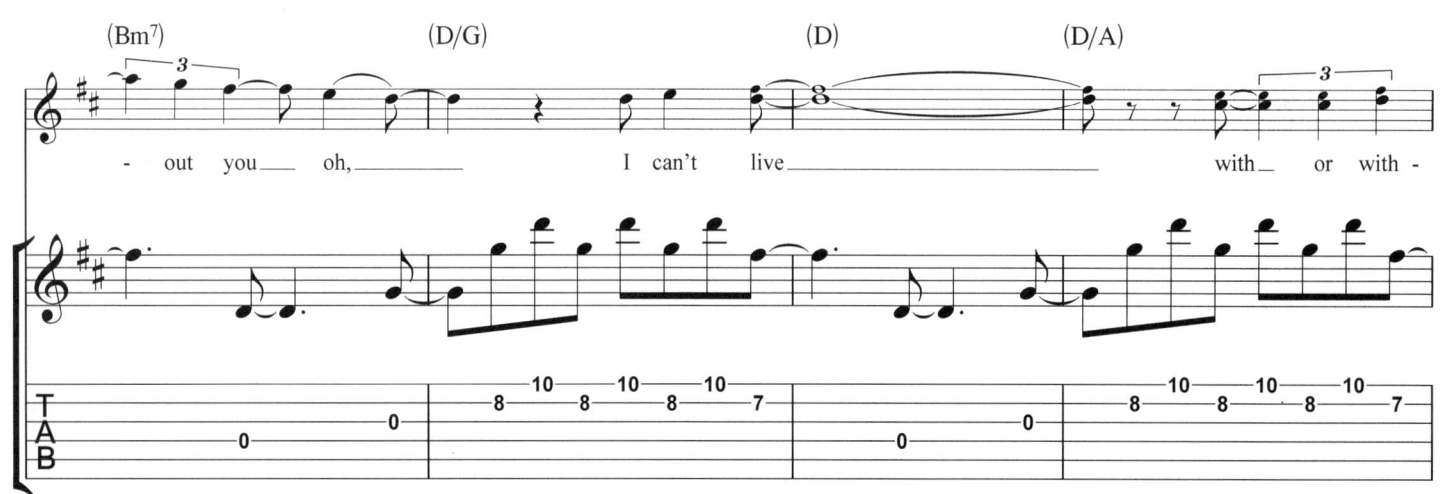

38

Vertigo

Words & Music by U2

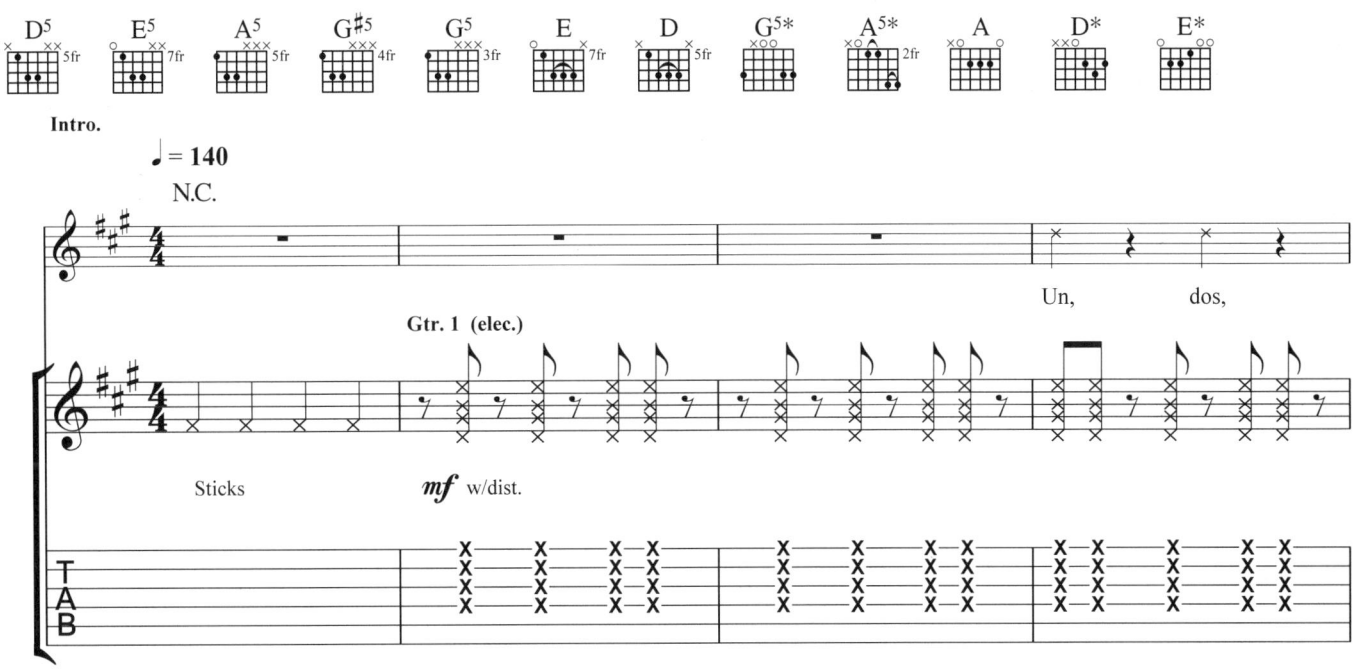

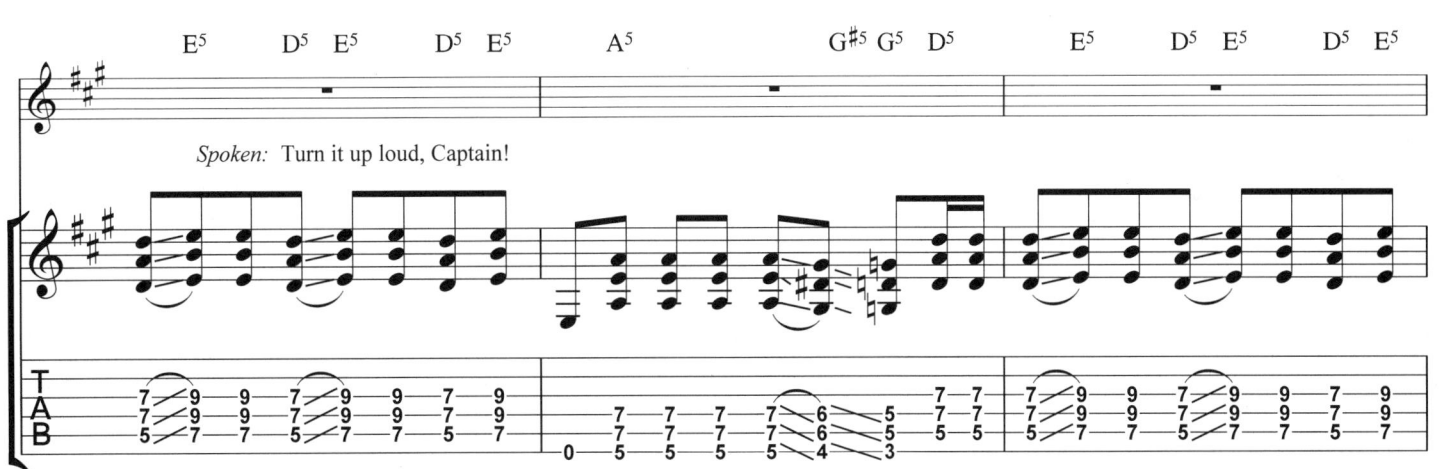

© Copyright 2004 Blue Mountain Music Limited.
All Rights Reserved. International Copyright Secured.

New Year's Day

Words & Music by U2

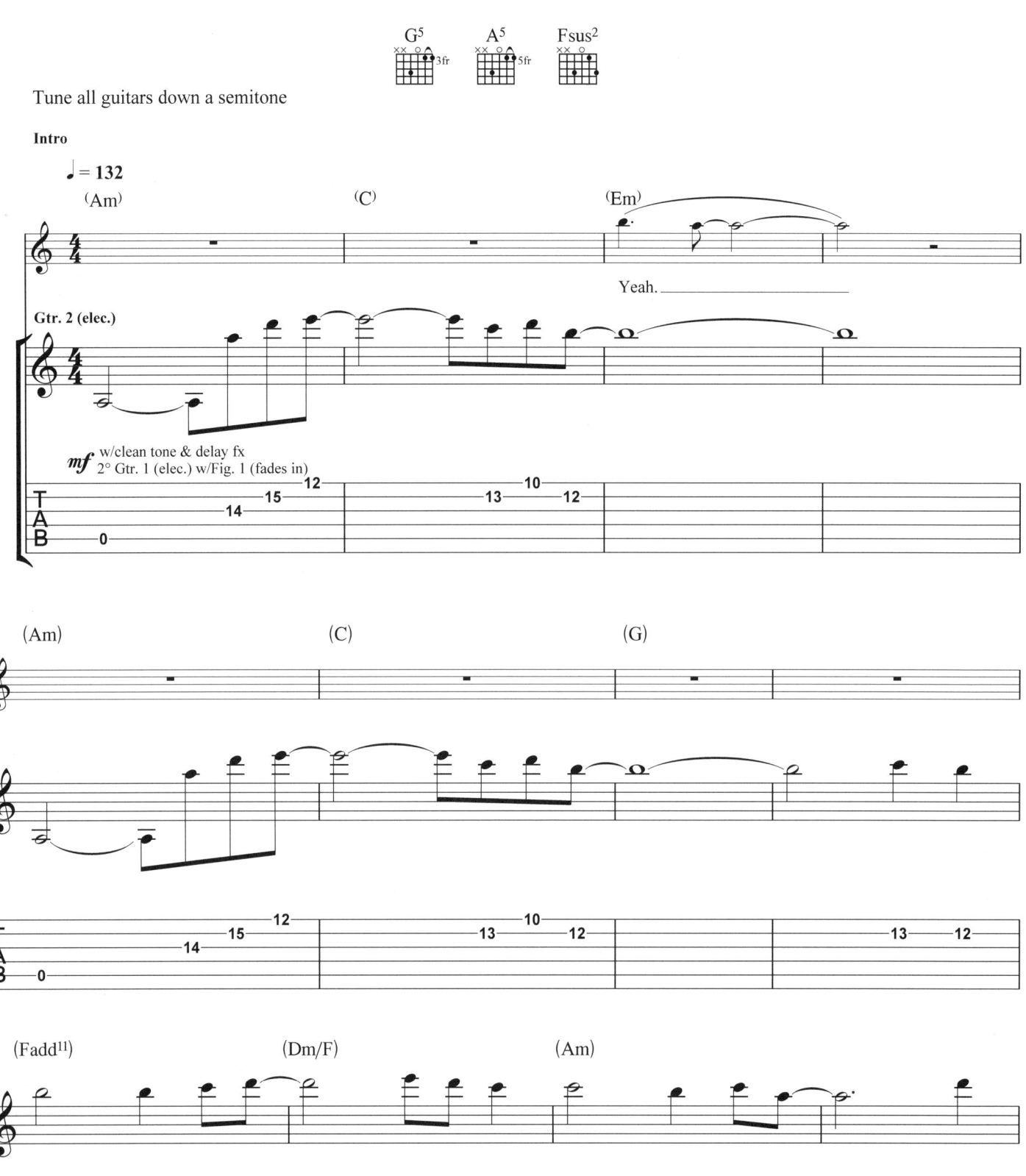

Tune all guitars down a semitone

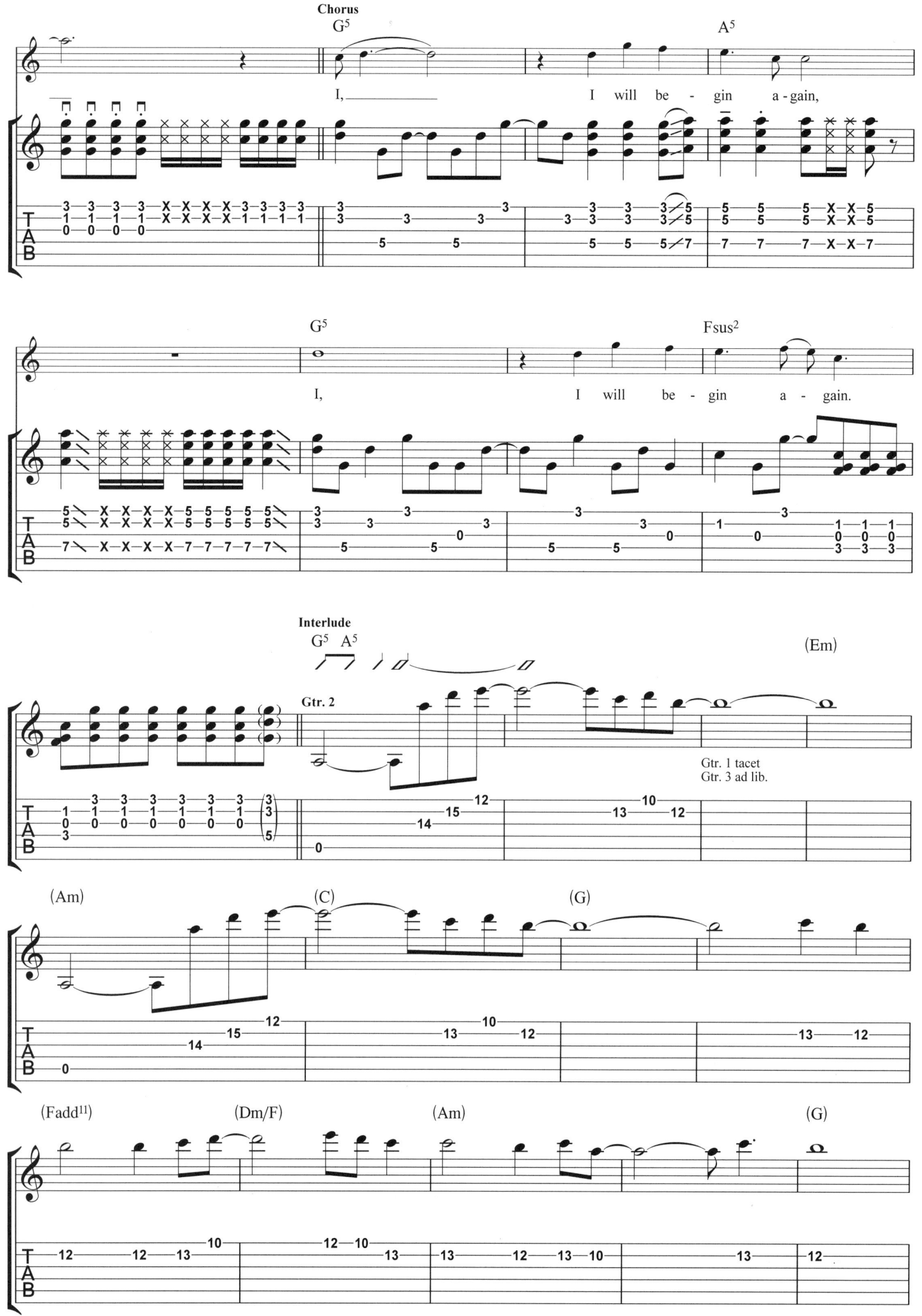

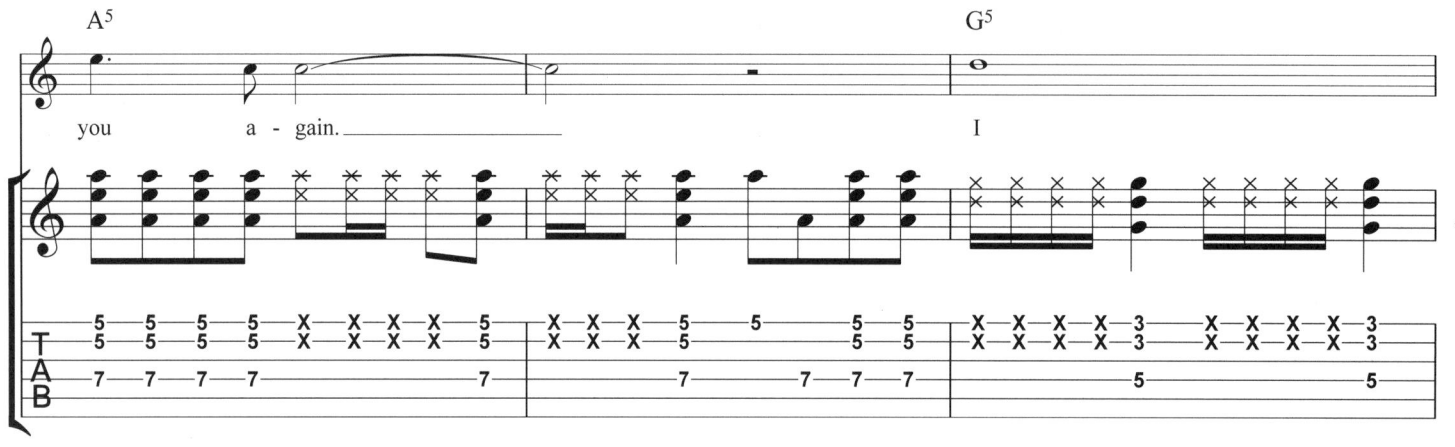
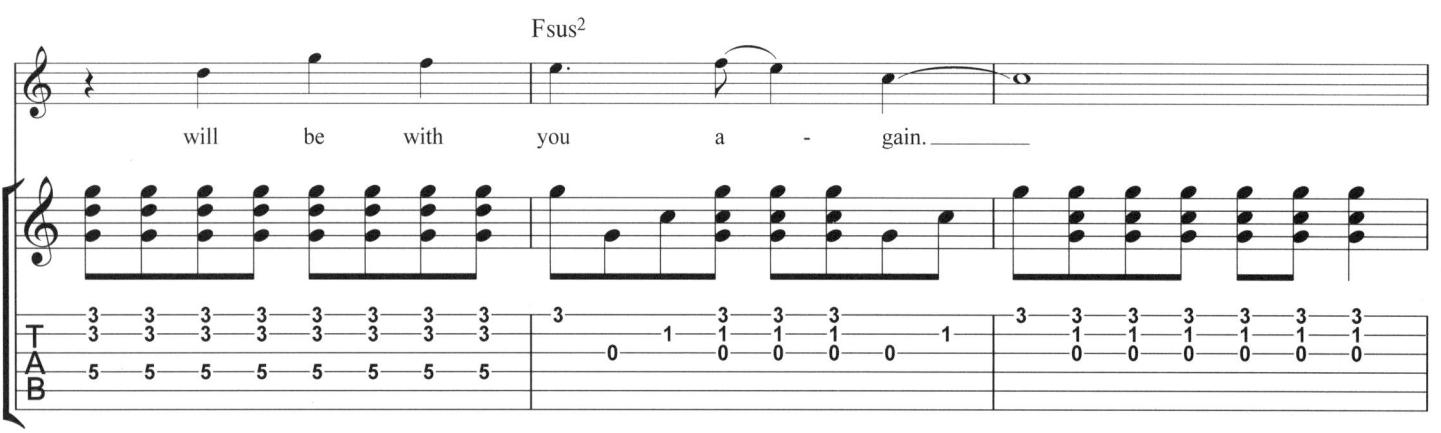
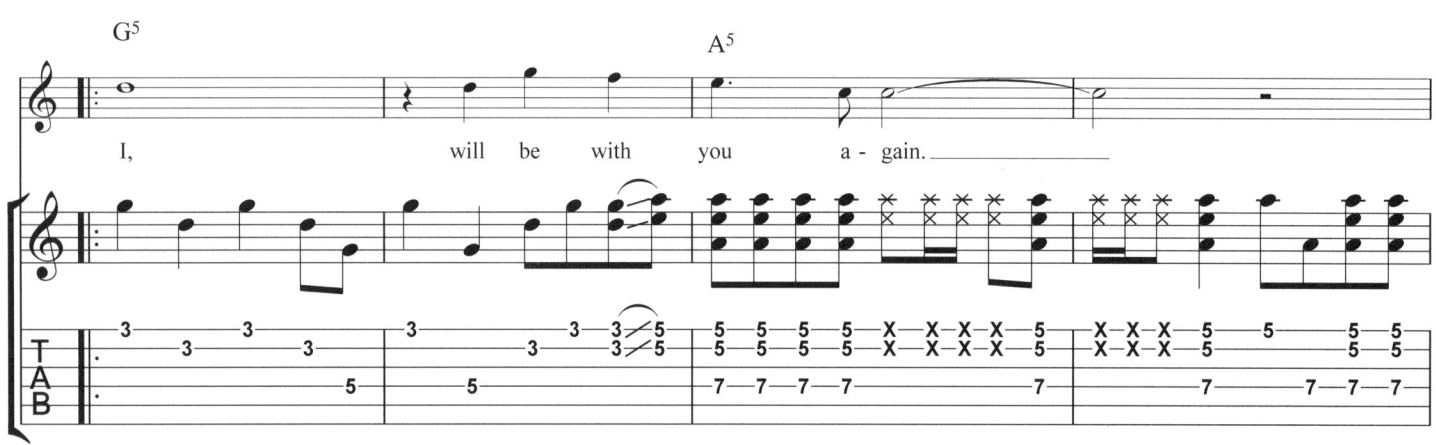

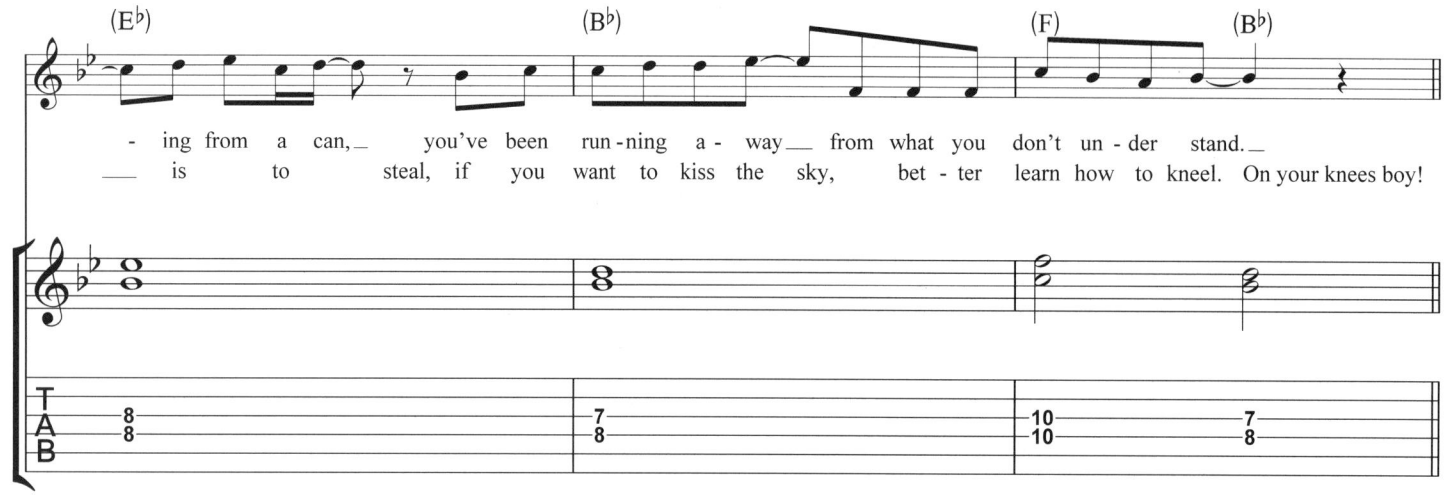
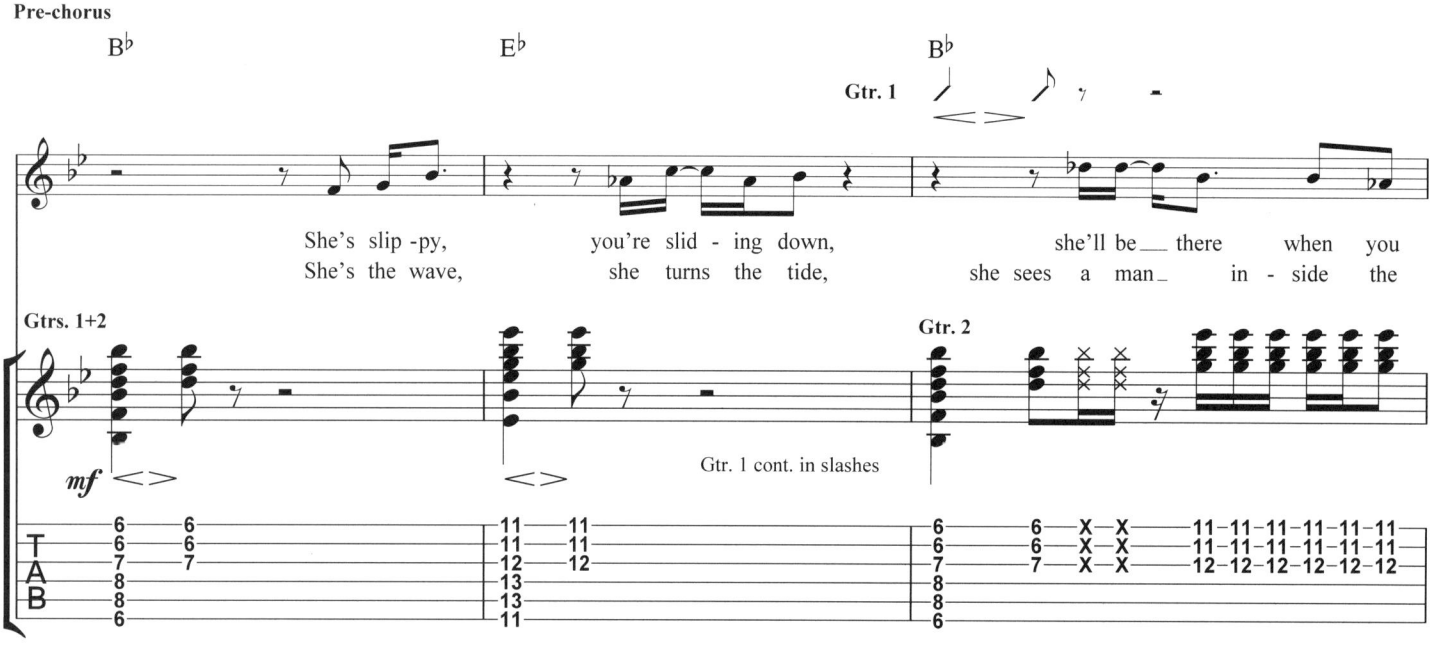
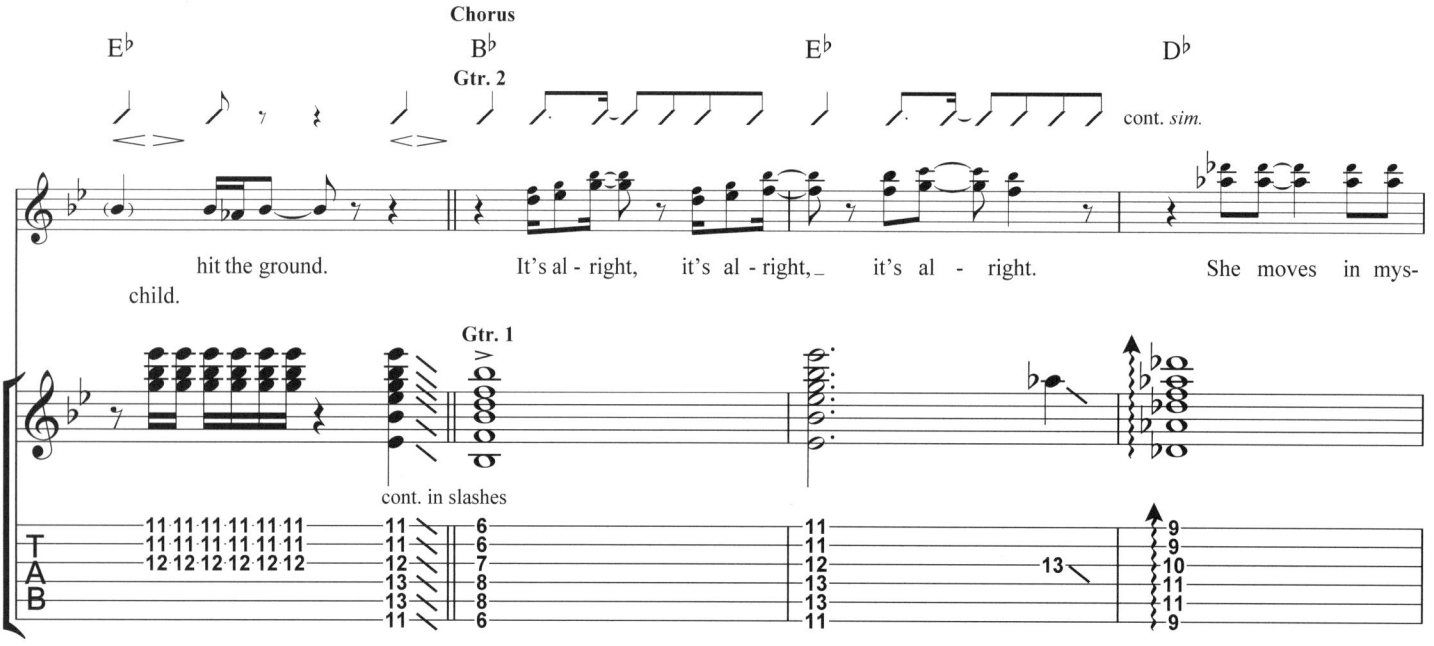

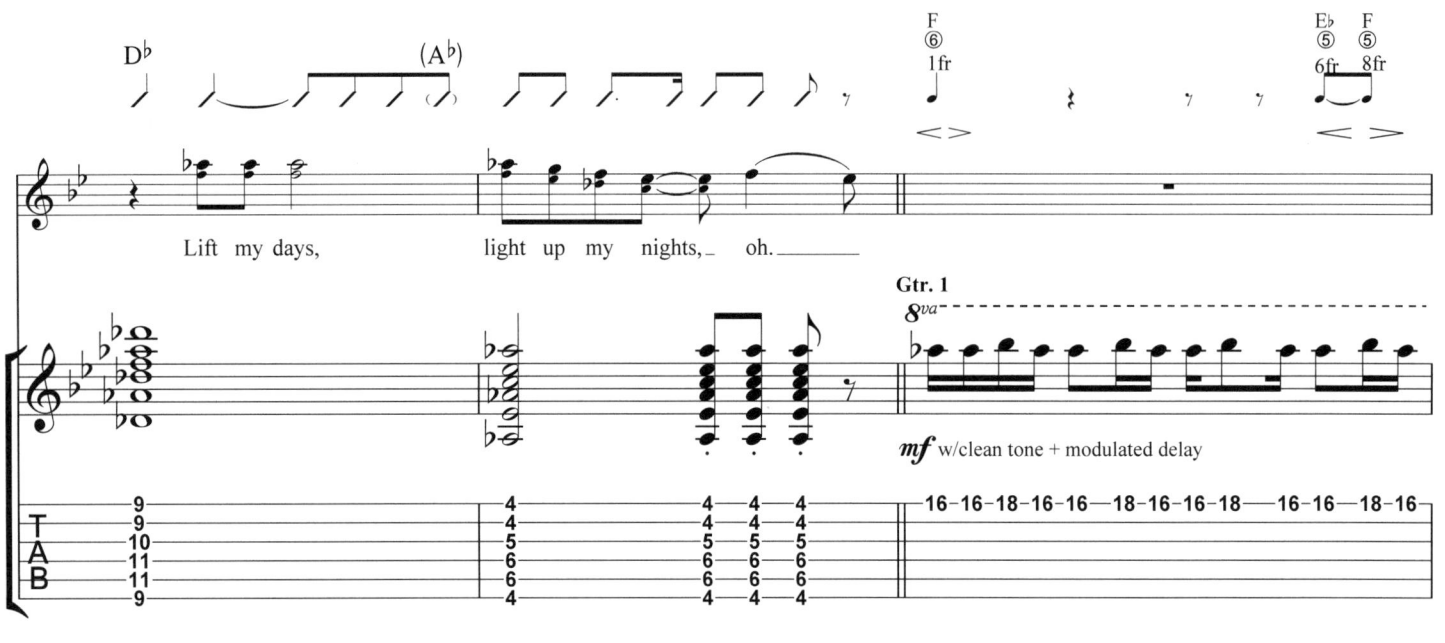
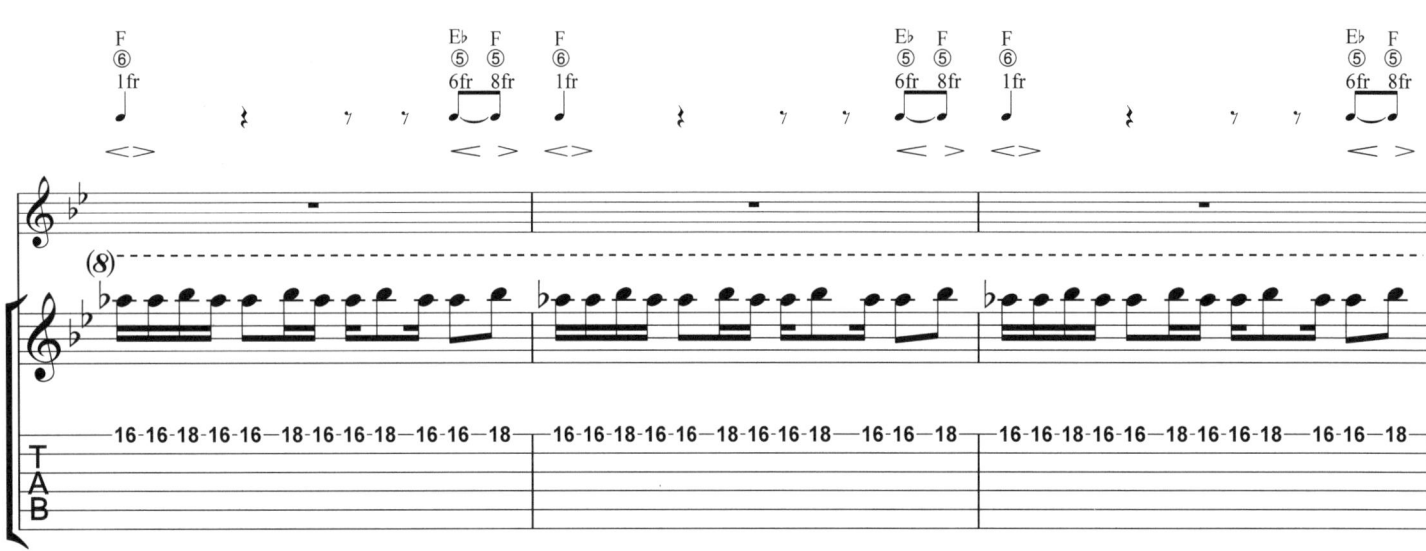
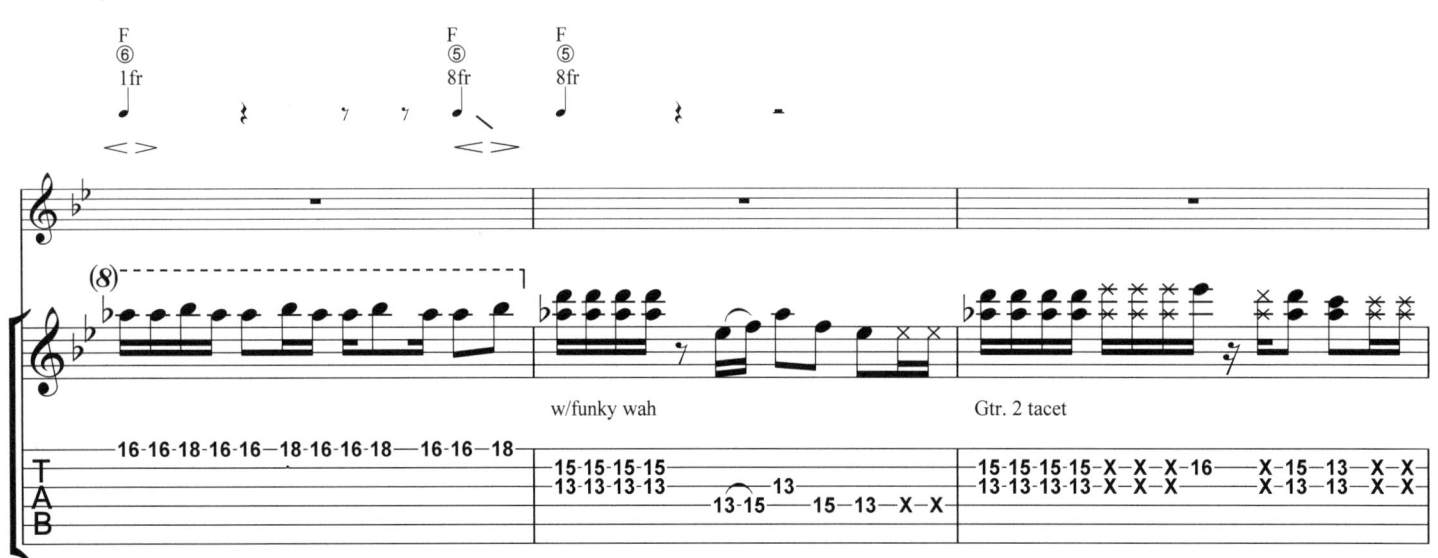

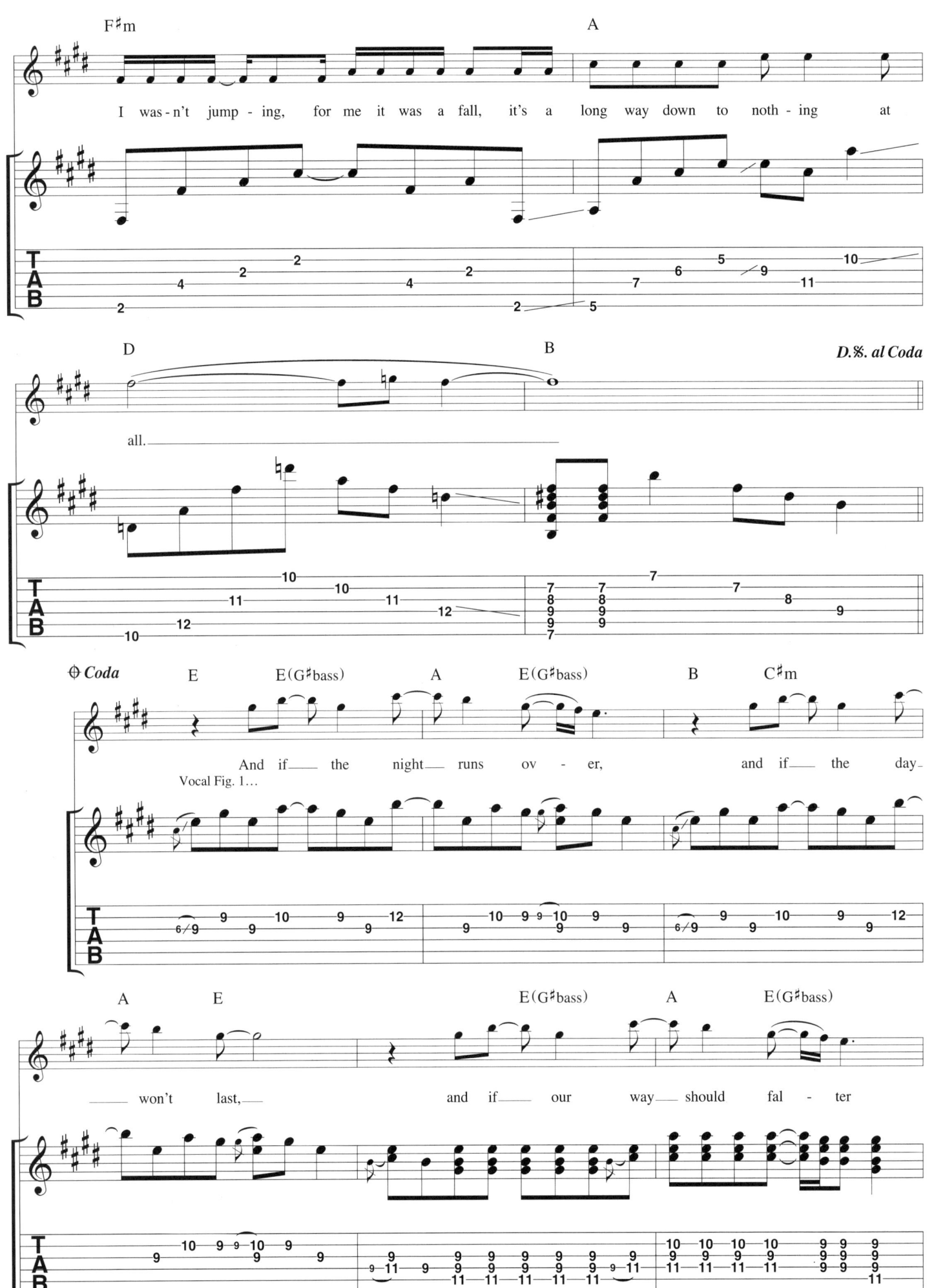

Where The Streets Have No Name

Words & Music by U2

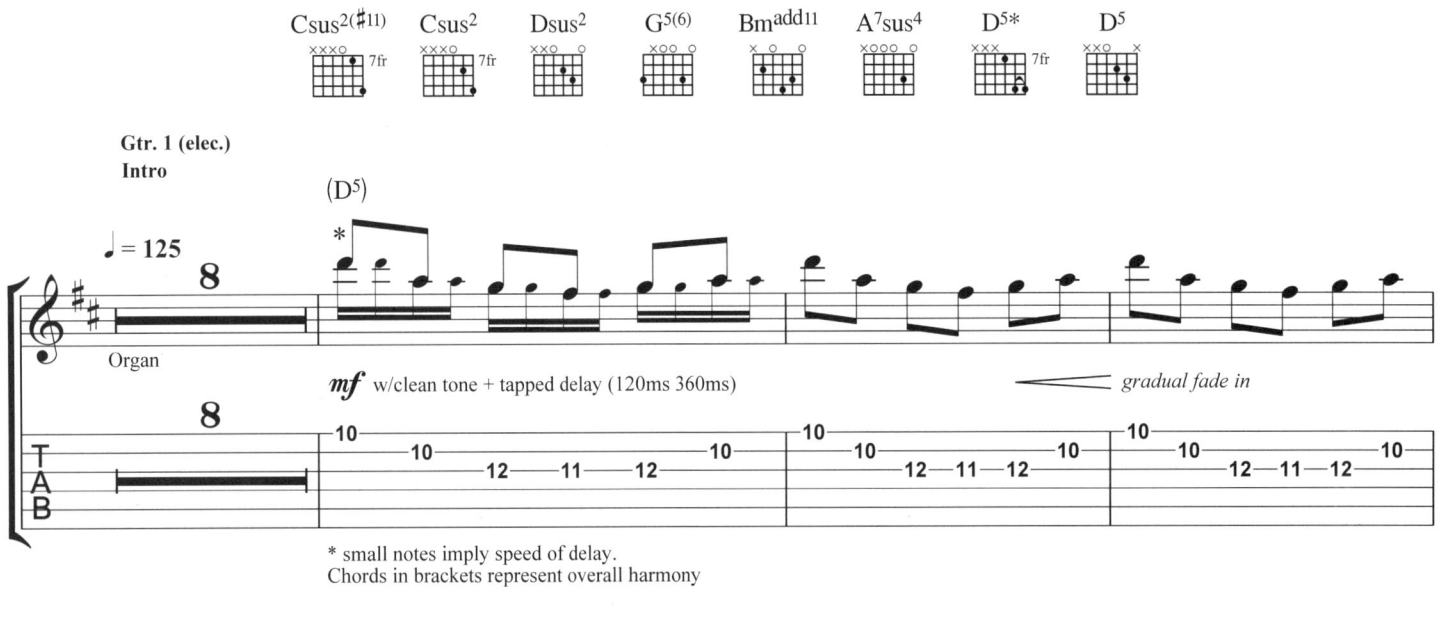

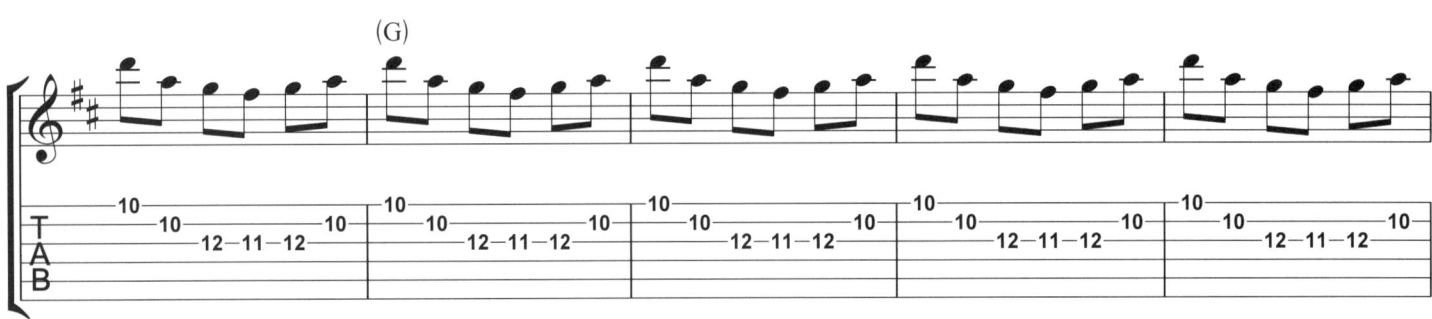

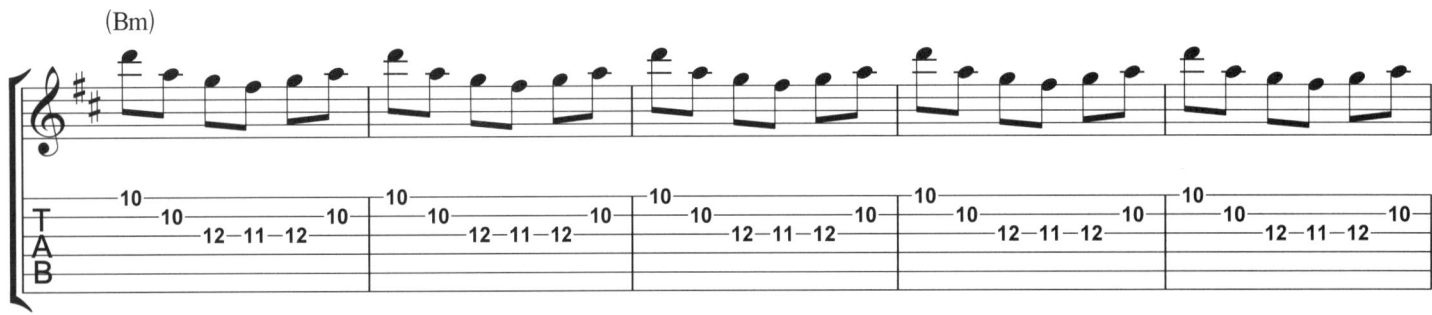

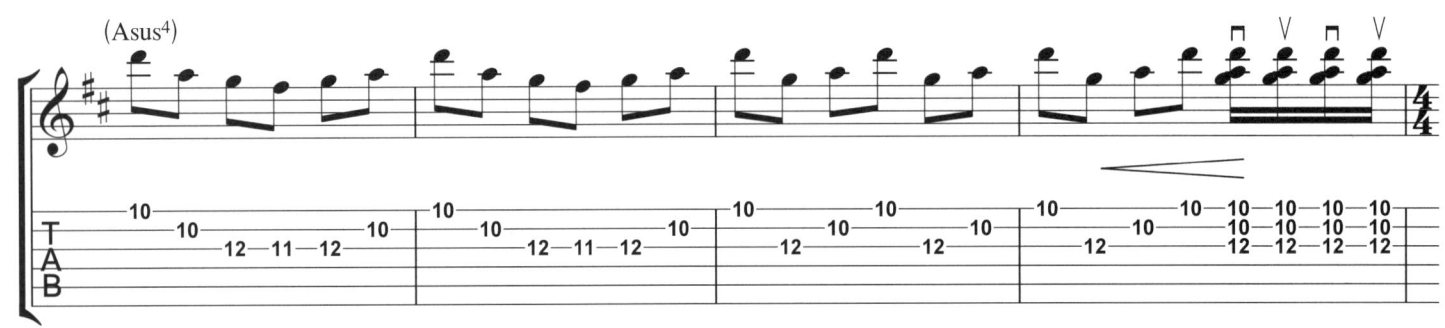

© Copyright 1987 Blue Mountain Music Limited/Mother Music Limited/
PolyGram International Music Publishing B.V.
All Rights Reserved. International Copyright Secured.

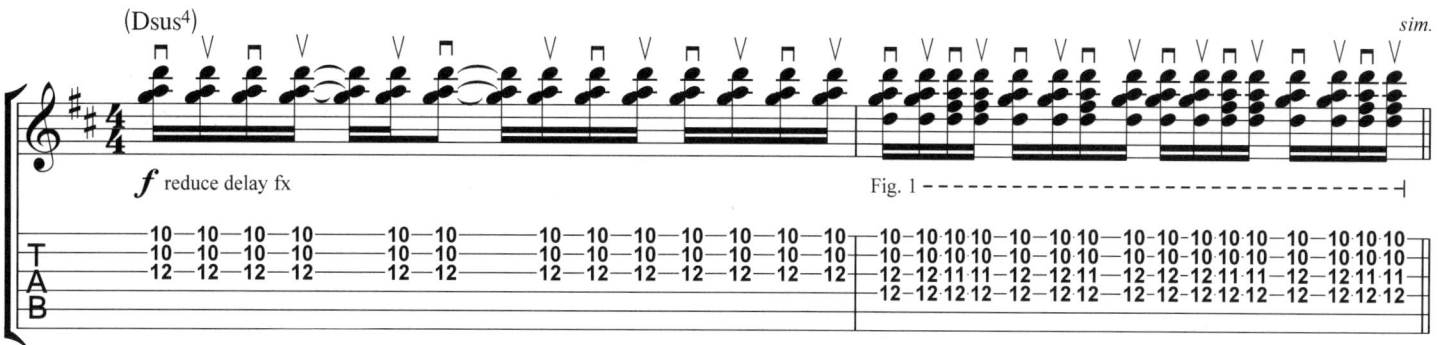

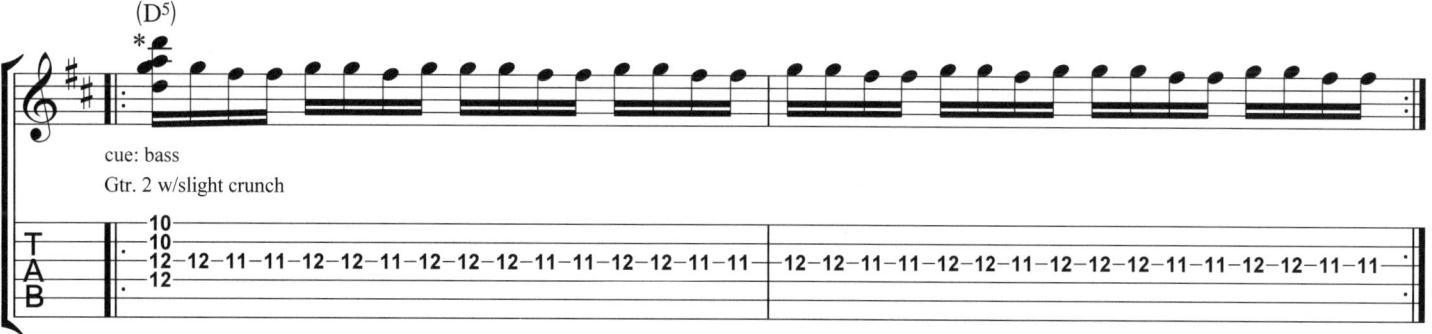

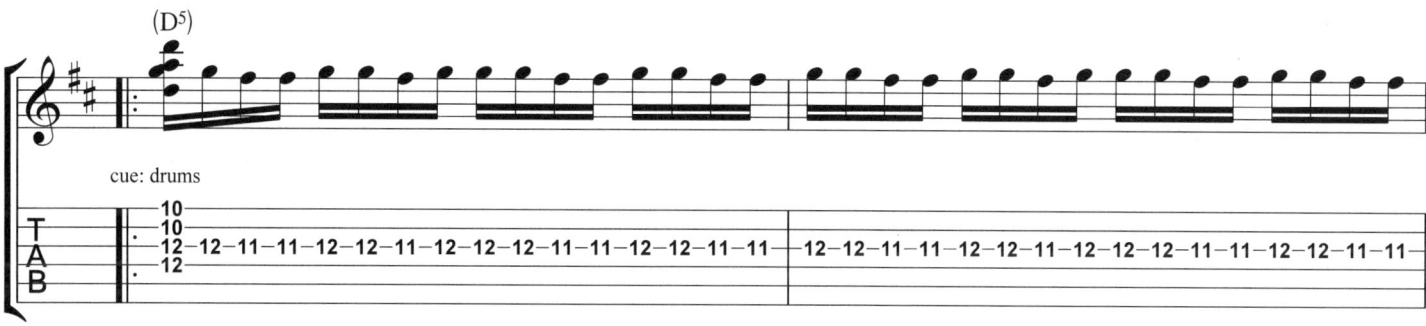

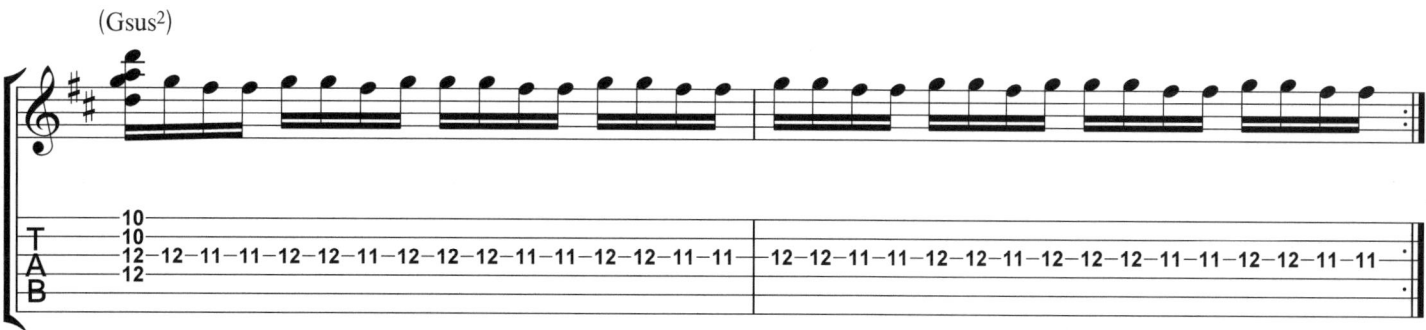

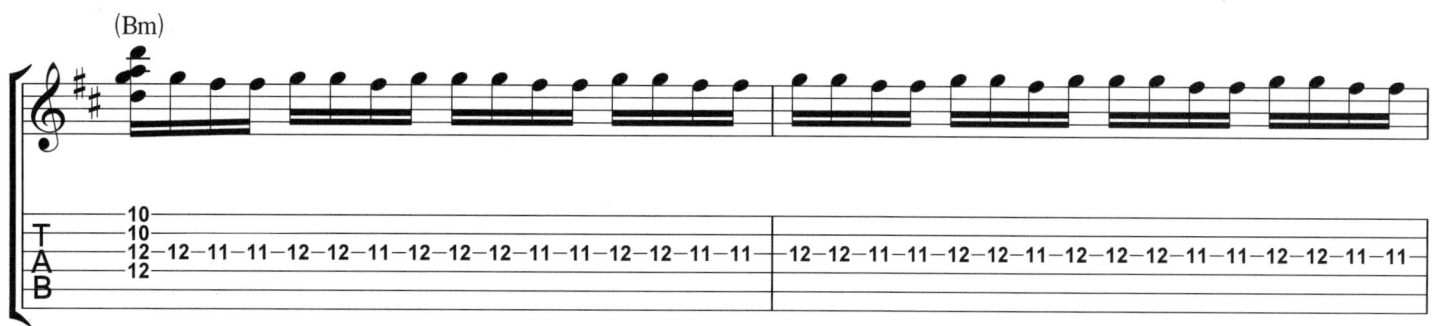

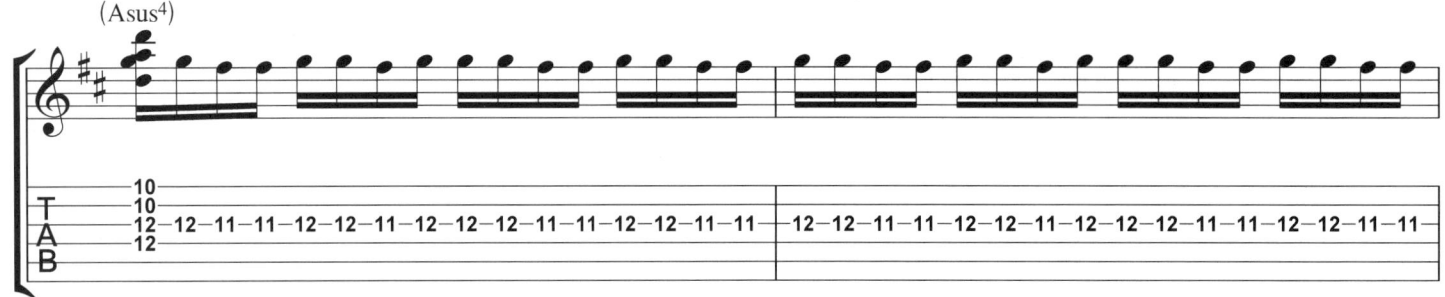
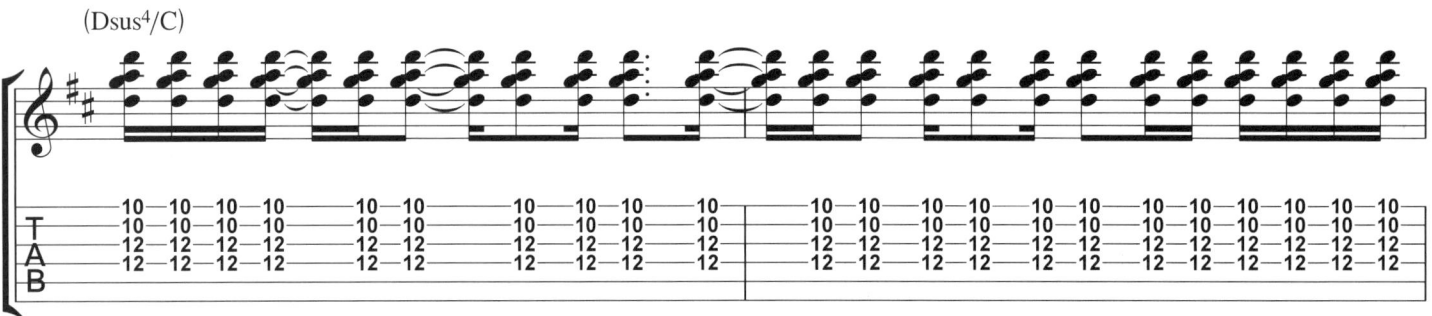
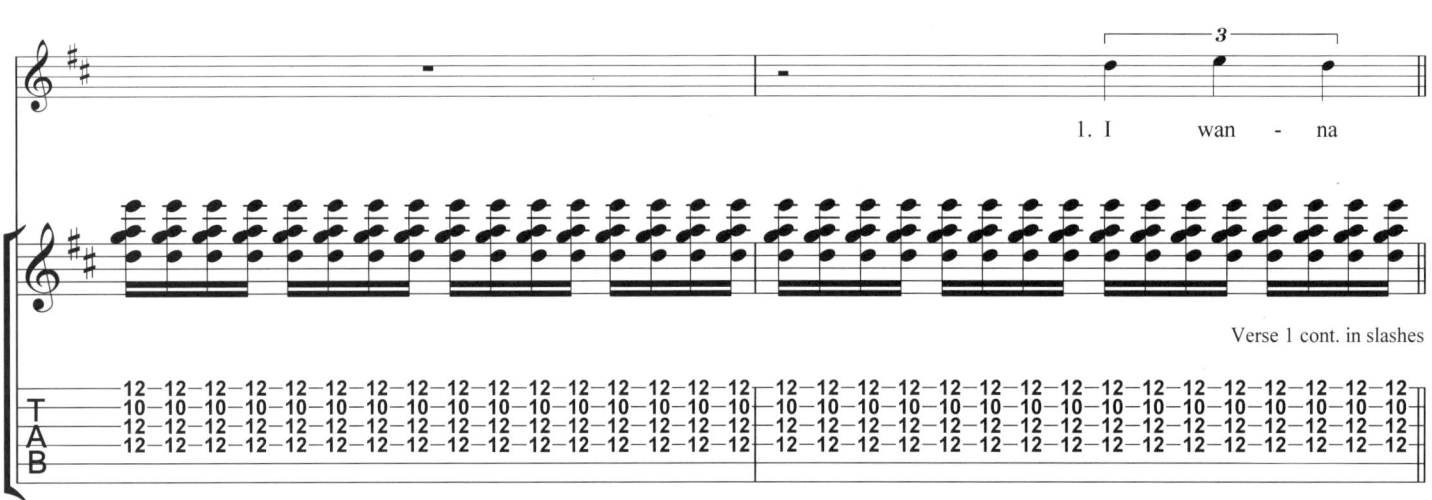
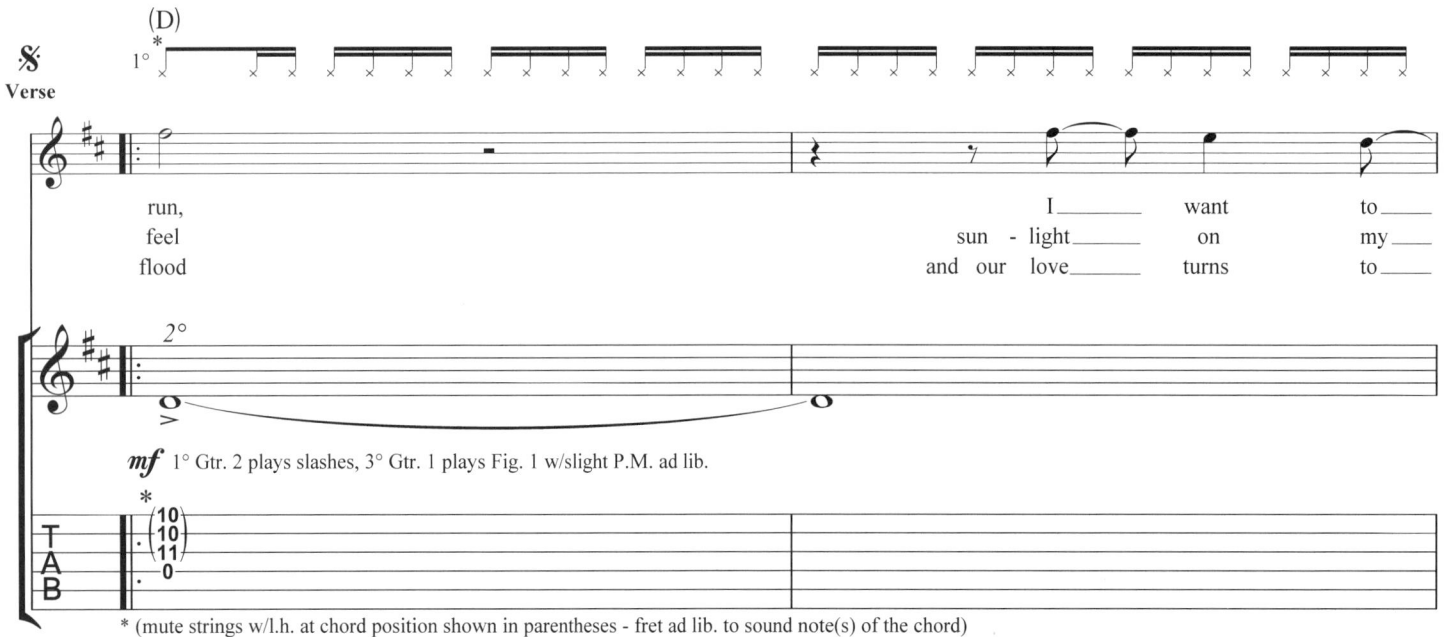

* (mute strings w/l.h. at chord position shown in parentheses - fret ad lib. to sound note(s) of the chord)

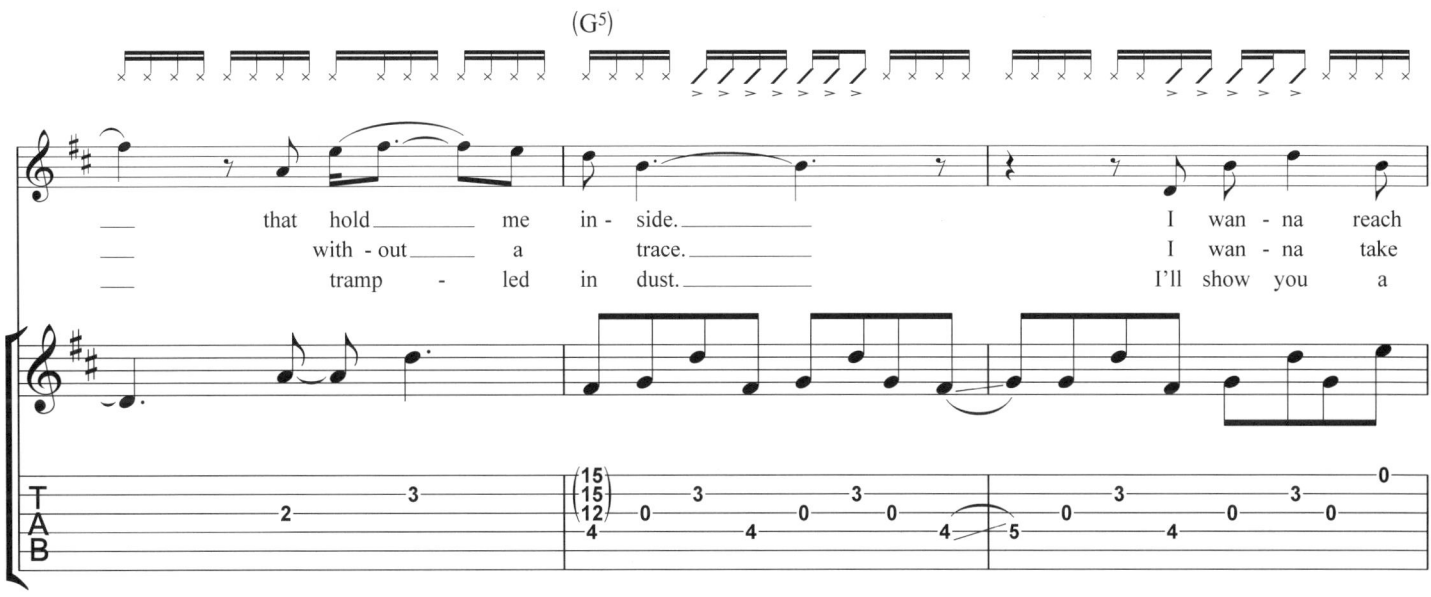
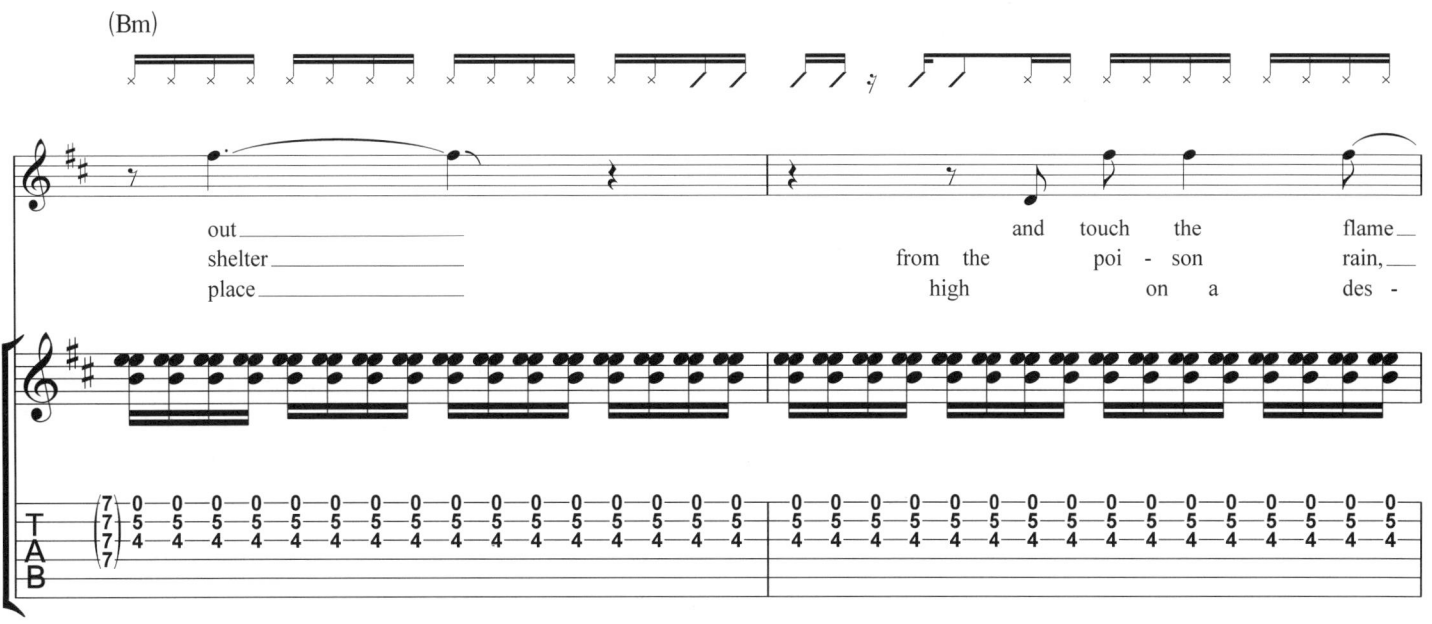

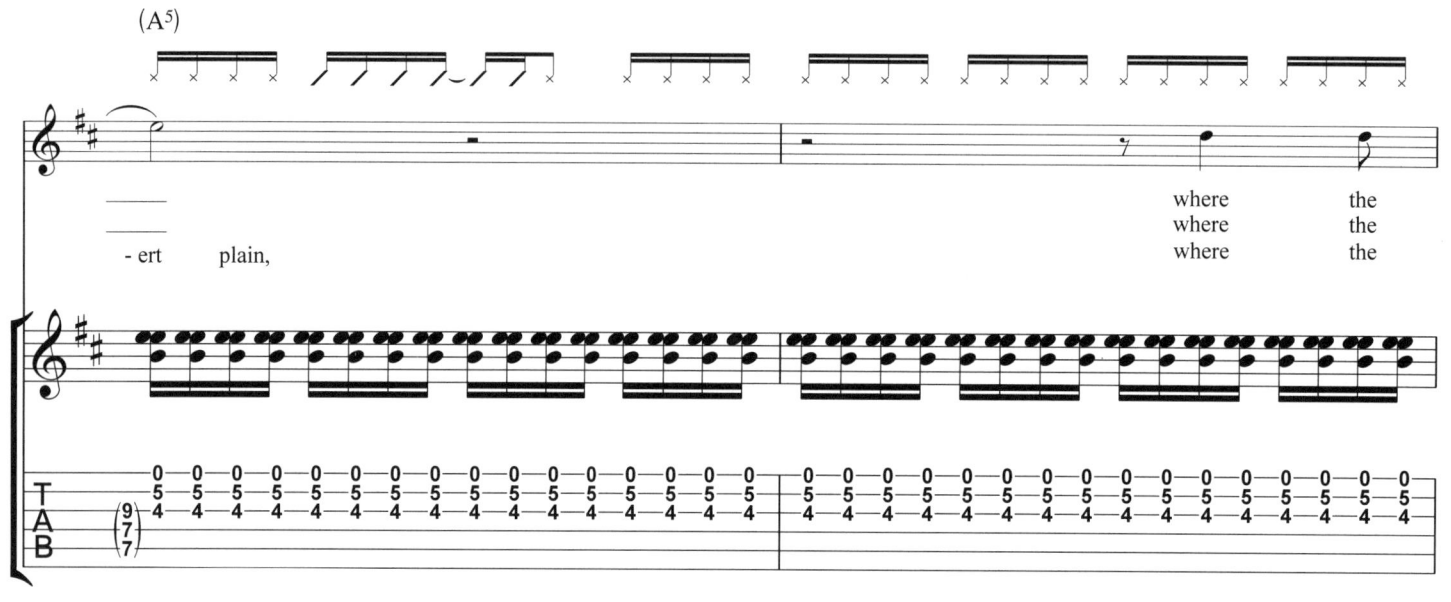
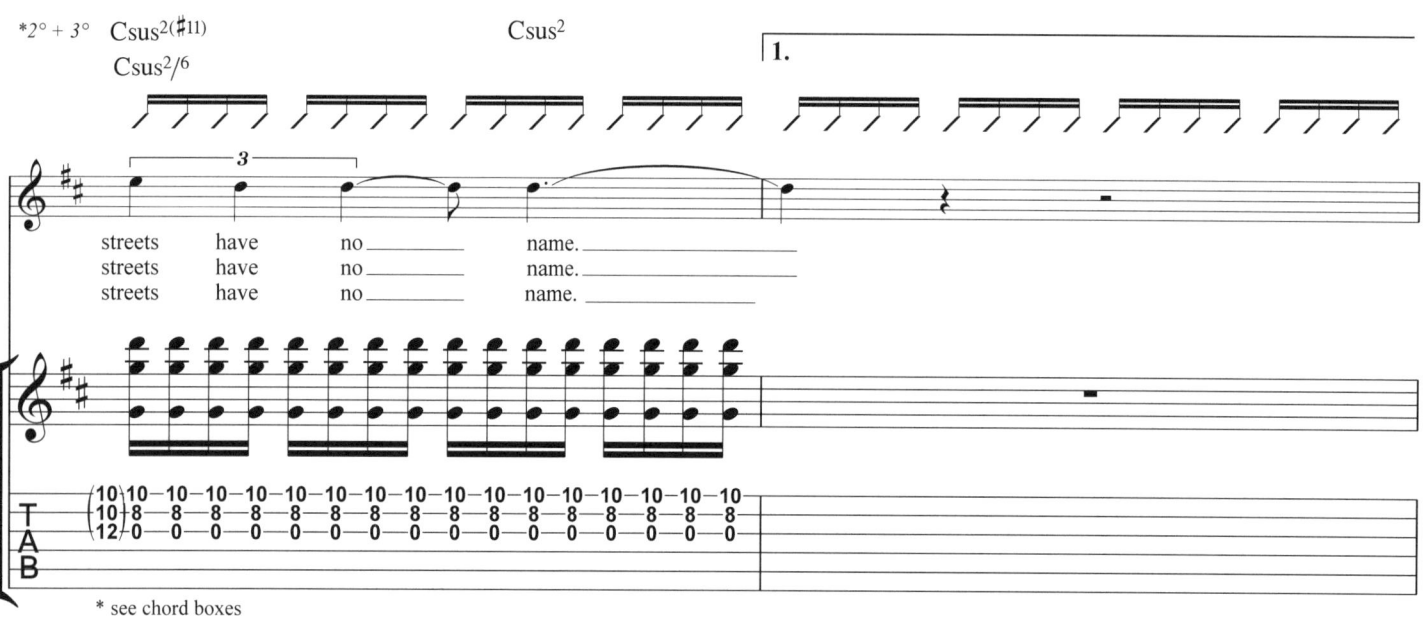

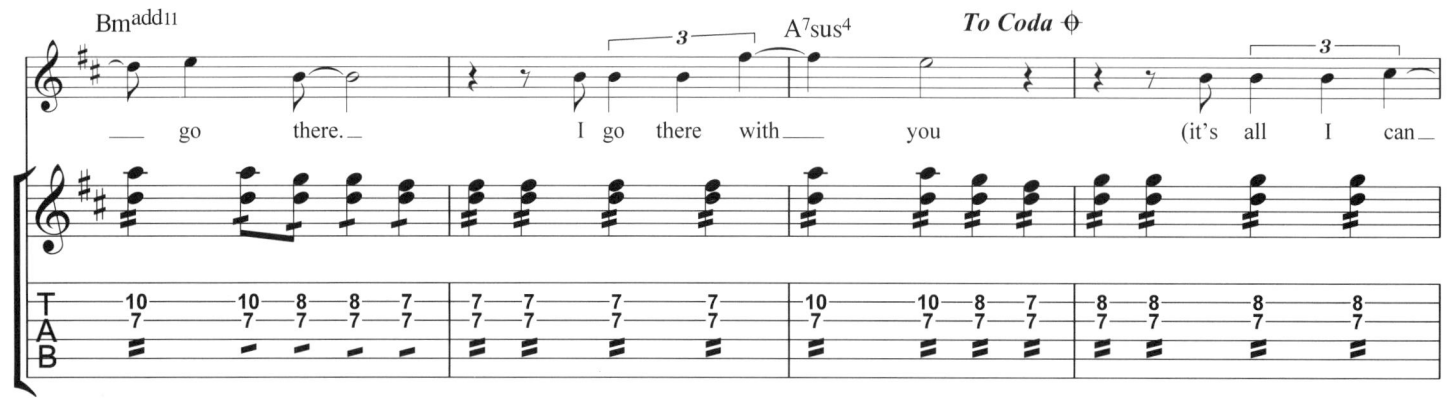
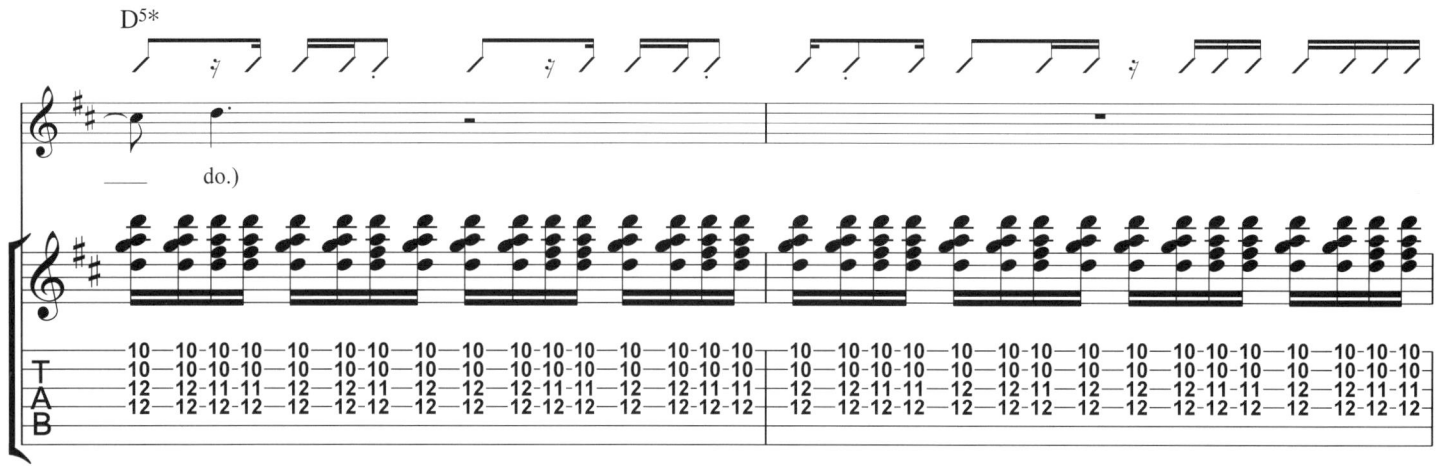
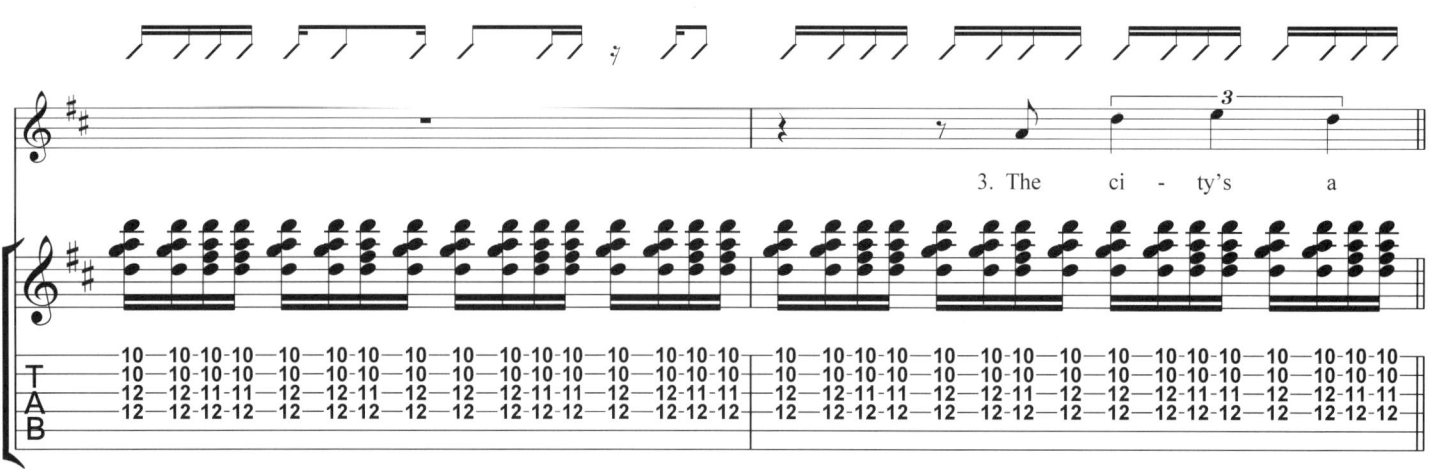
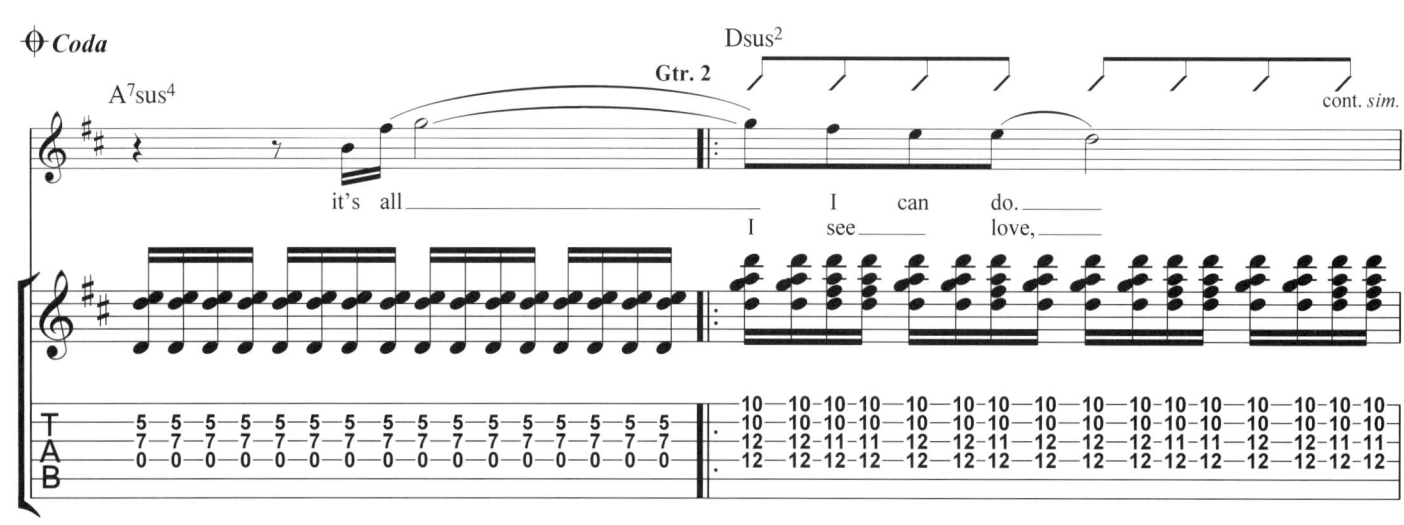

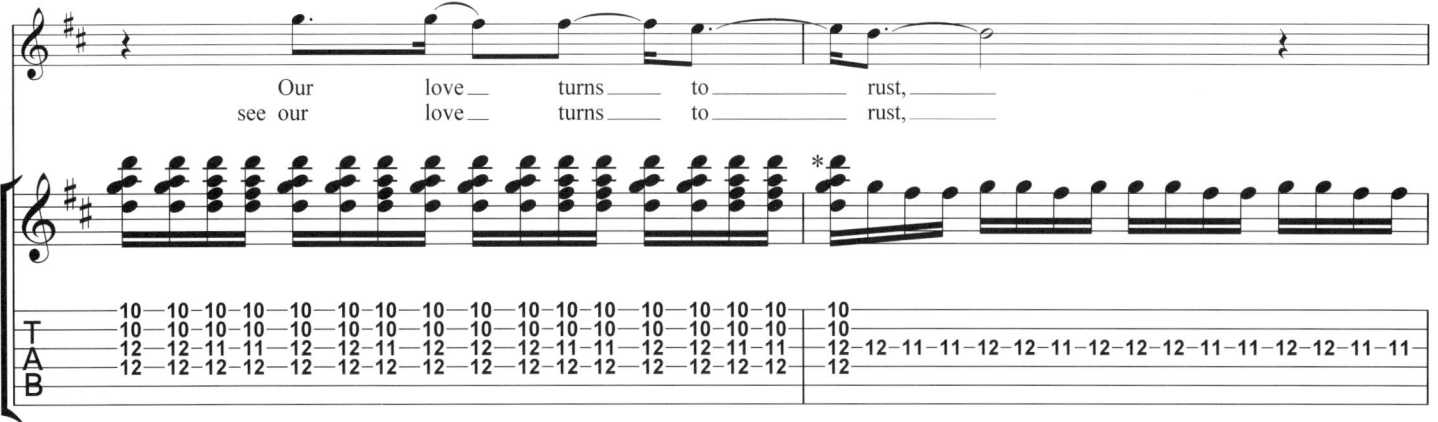
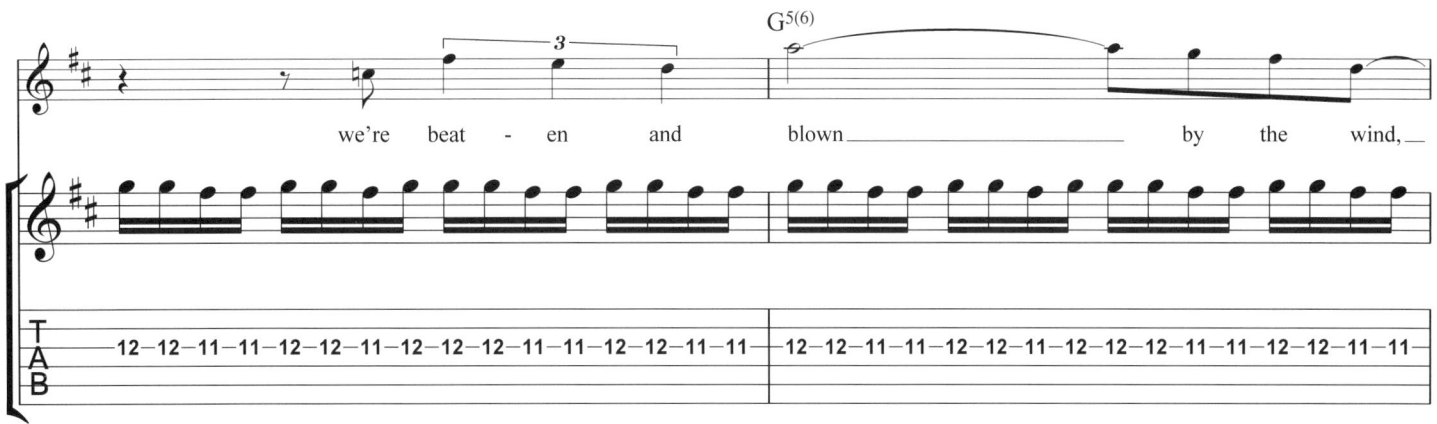
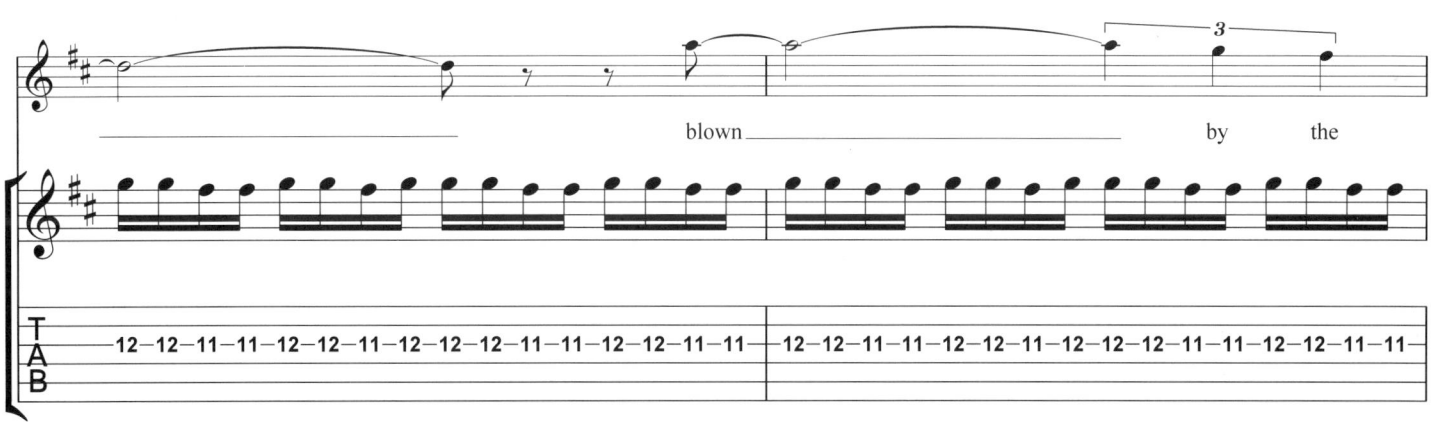
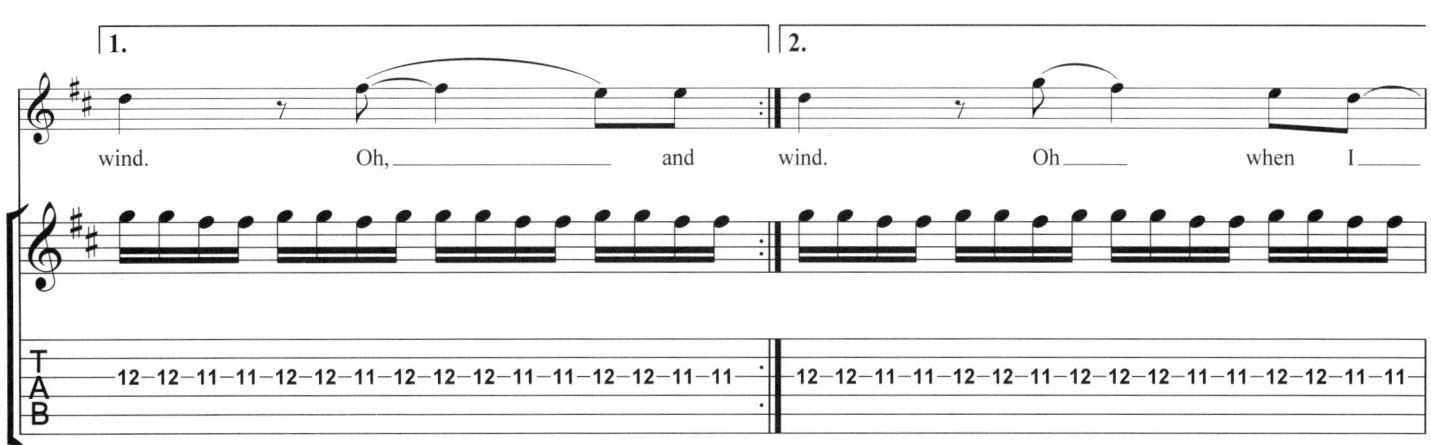

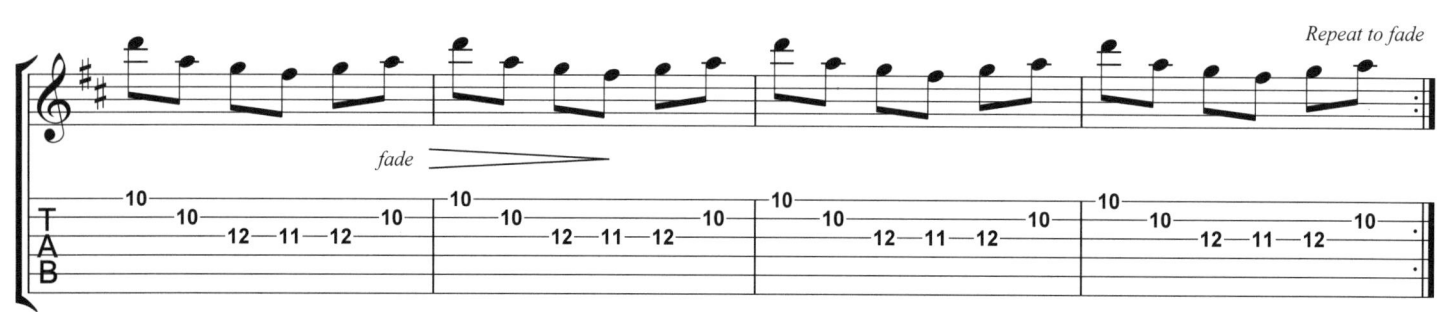

Sweetest Thing

Words & Music by U2

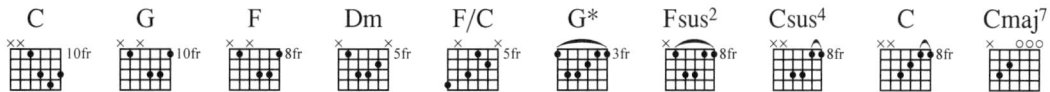
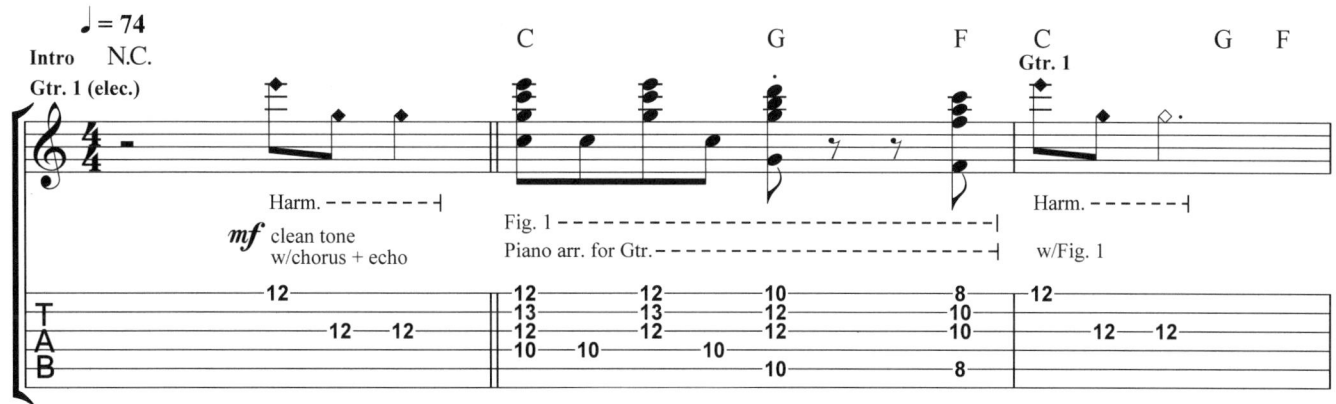
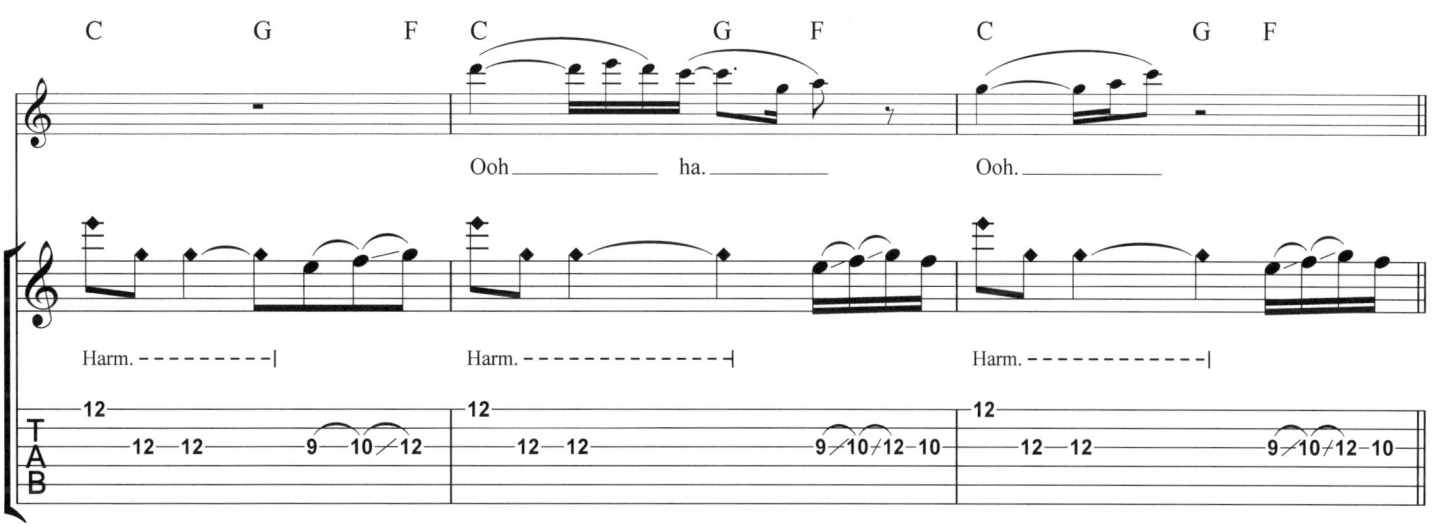
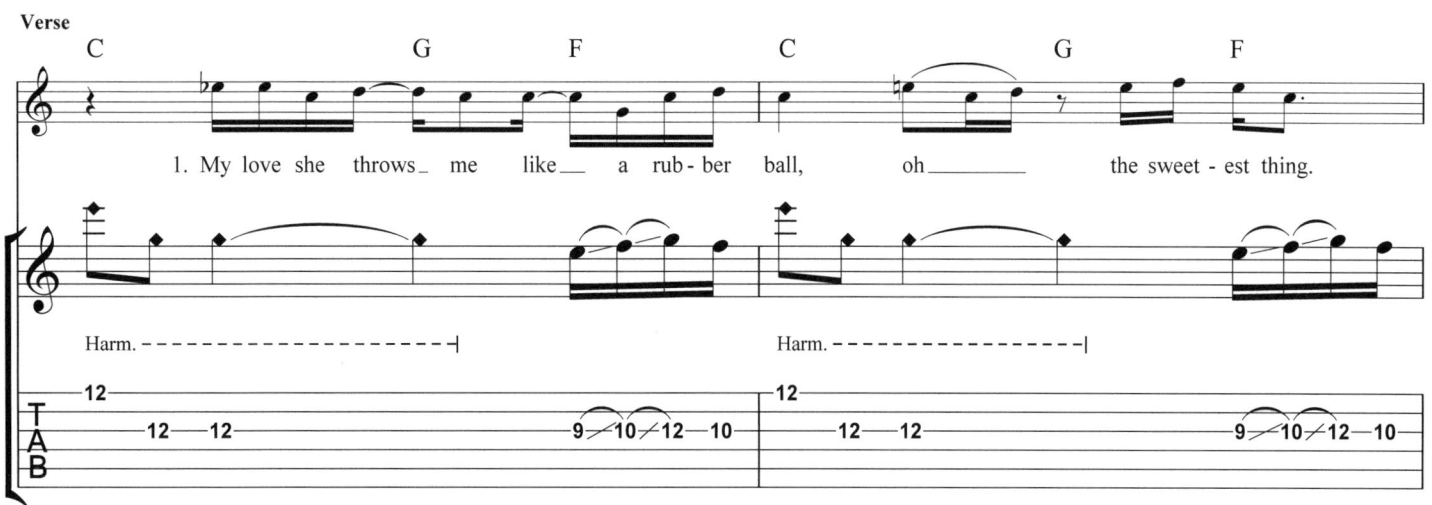

© Copyright 1987 Blue Mountain Music Limited/Mother Music Limited/
PolyGram International Music Publishing B.V.
All Rights Reserved. International Copyright Secured.

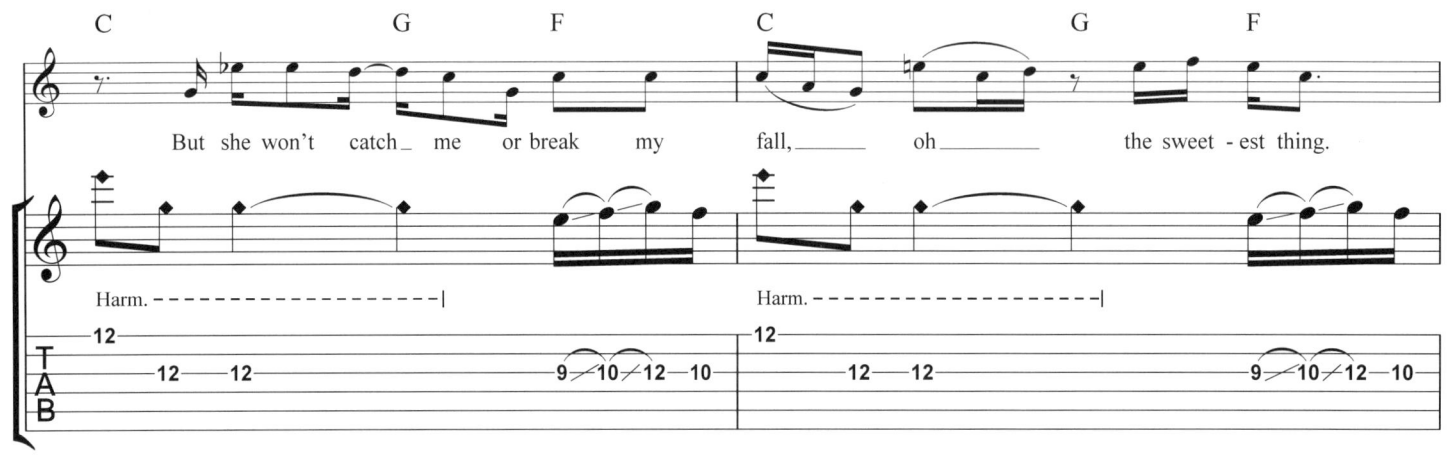
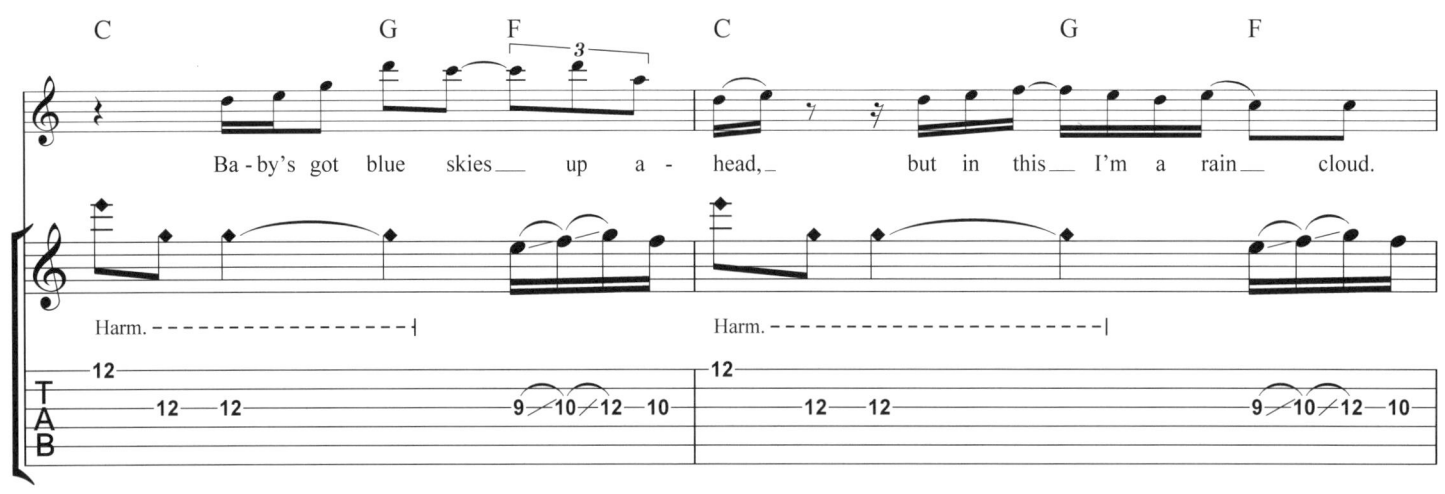

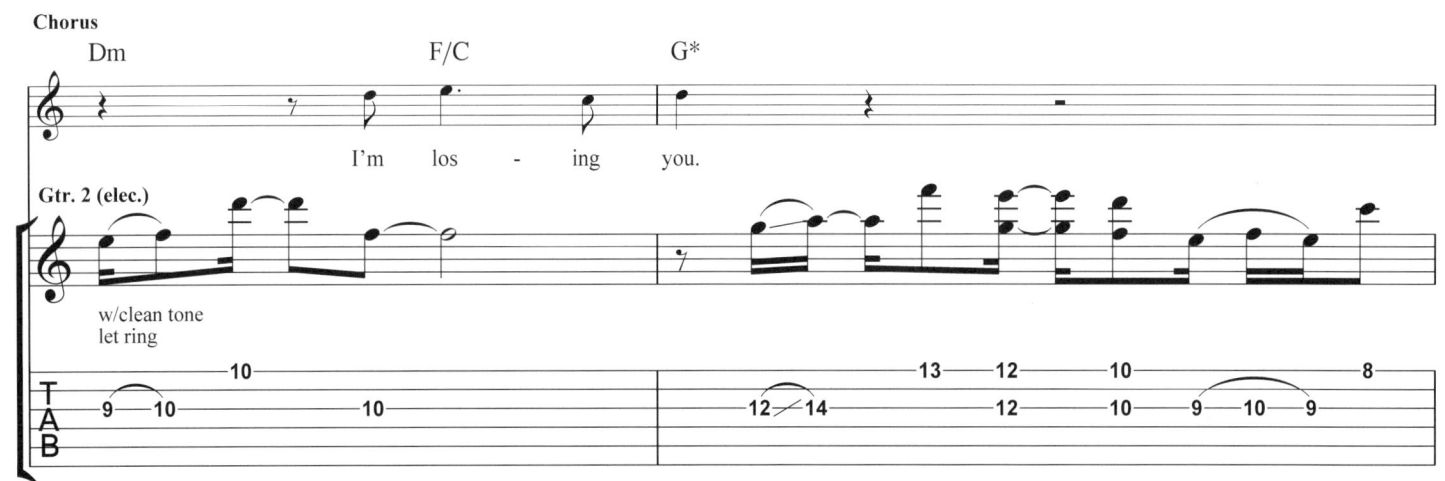

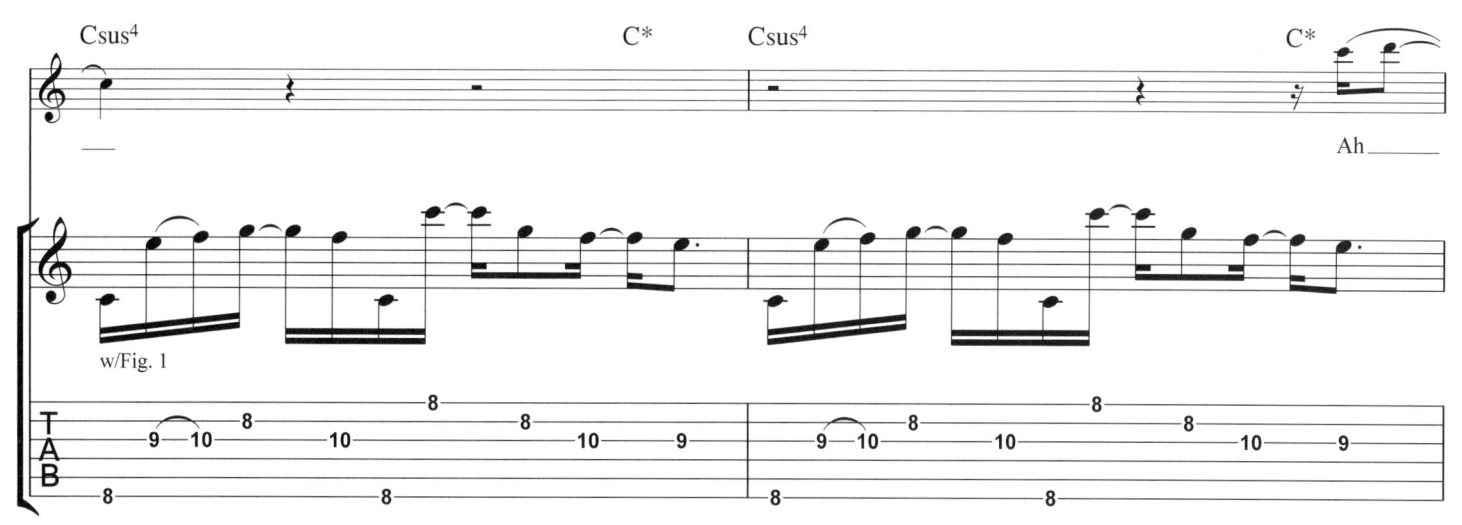

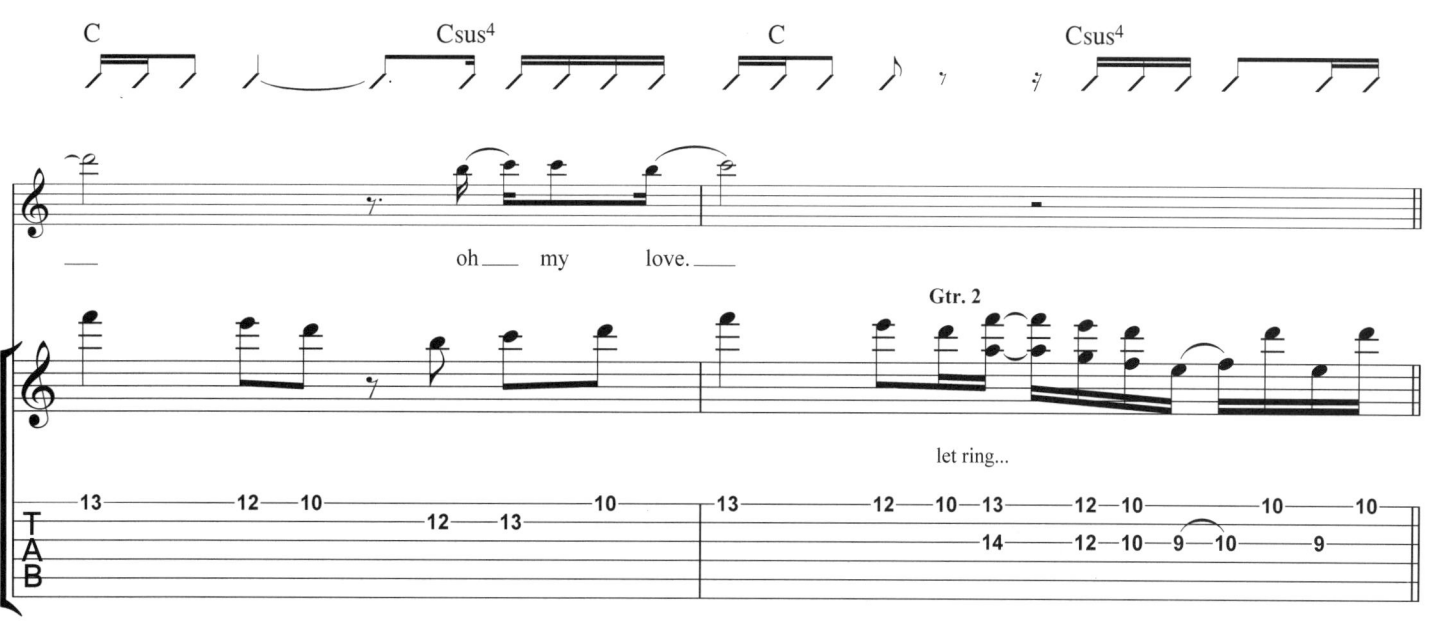

83

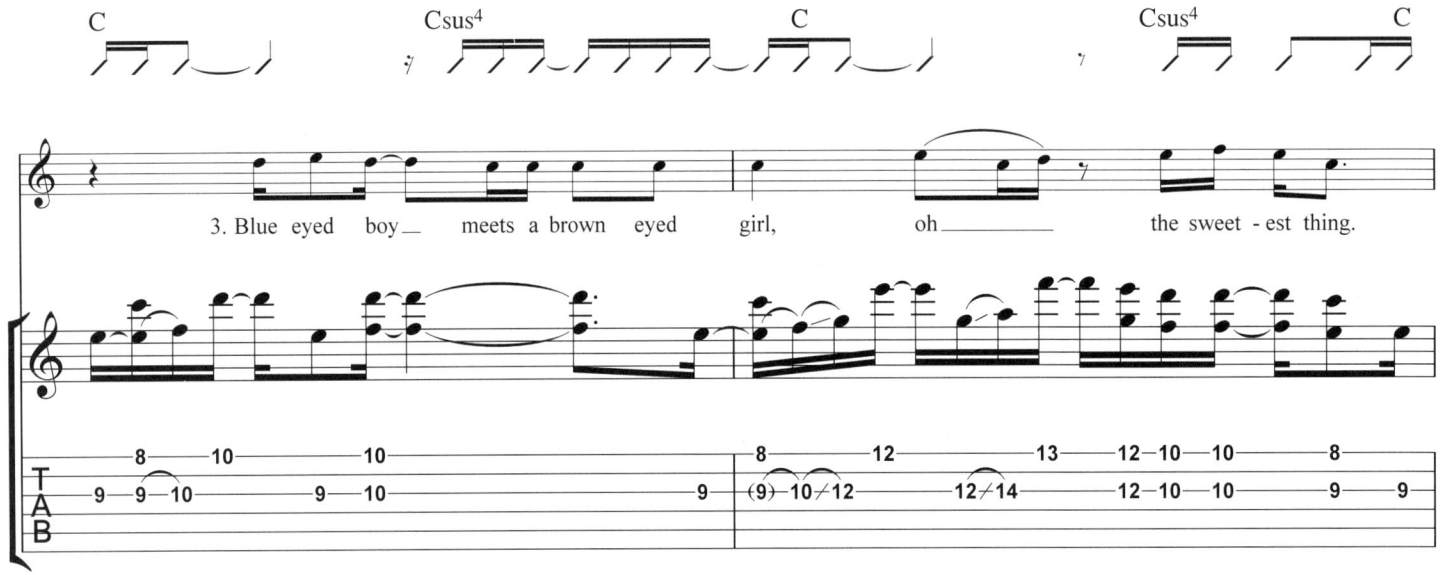
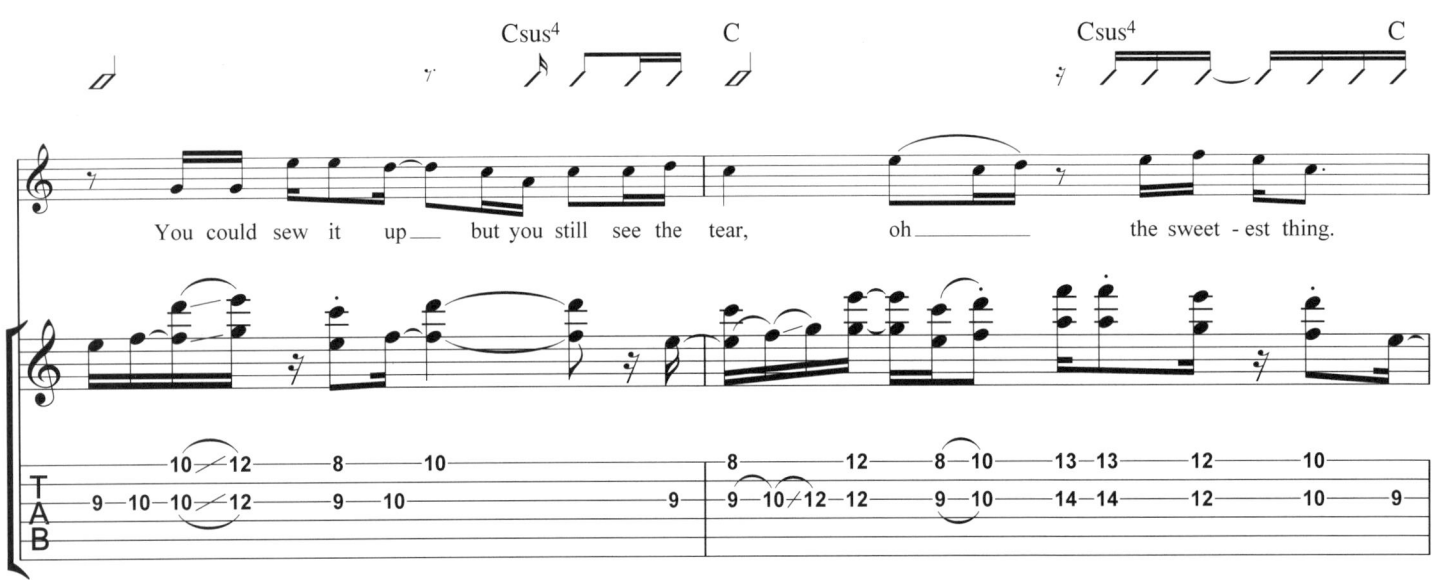
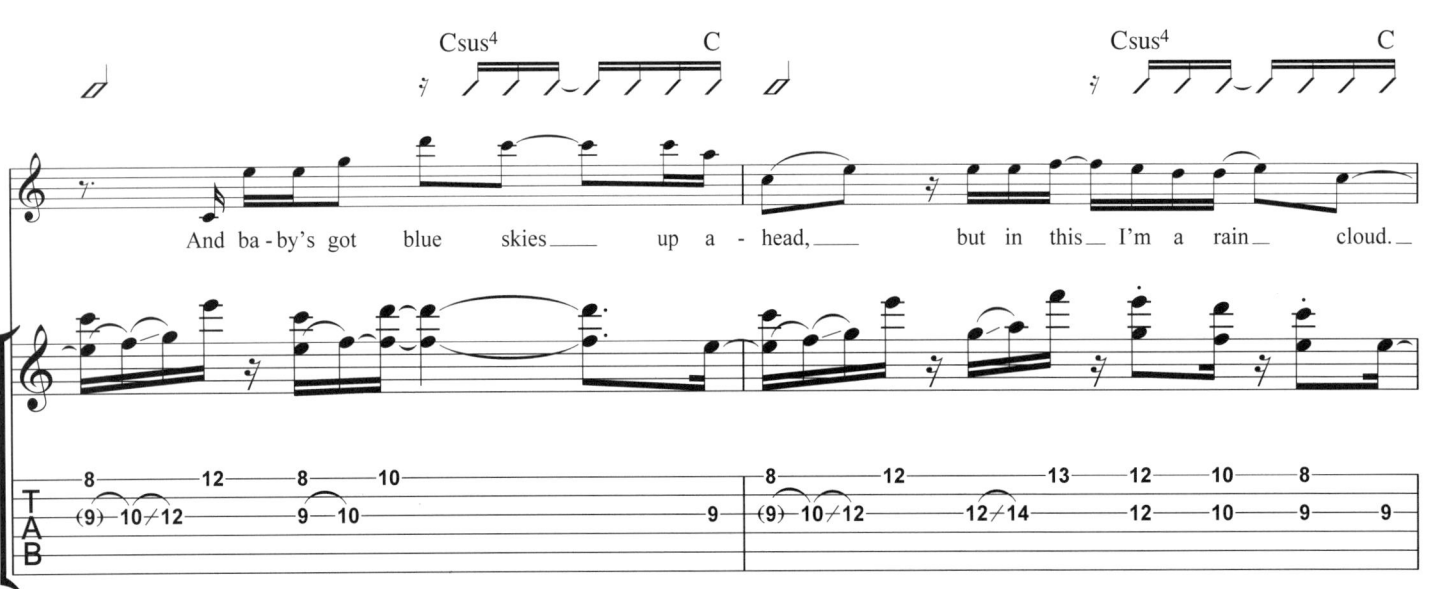

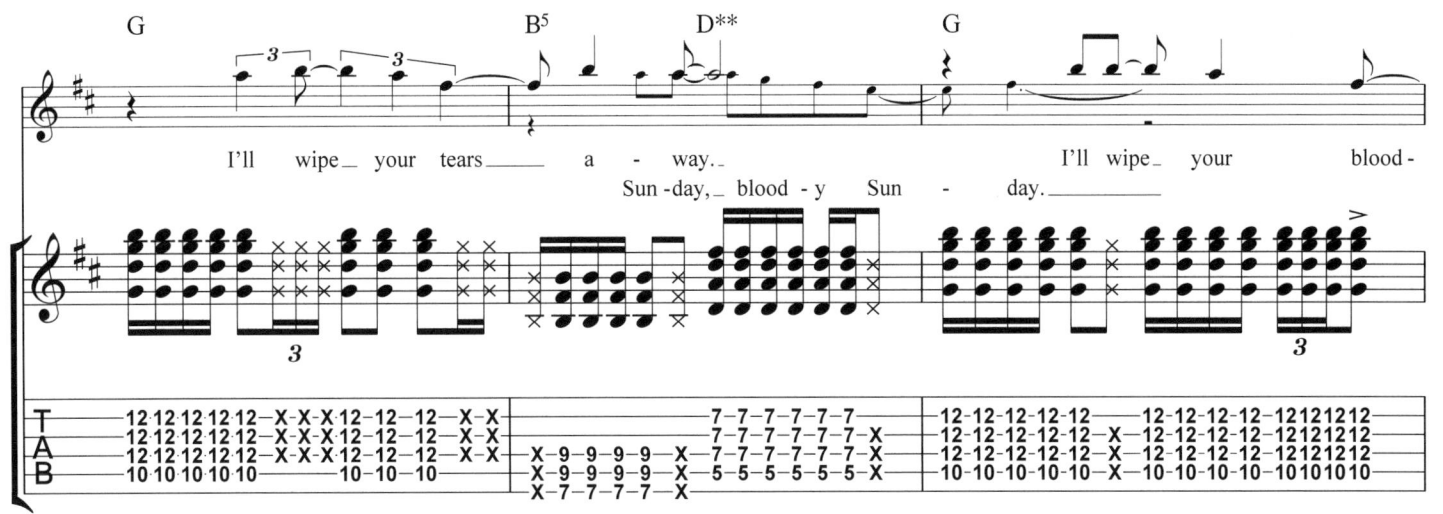
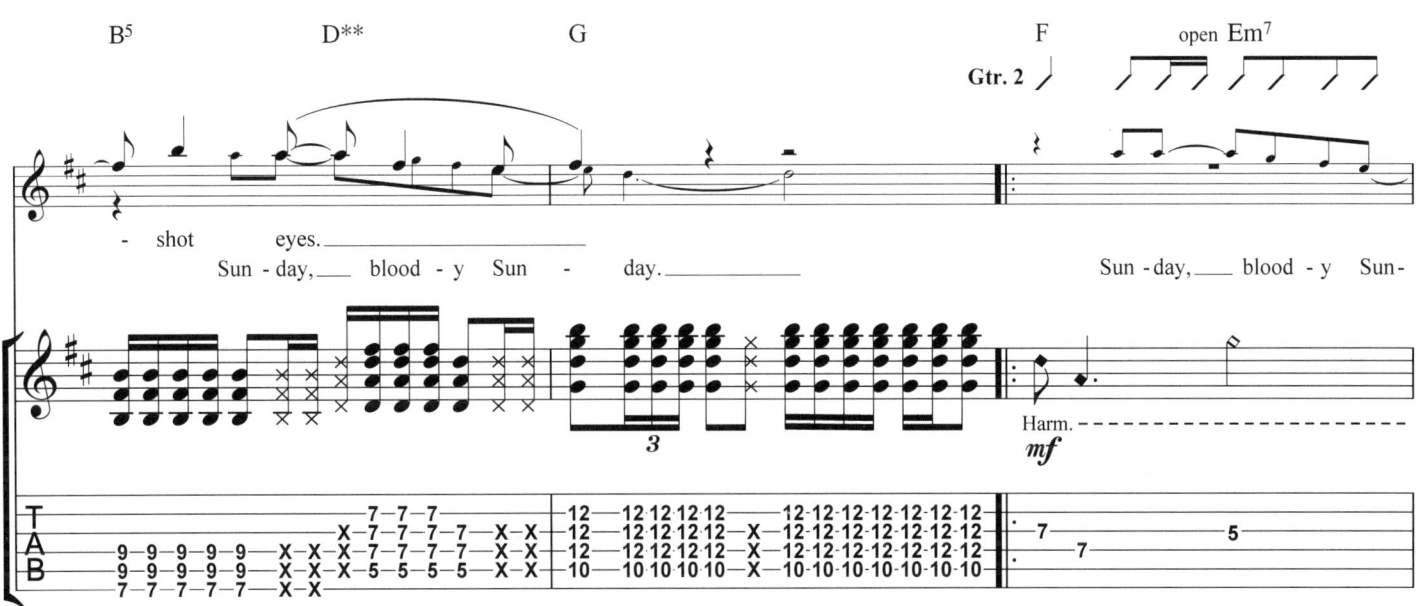

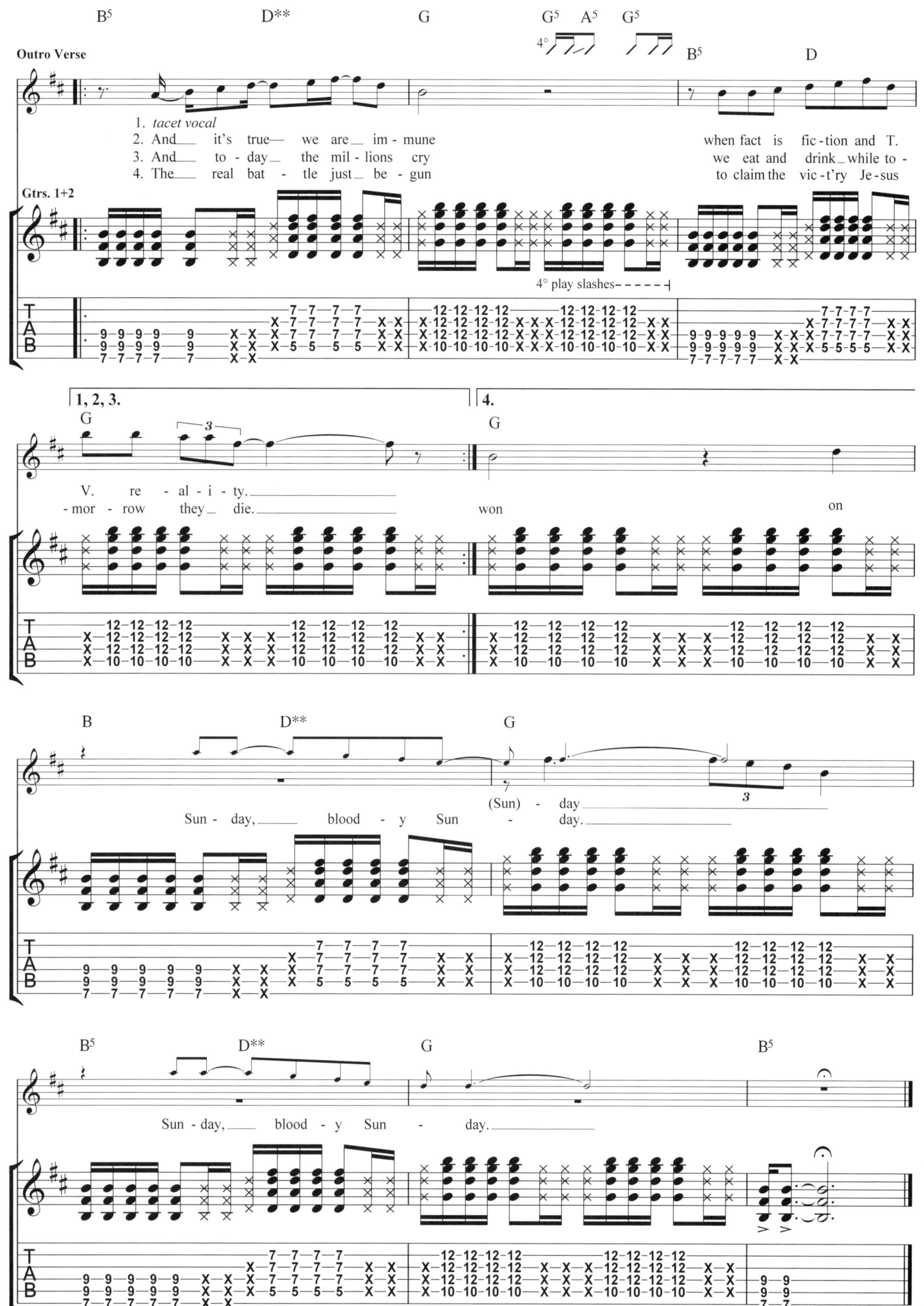

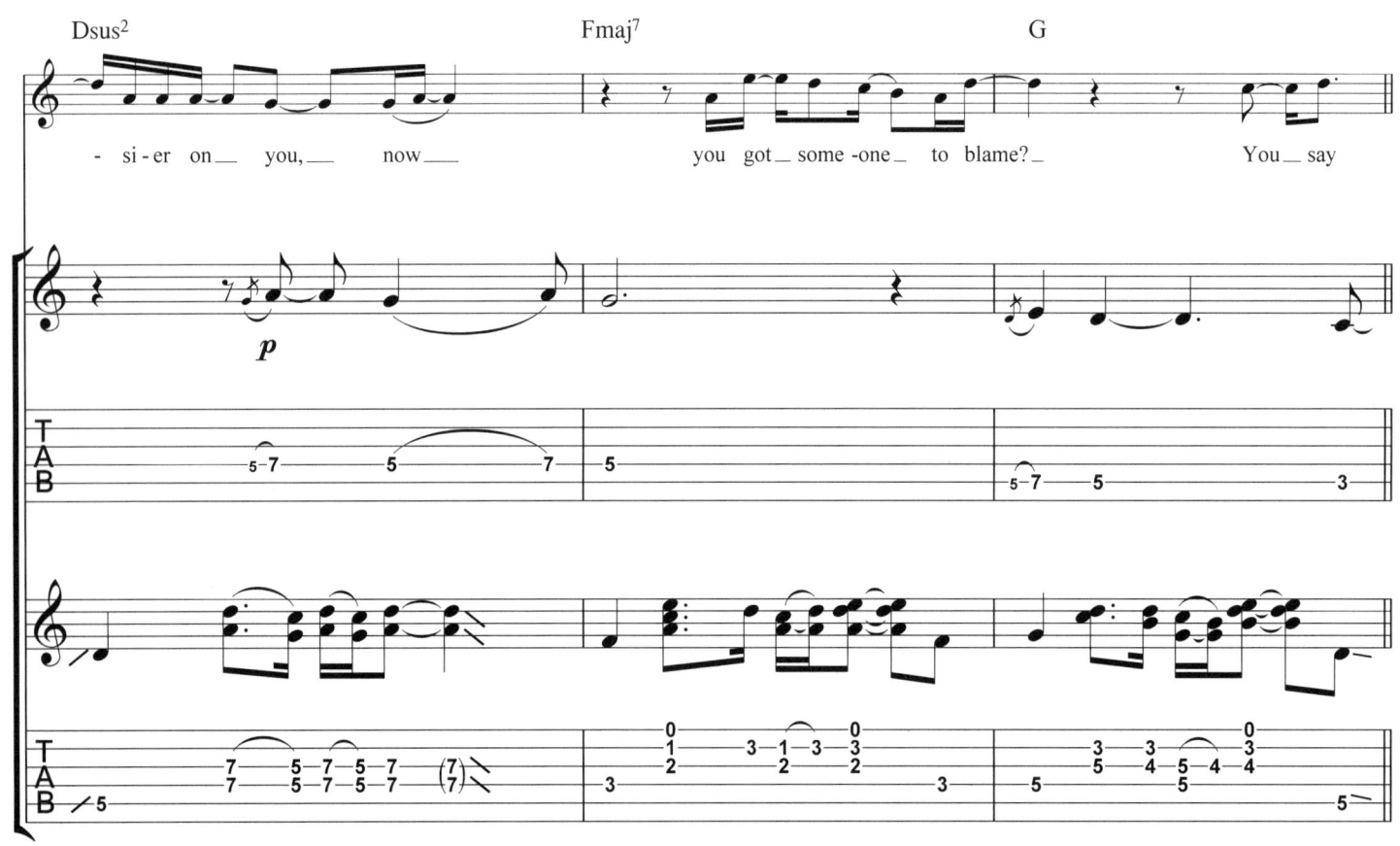

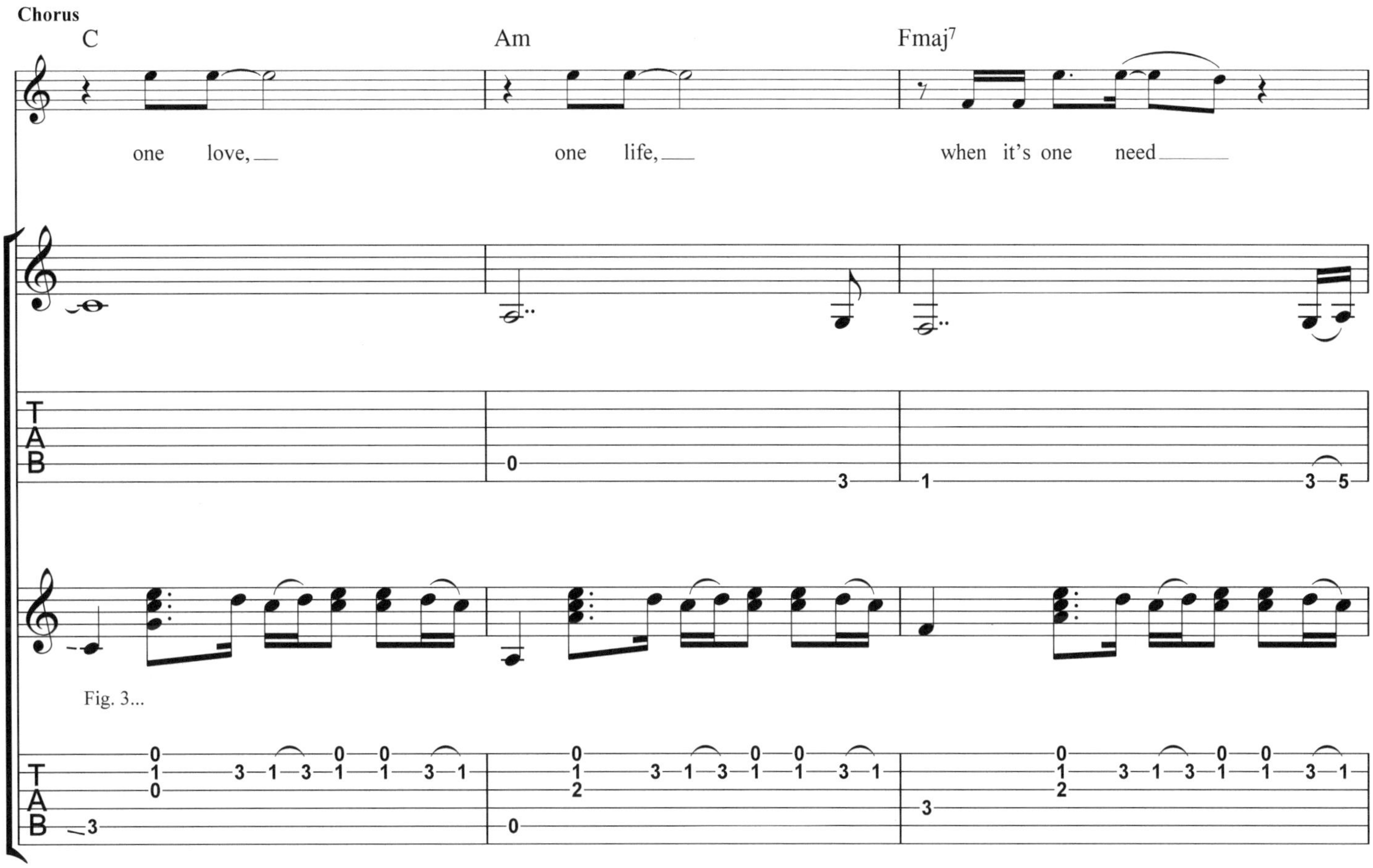
Chorus
C
Am
Fmaj7
one love,
one life,
when it's one need
Fig. 3...

C
Am
in the night.
One love,
we get to share it,
...Fig. 3 ends
Fig. 1

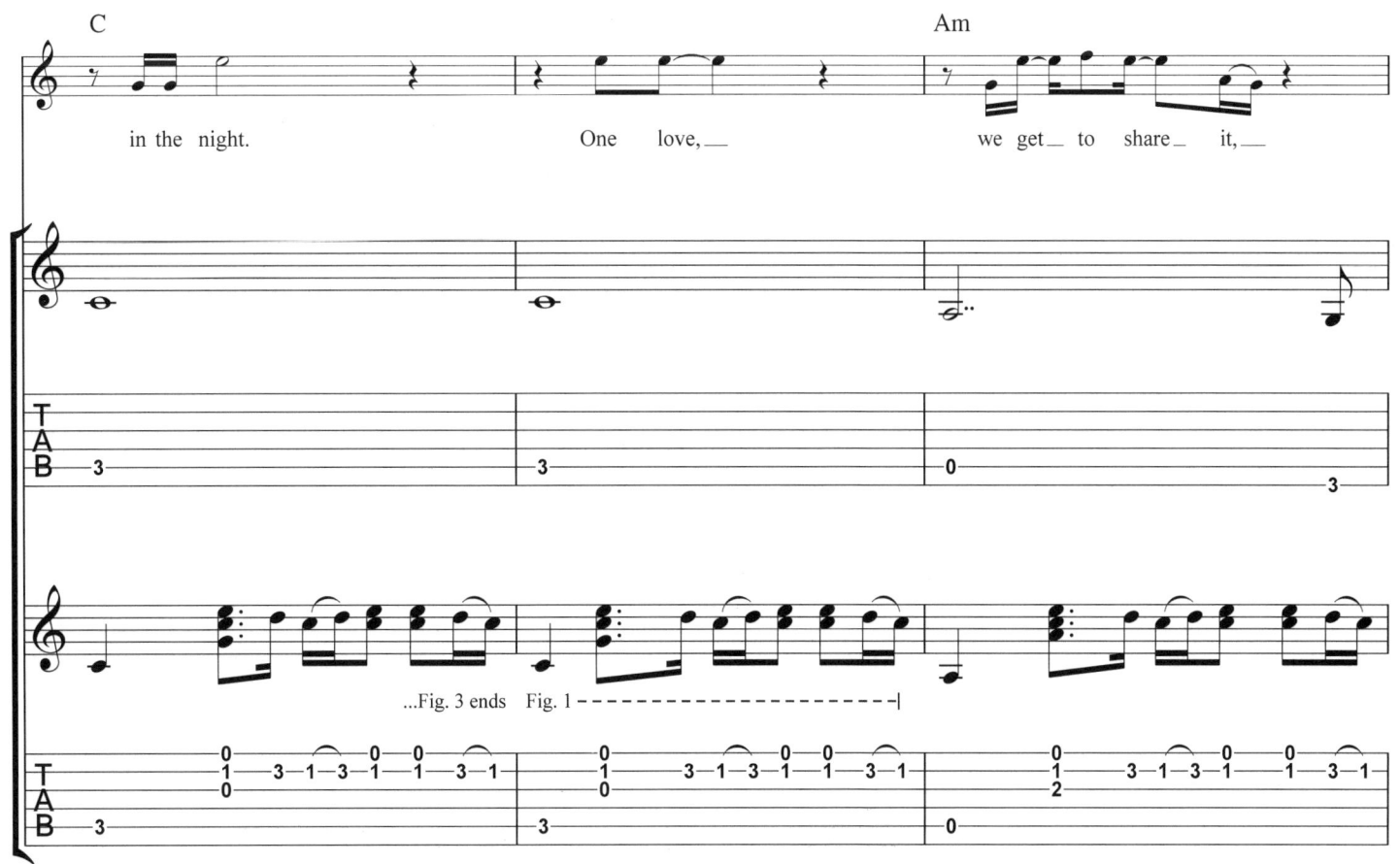

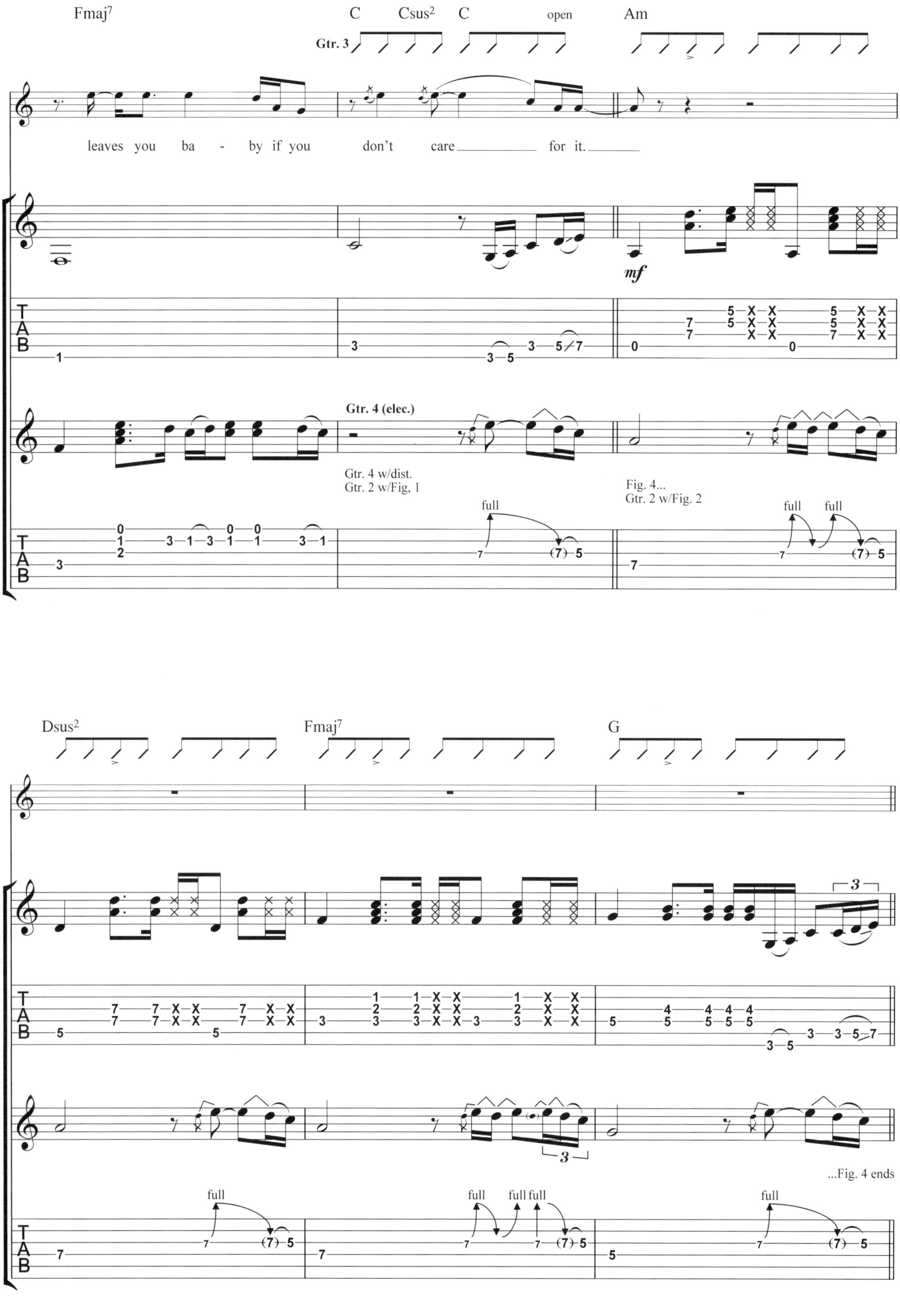
Fmaj7
C Csus2 C open Am
Gtr. 3
leaves you ba - by if you don't care for it.
mf
Gtr. 4 (elec.)
Gtr. 4 w/dist.
Gtr. 2 w/Fig, 1
Fig. 4...
Gtr. 2 w/Fig. 2
full
Dsus2
Fmaj7
G
...Fig. 4 ends

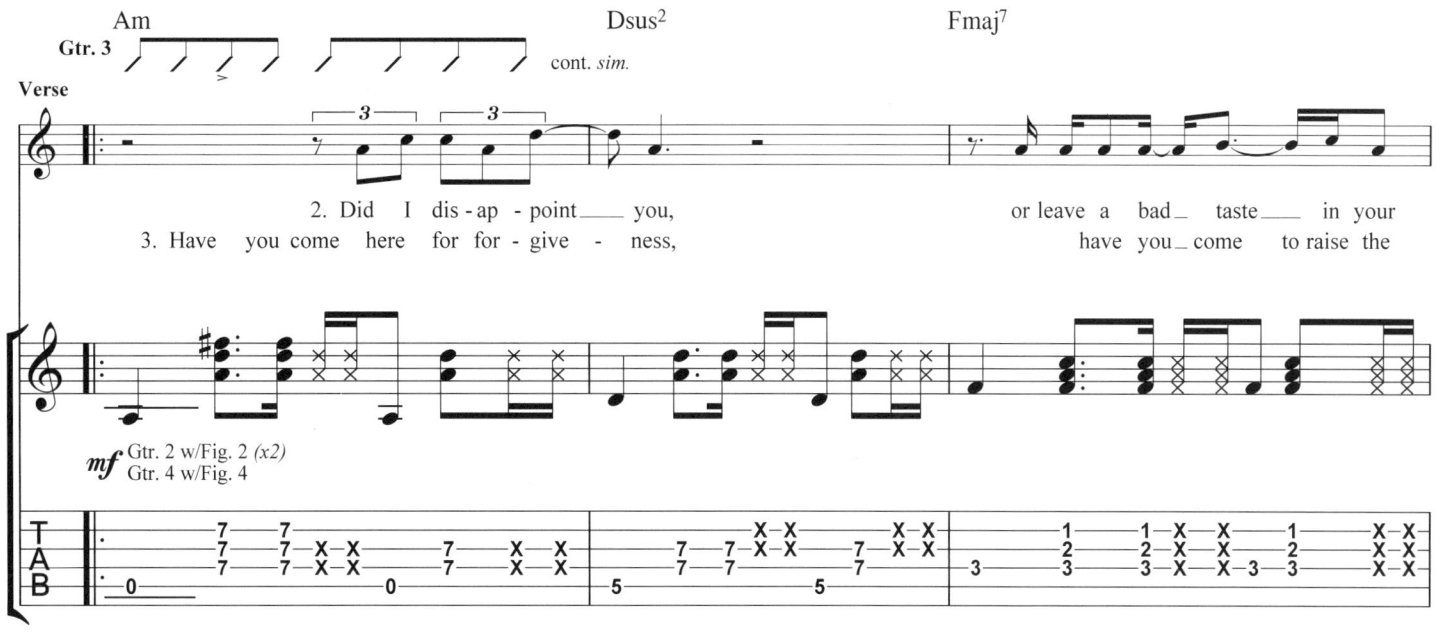

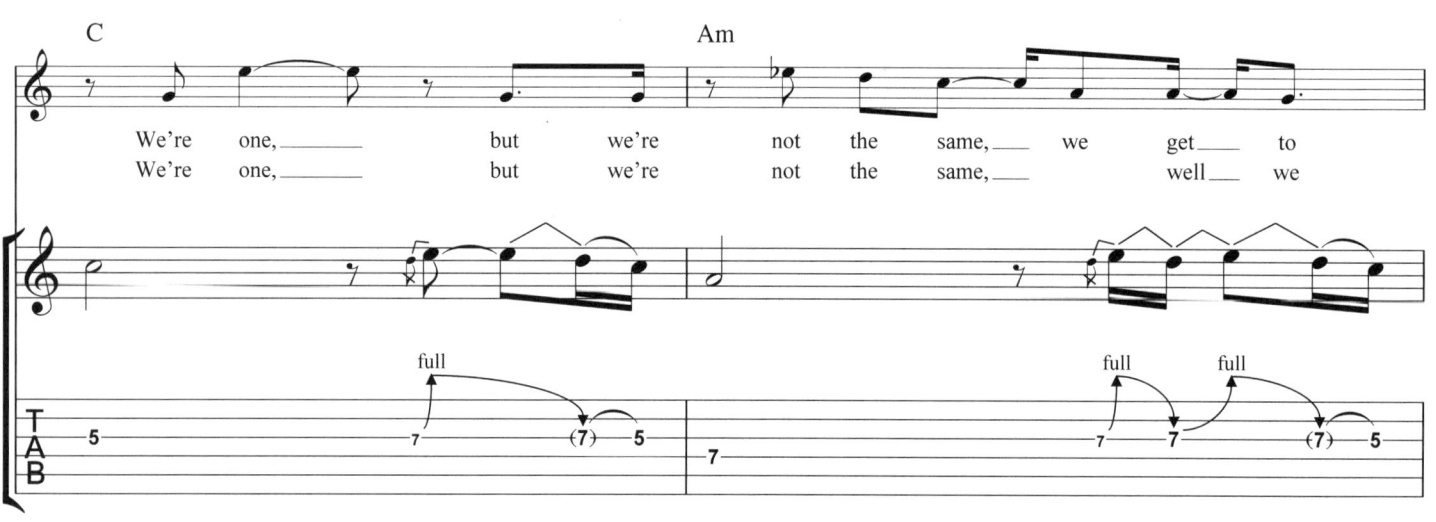
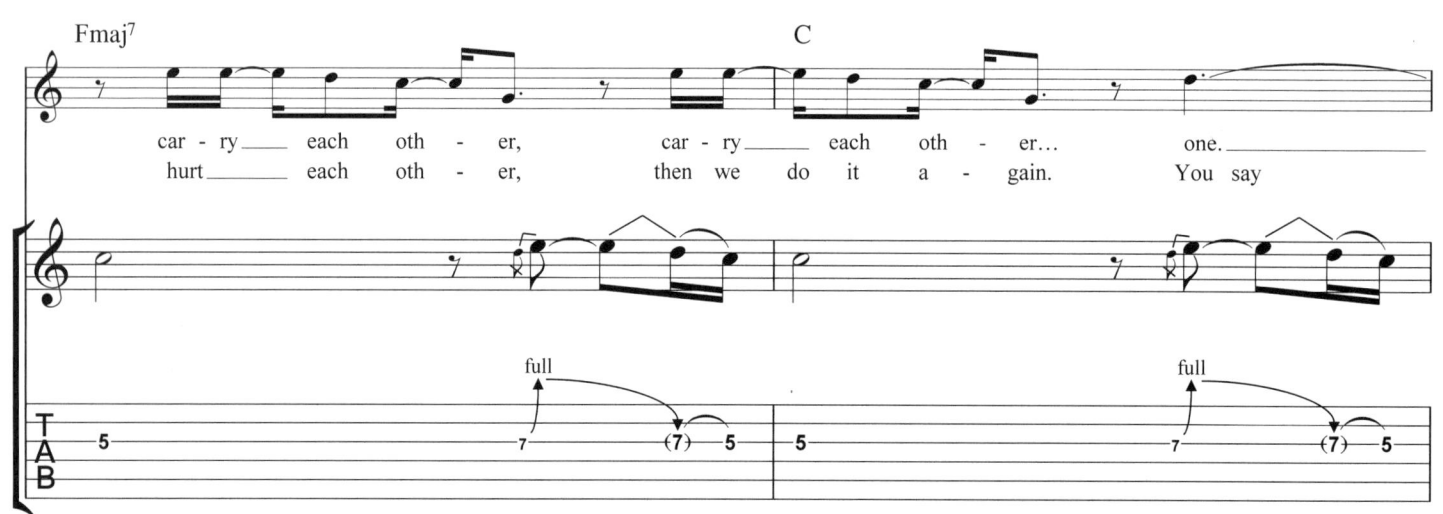

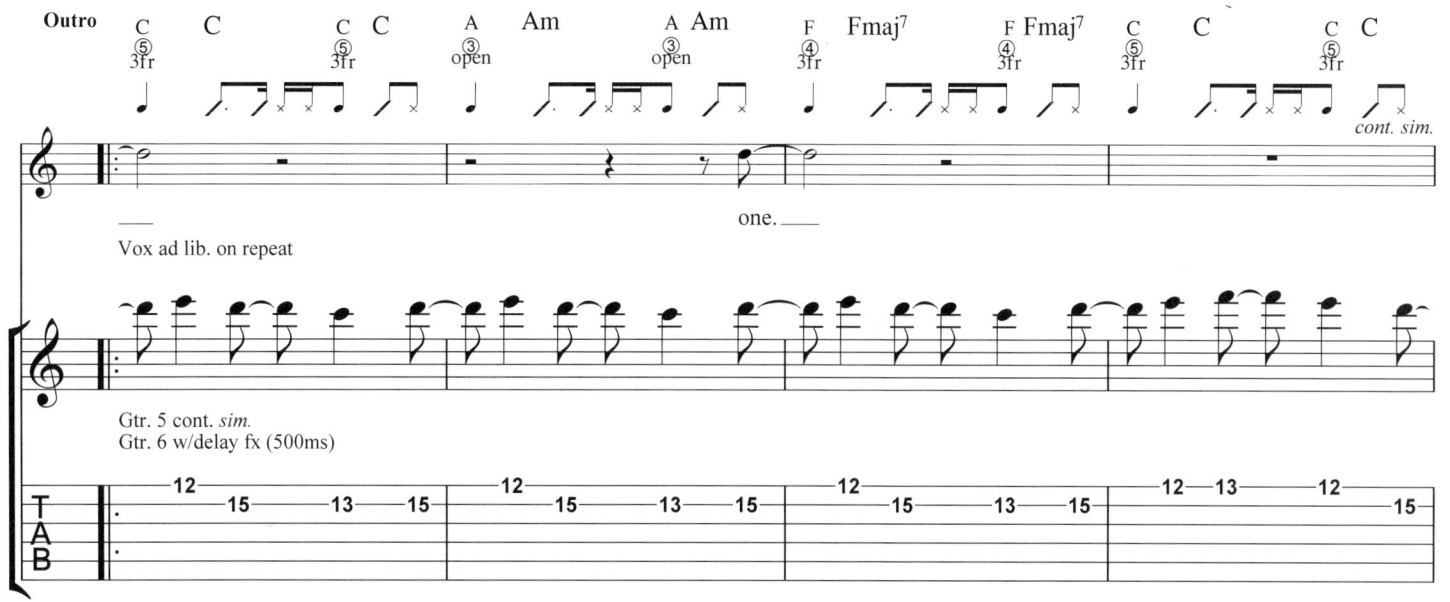
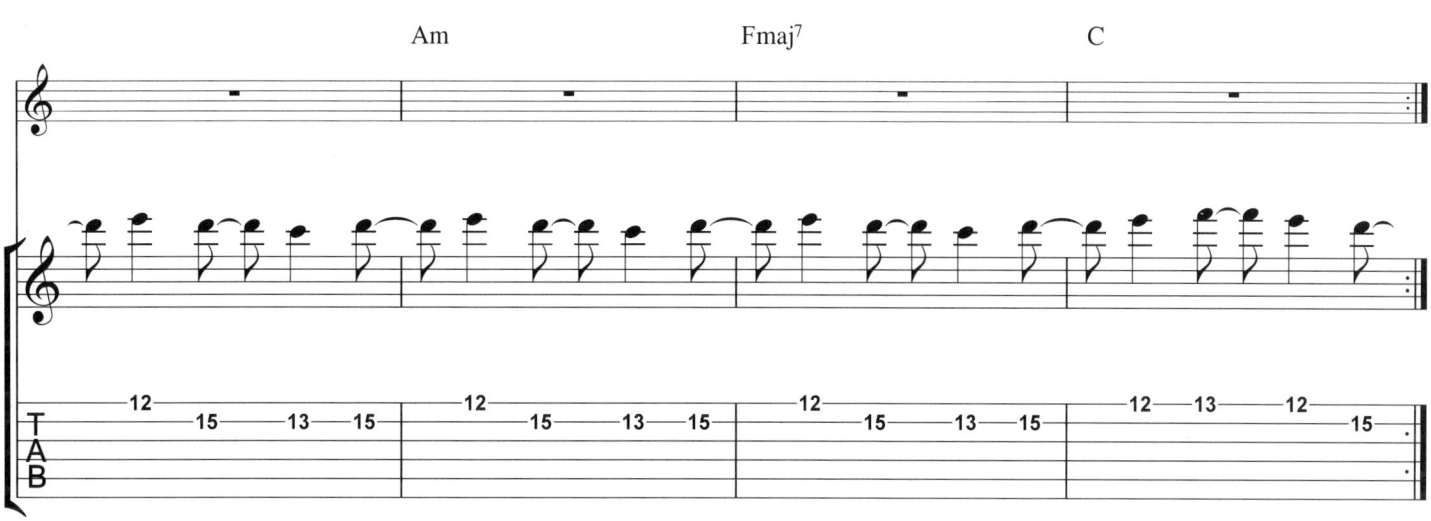
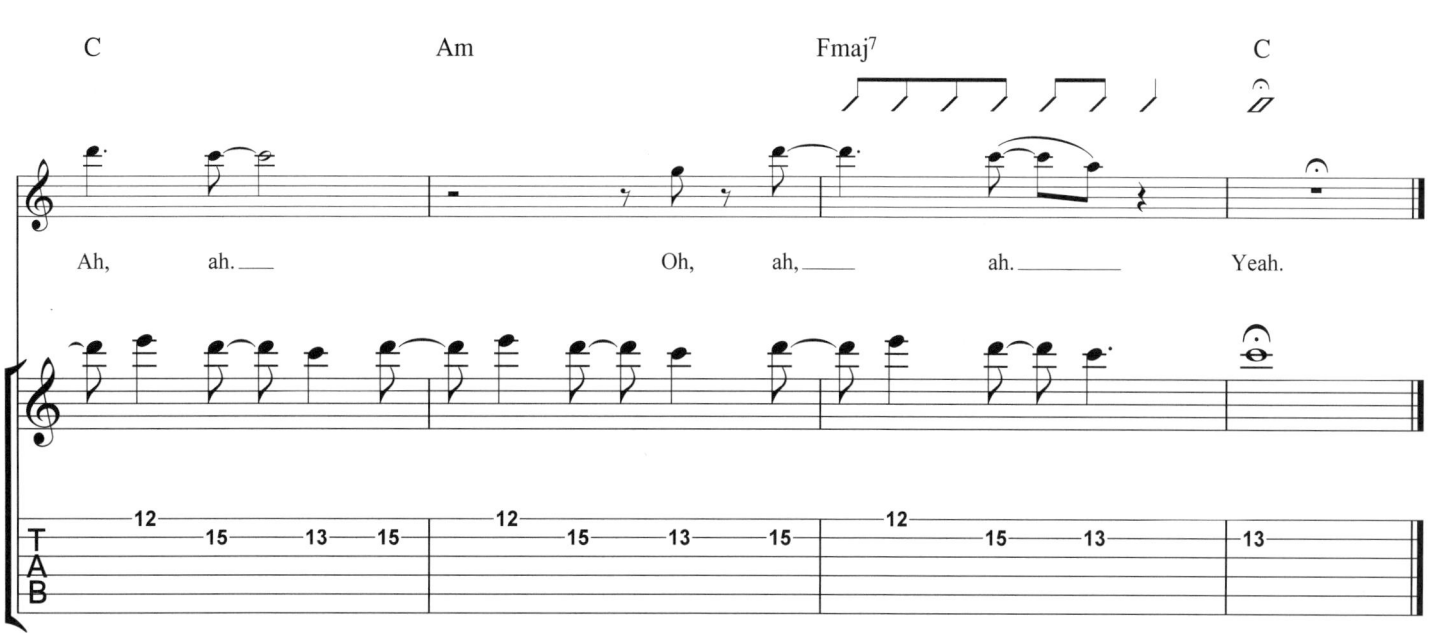

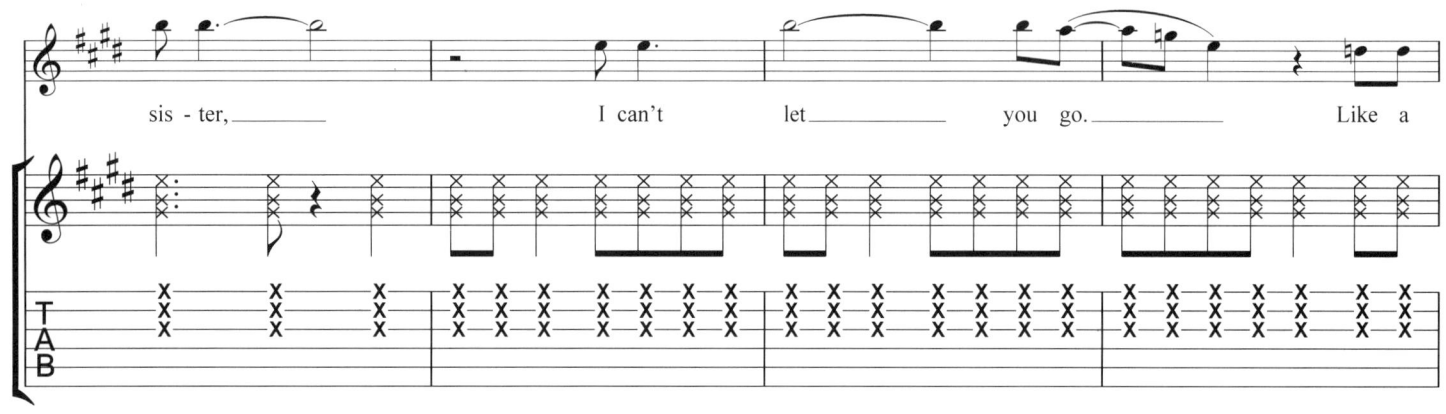
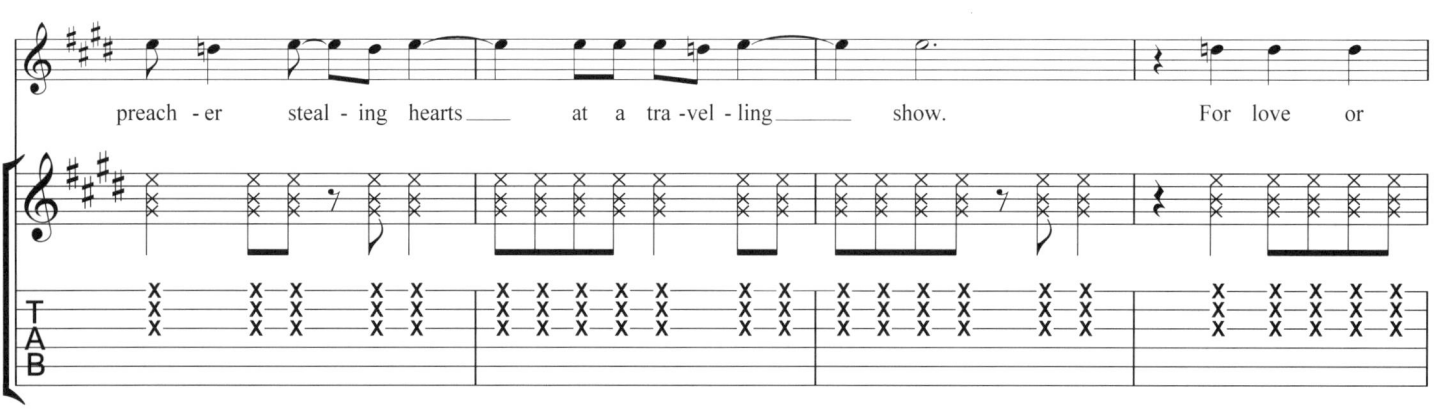
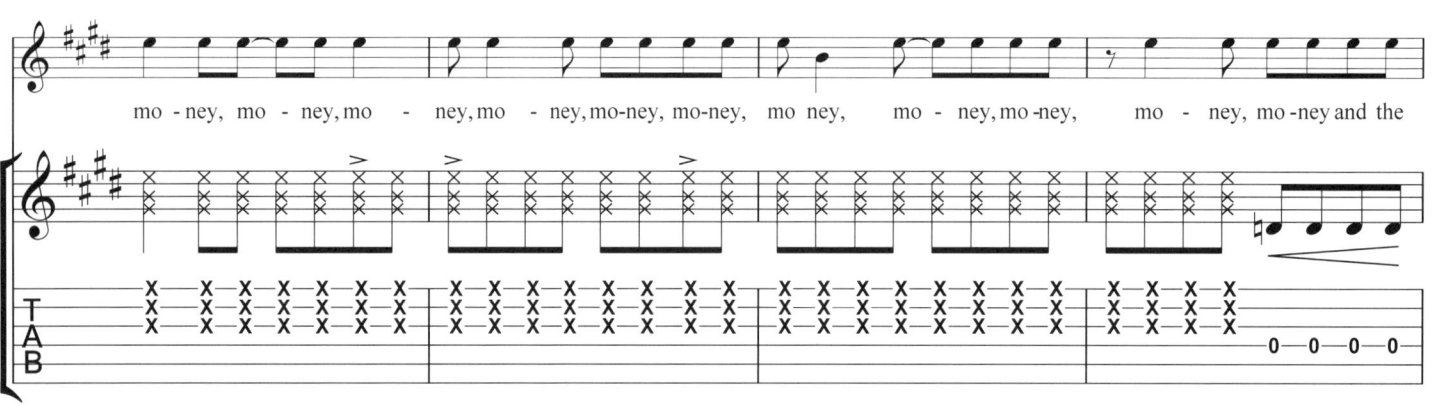
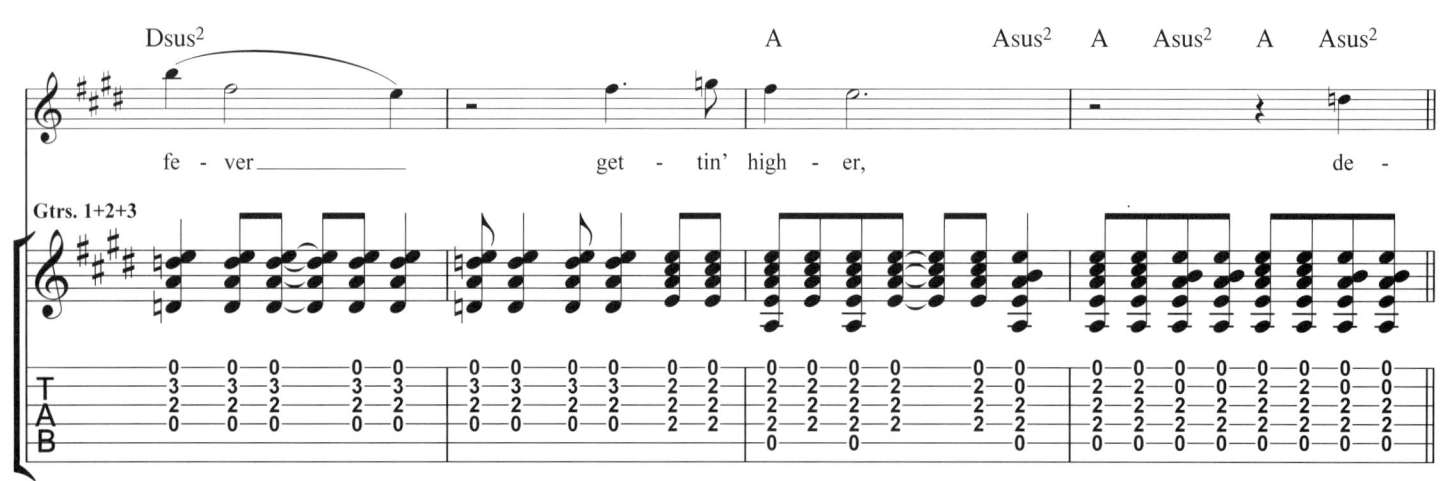

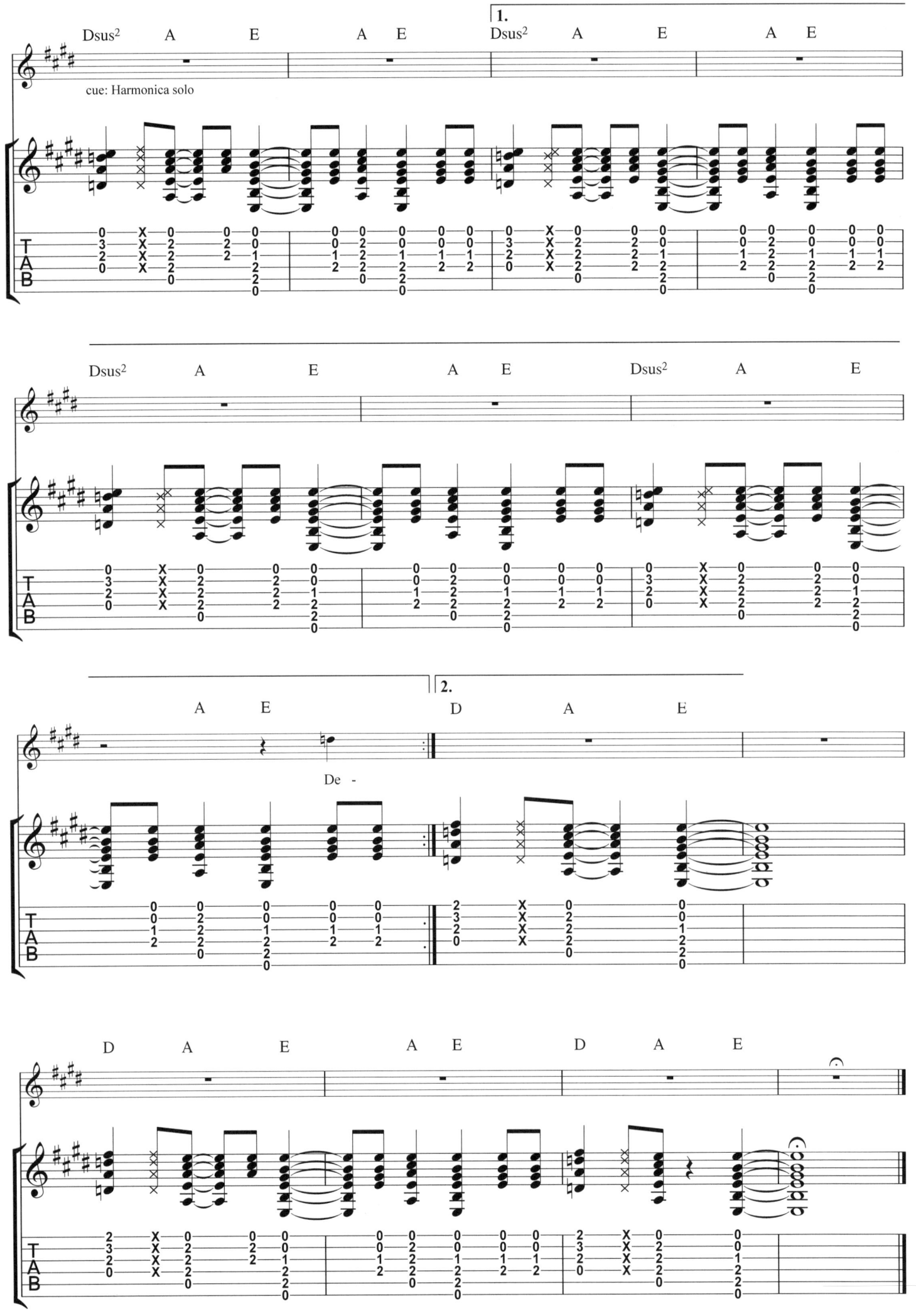

113

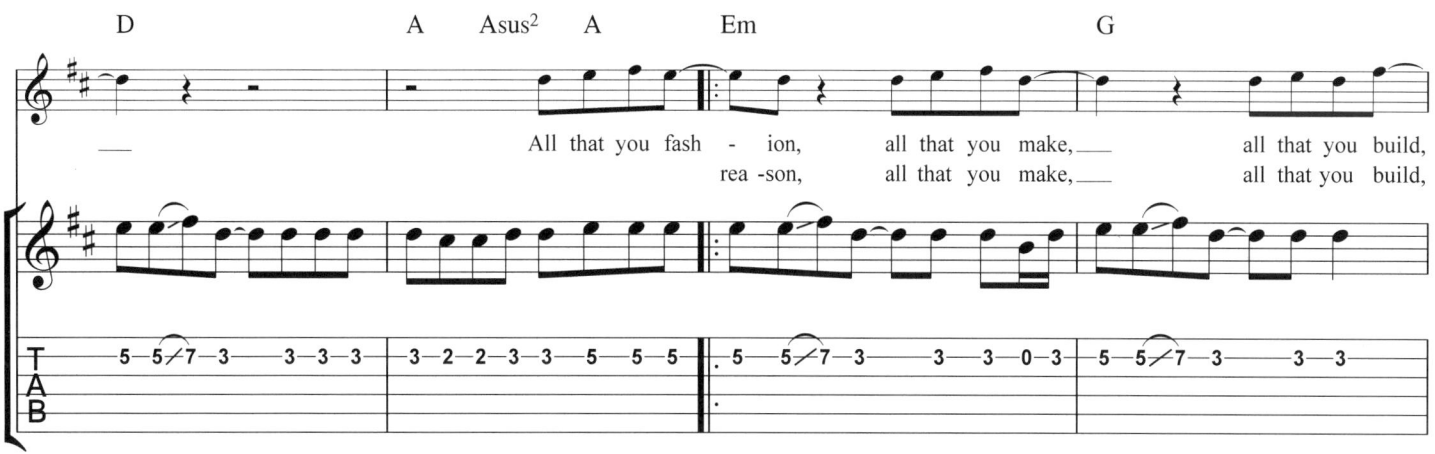
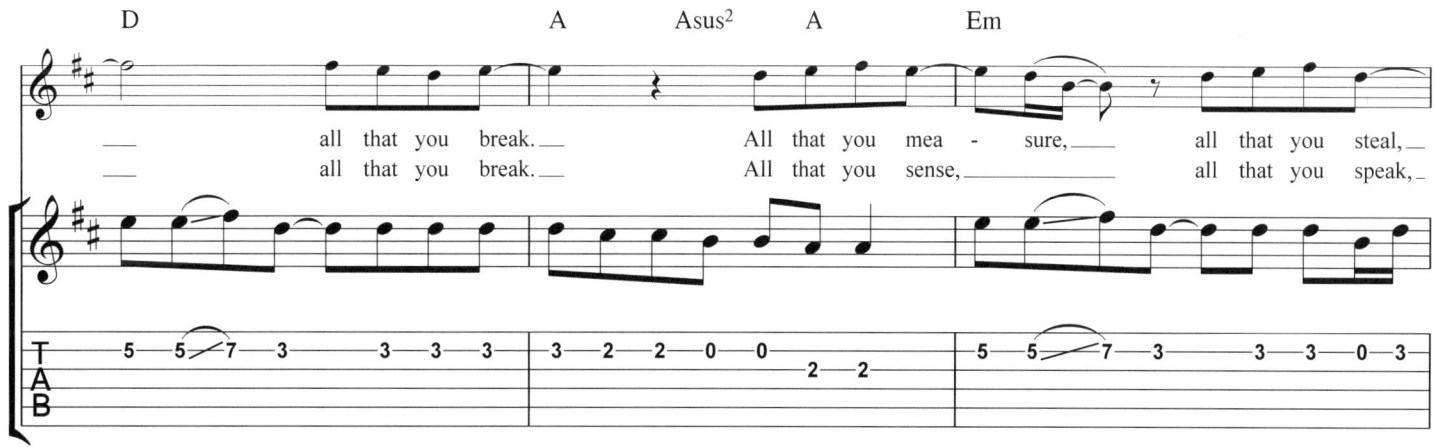
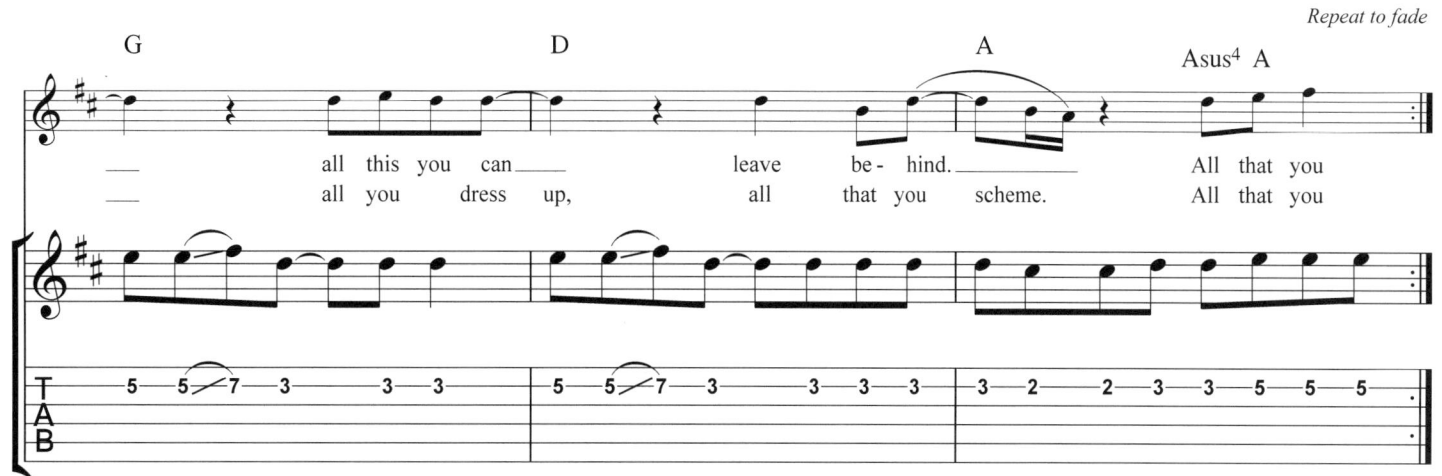

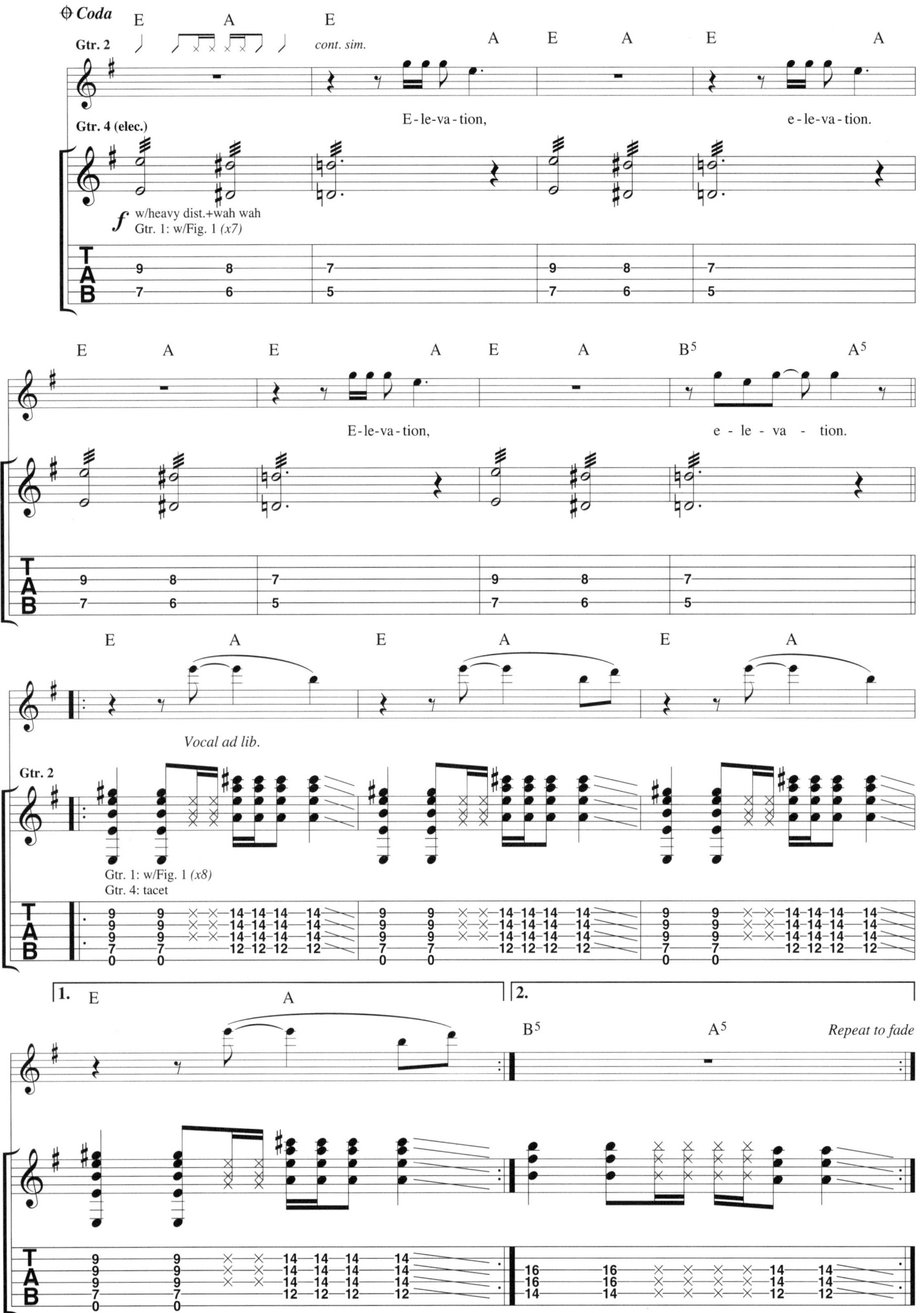

Sometimes You Can't Make It On Your Own

Words by Bono
Music by U2

Verse
A
Asus4
A
Asus4
A
fight
you
all the time,
Gtr. 2 (elec.) (1°)
let ring...
w/clean tone
Fig. 2
Gtr. 4 (elec.) (2°)
Gtr. 4 w/octivider (8va)
1°+2° Gtr. 1 w/Fig. 1 (x4)
Gtr. 3 (2°)
Gtr. 2 (2°)
Fig. 3
A/G
Asus4/G
A/G
Asus4/G
A/G
F#m7
F#m7#5
think you've got the stuff,
you're tell - ing me and
you and I,
that's al - right.
1° Gtr. 1 w/Fig. 2 (x7)
2° Gtrs. 2+3 w/Fig. 3 (x7)

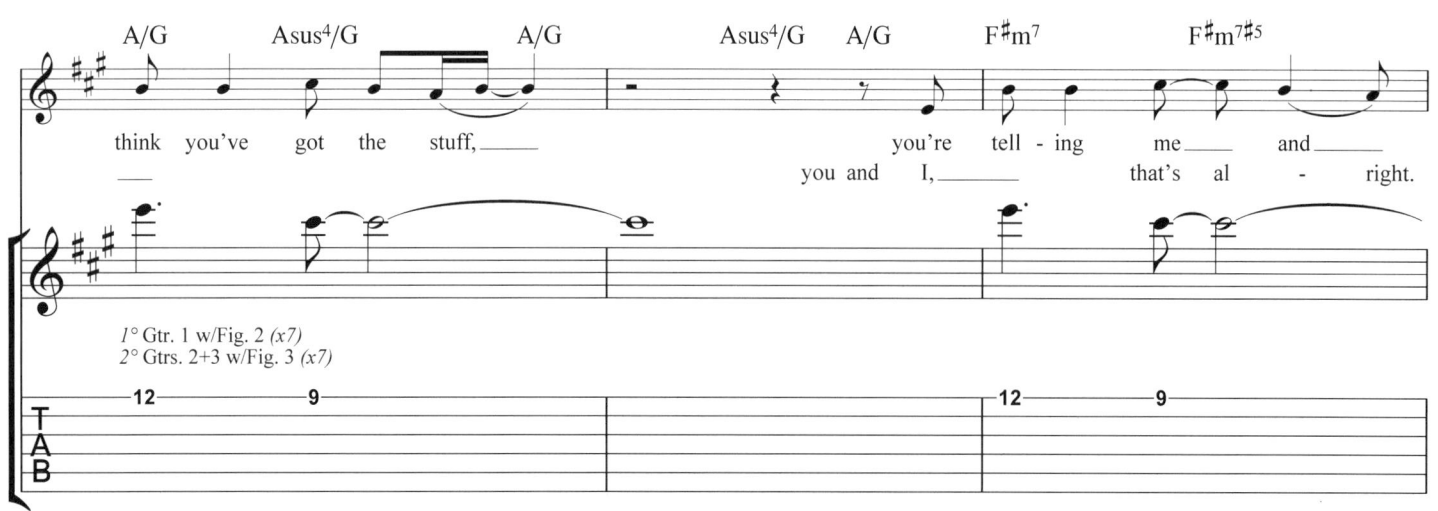

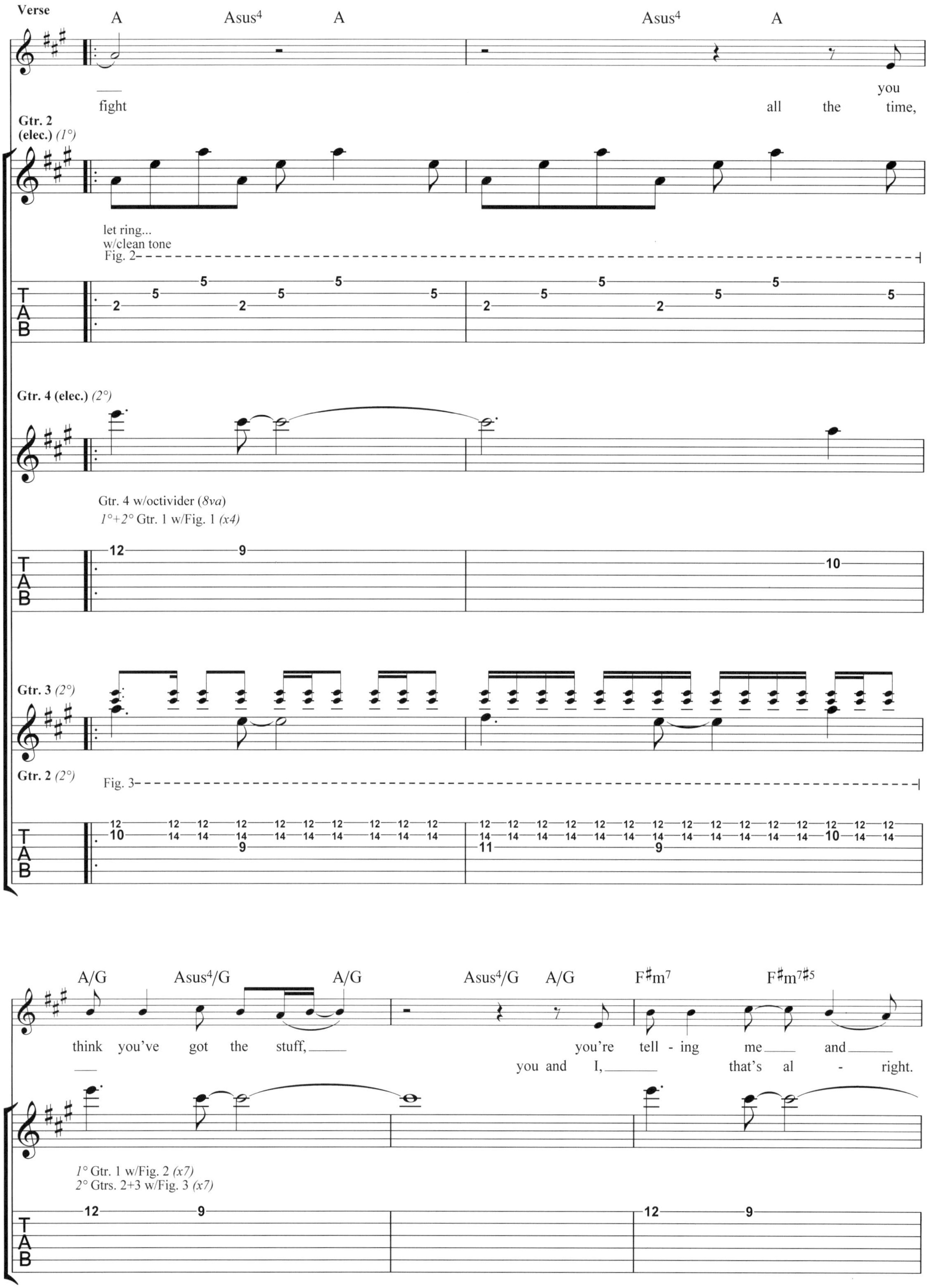

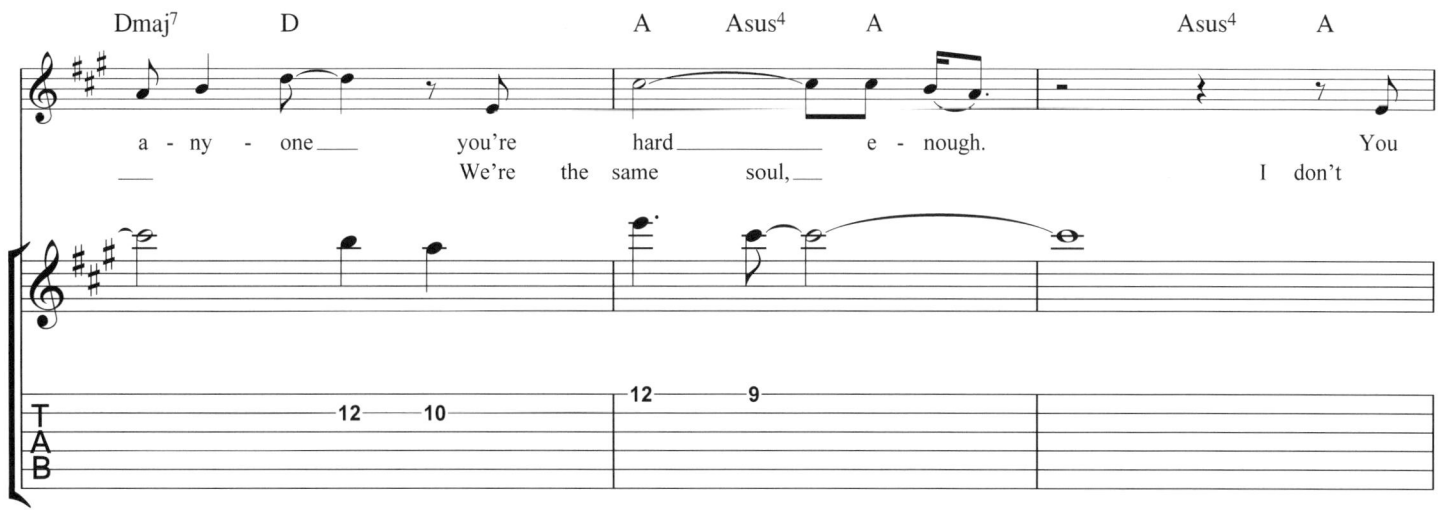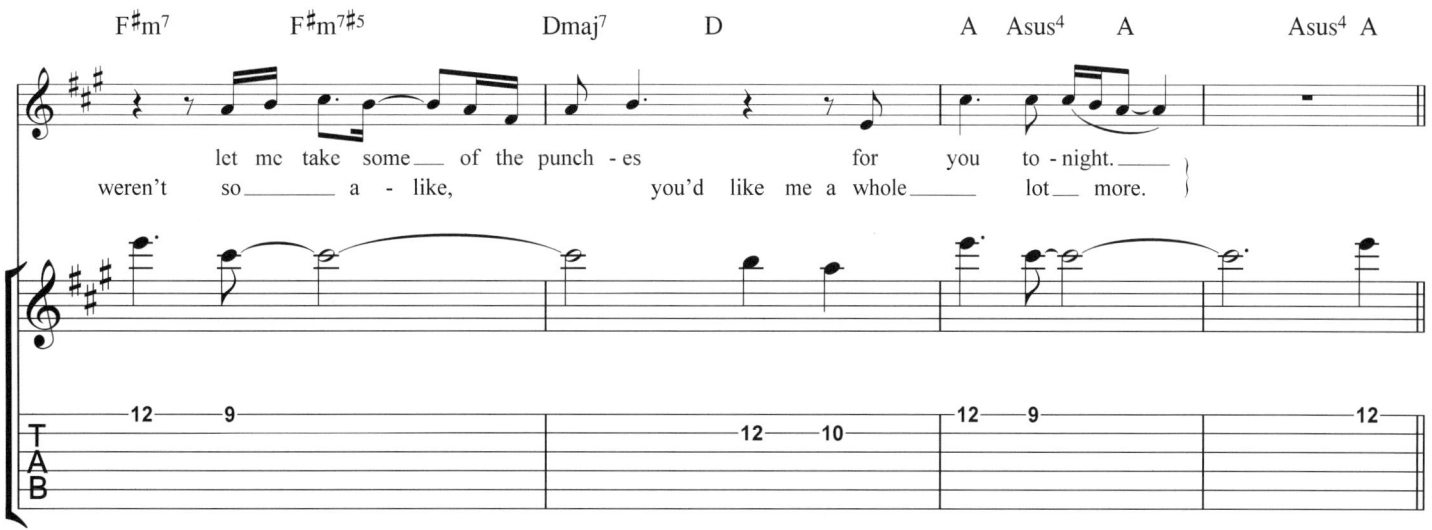

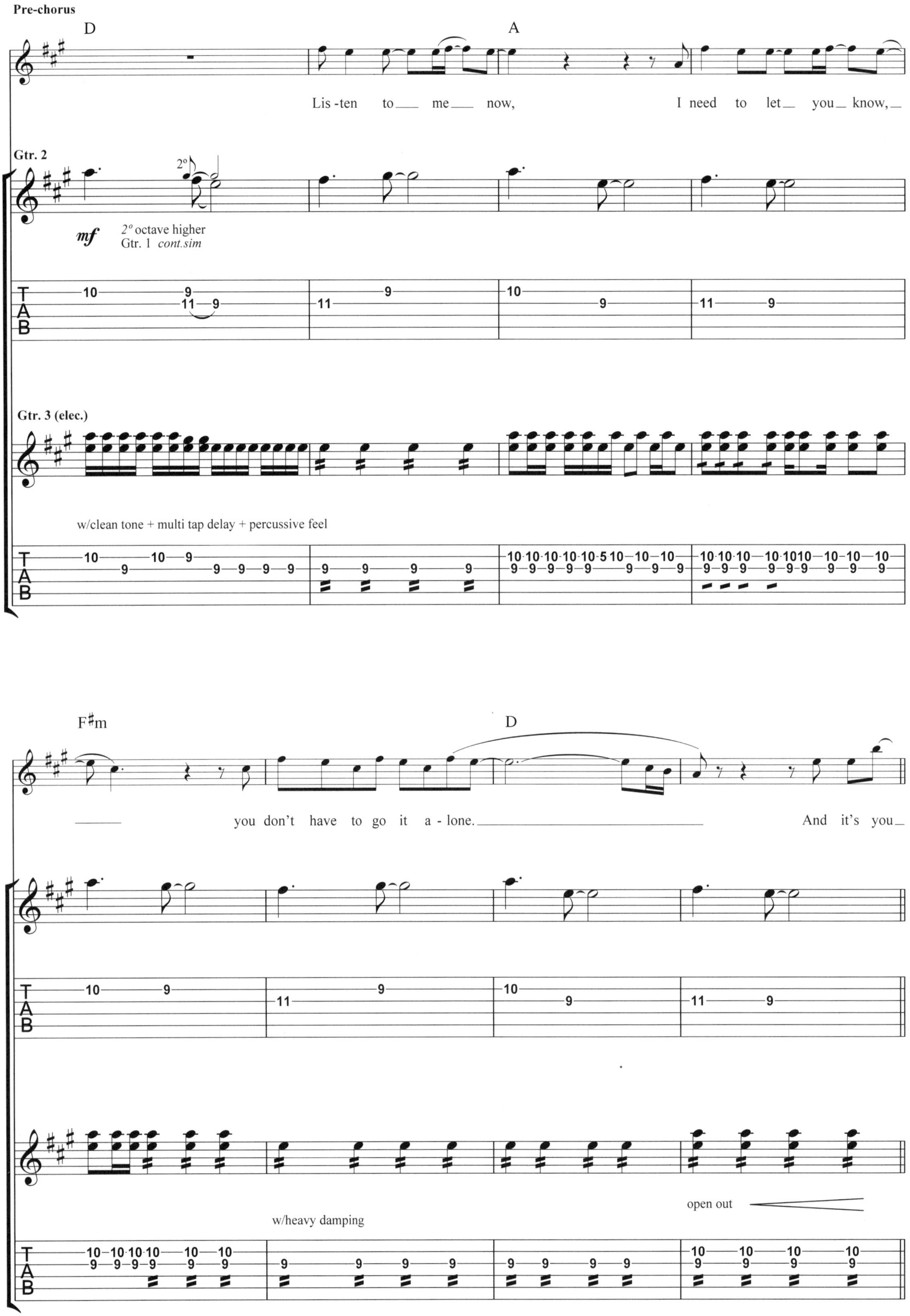
Pre-chorus
D
A
Lis-ten to me now, I need to let you know,
Gtr. 2
mf
2º octave higher
Gtr. 1 cont.sim
Gtr. 3 (elec.)
w/clean tone + multi tap delay + percussive feel
F♯m
D
you don't have to go it a-lone. And it's you
w/heavy damping
open out

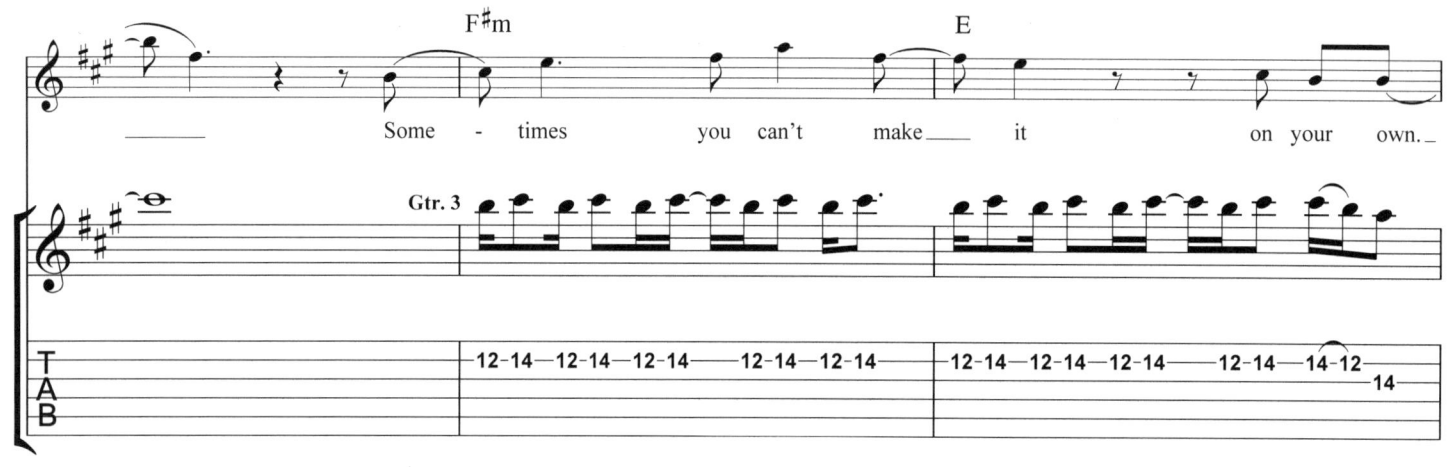
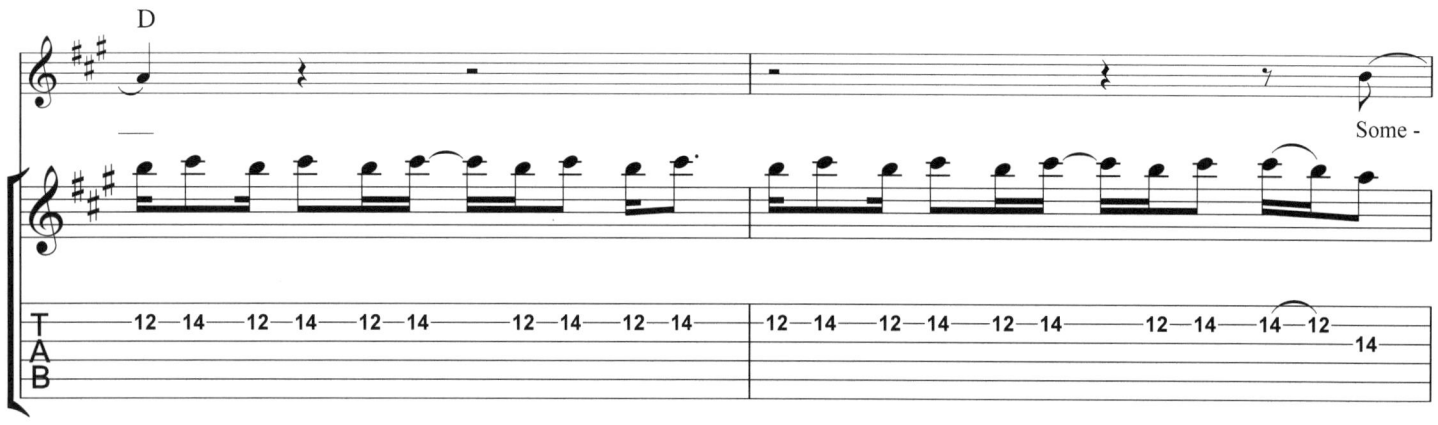
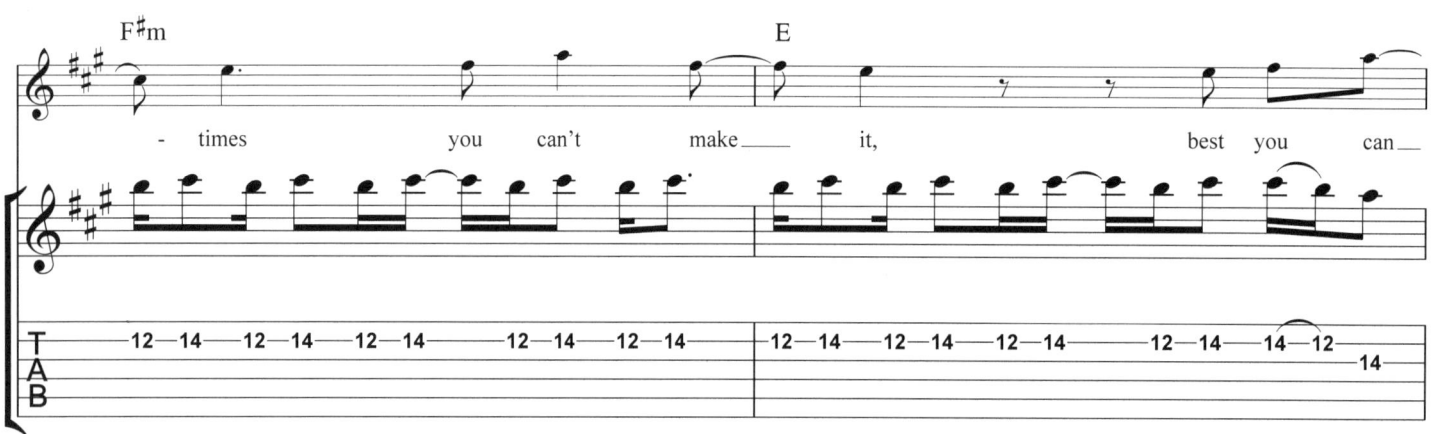
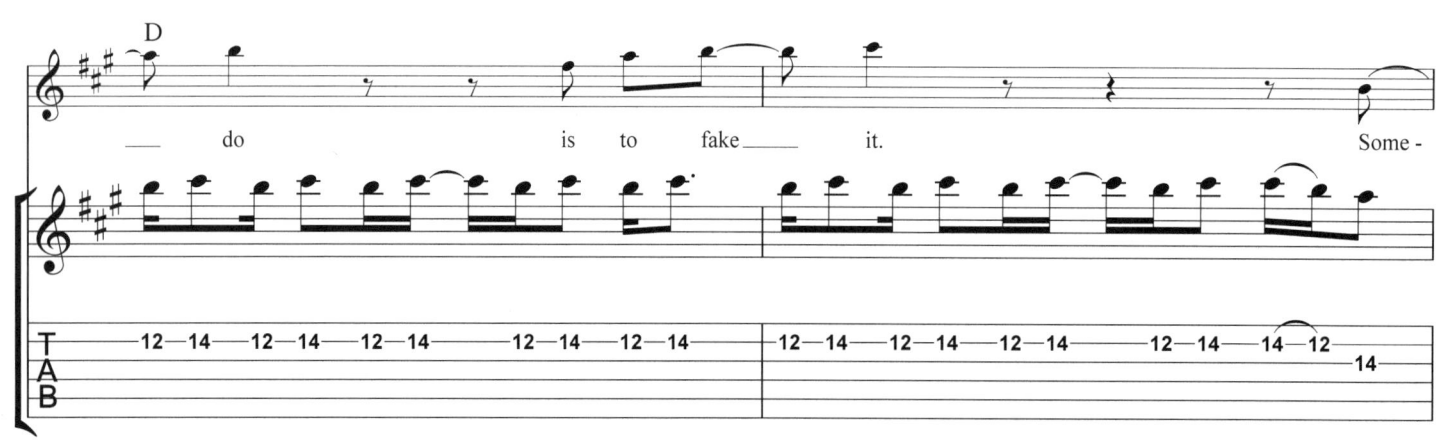

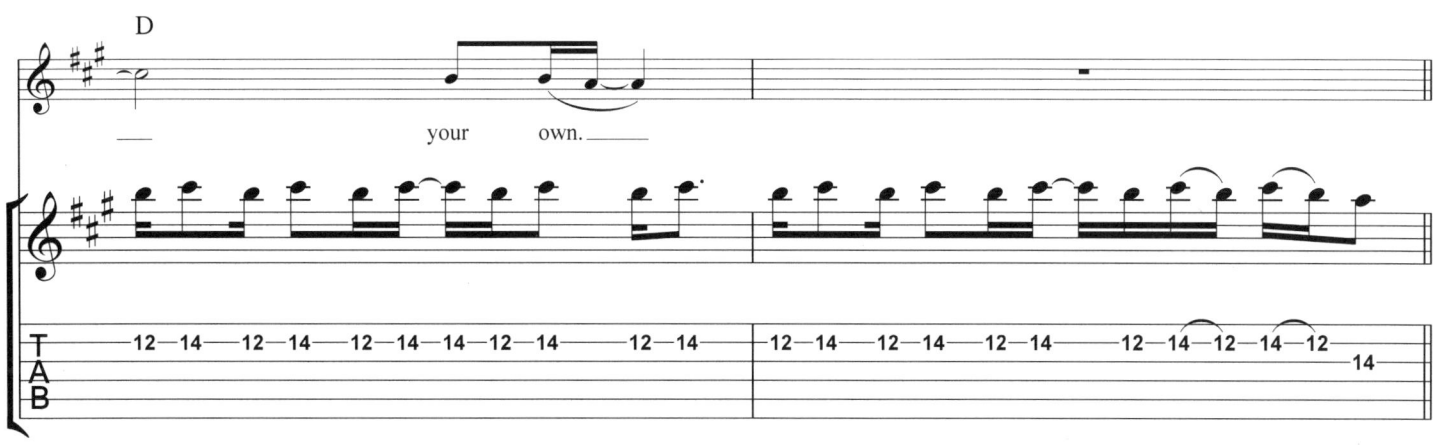
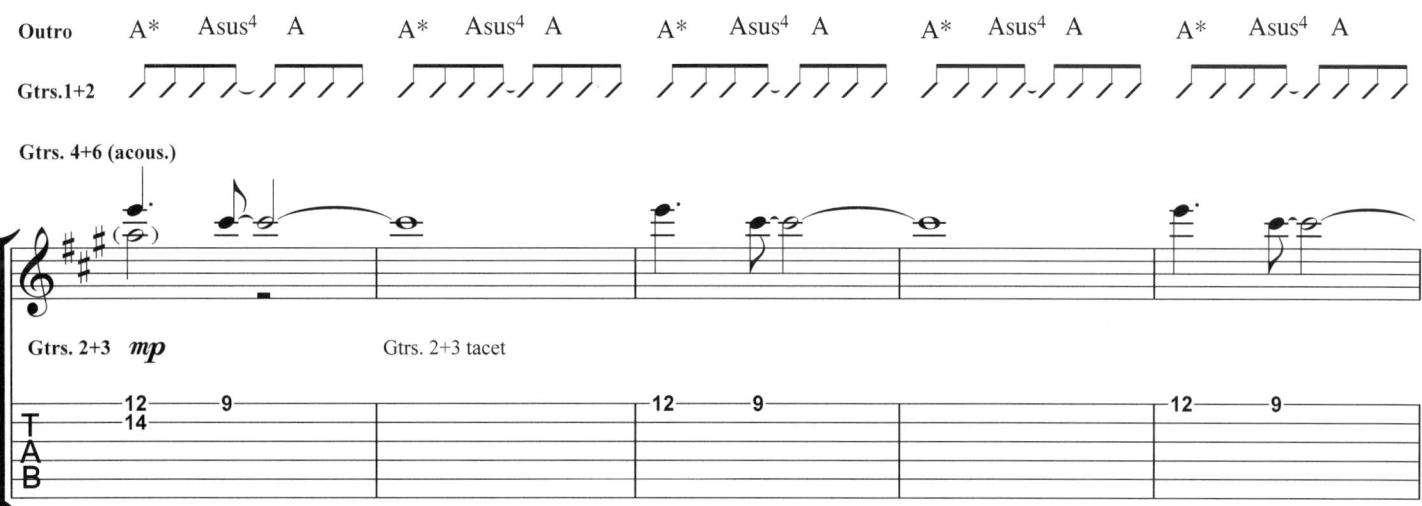
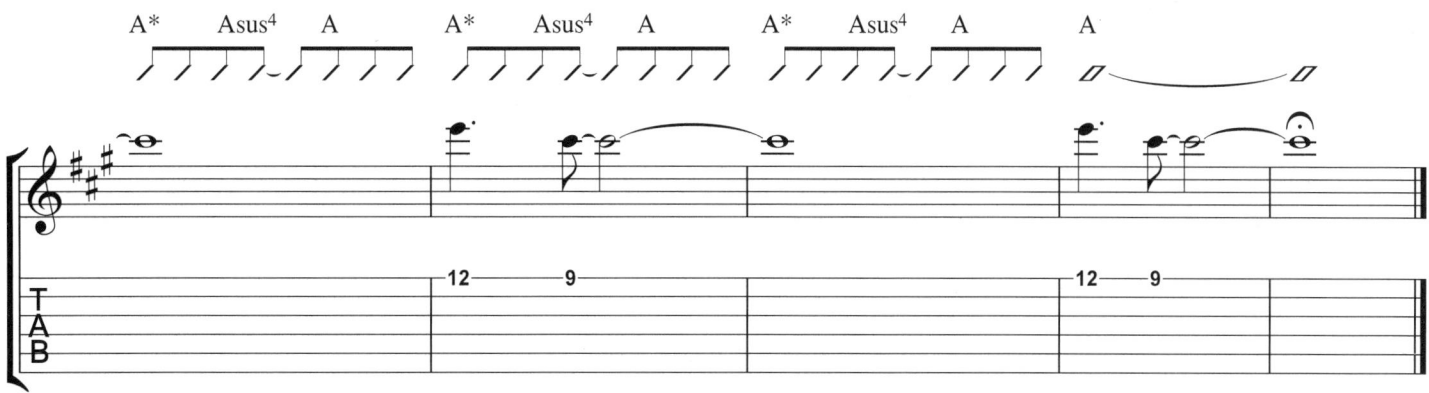

131

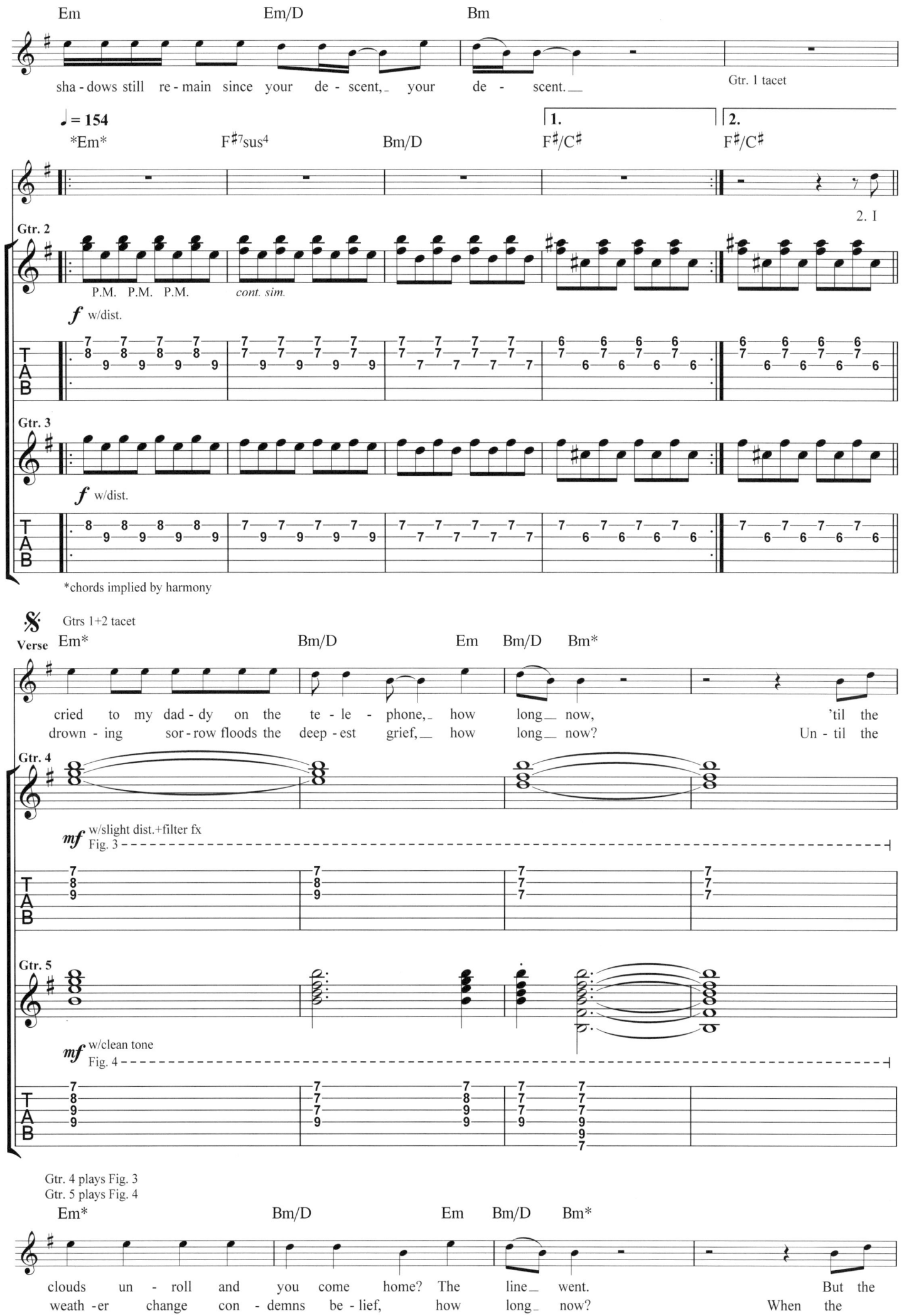

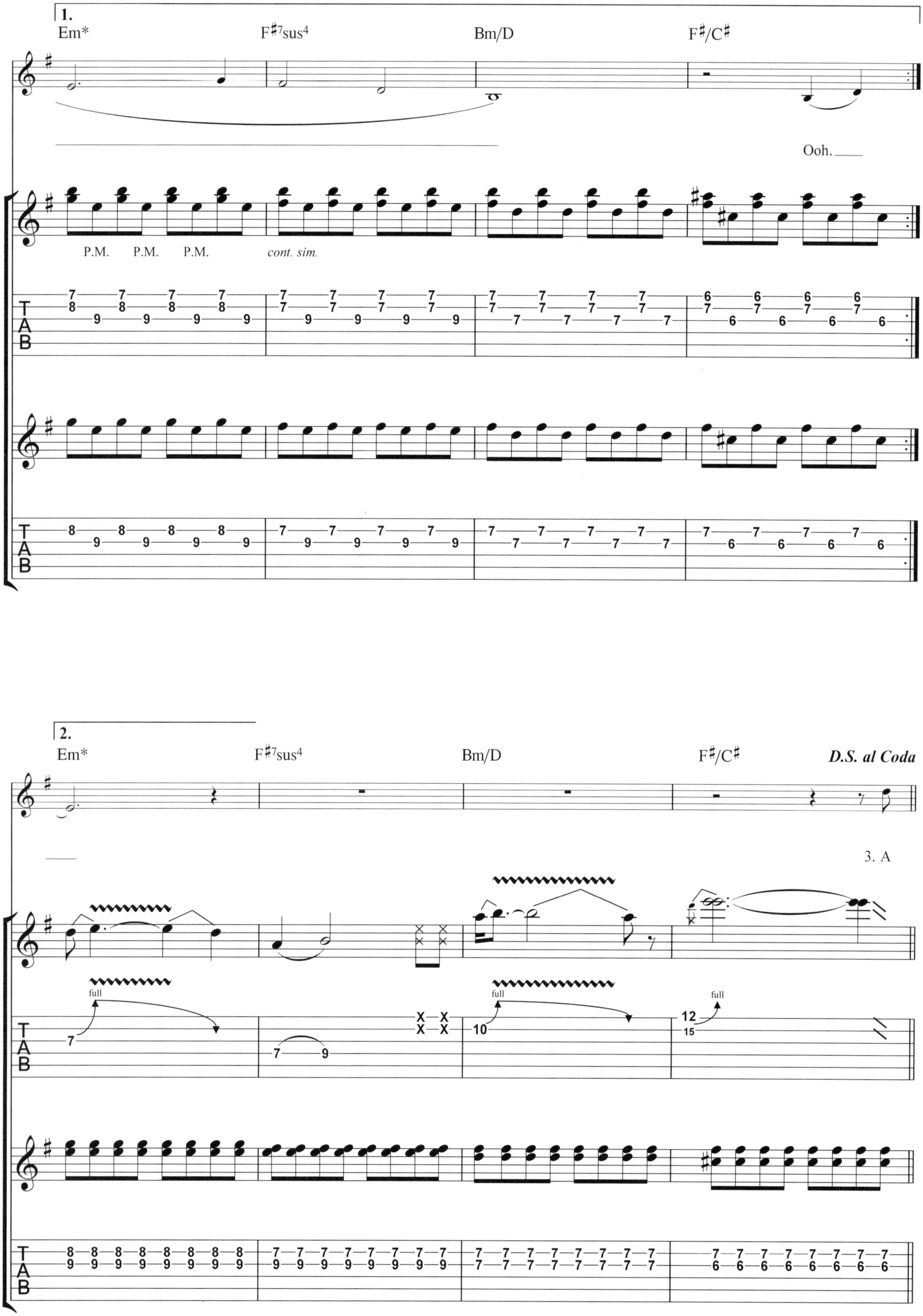
1.
Em*
F♯7sus4
Bm/D
F♯/C♯
Ooh.
P.M.
P.M.
P.M.
cont. sim.
2.
Em*
F♯7sus4
Bm/D
F♯/C♯
D.S. al Coda
3. A
full
full
full

Coda
Em/G
Em
Em/G
re - al - ise there's no re - ply. I say no mat - ter how I try, I re - al - ise there's no re - ply. I
Em
Em/G
Em
say no mat - ter how I try, I re - al - ise there's no re - ply.

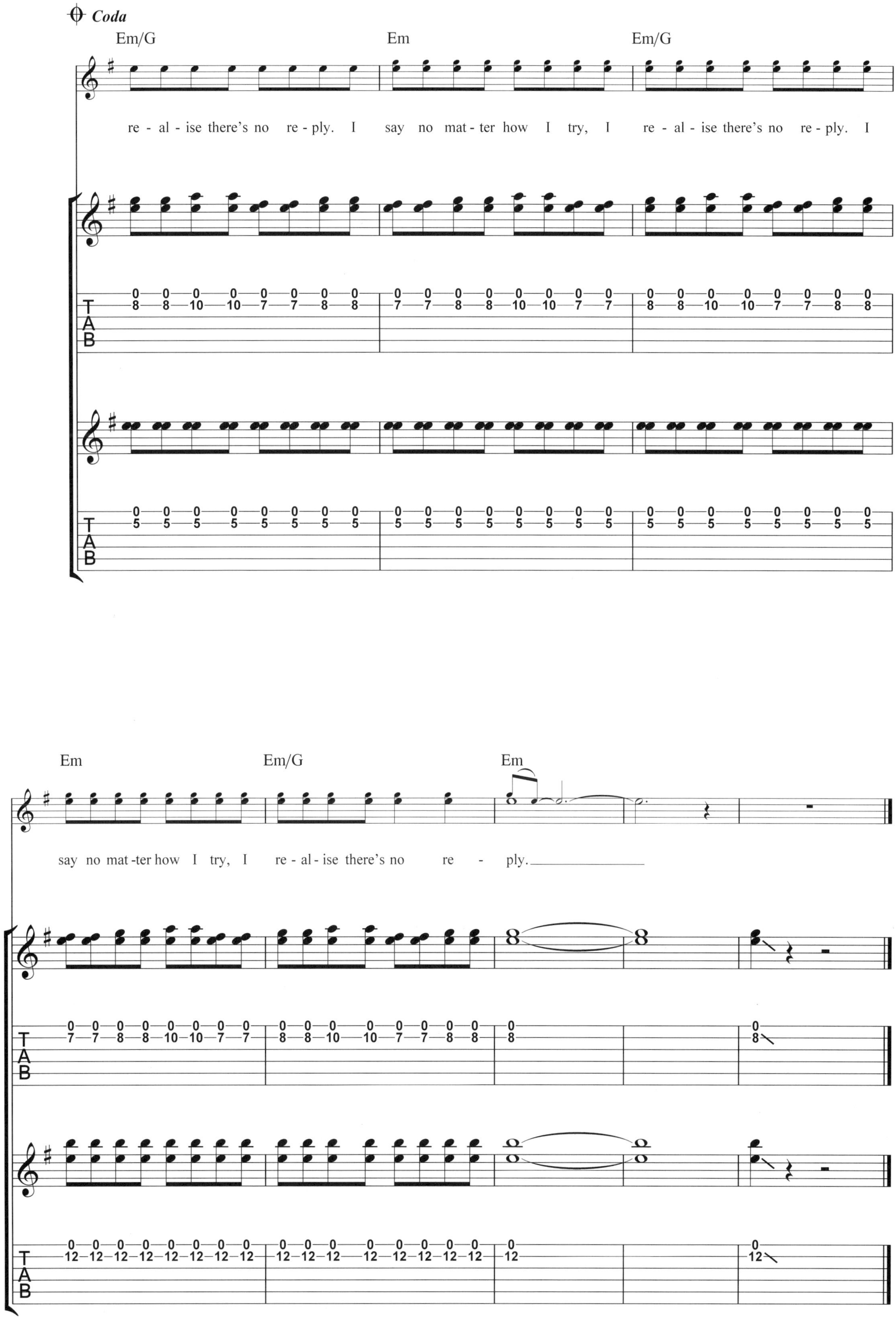

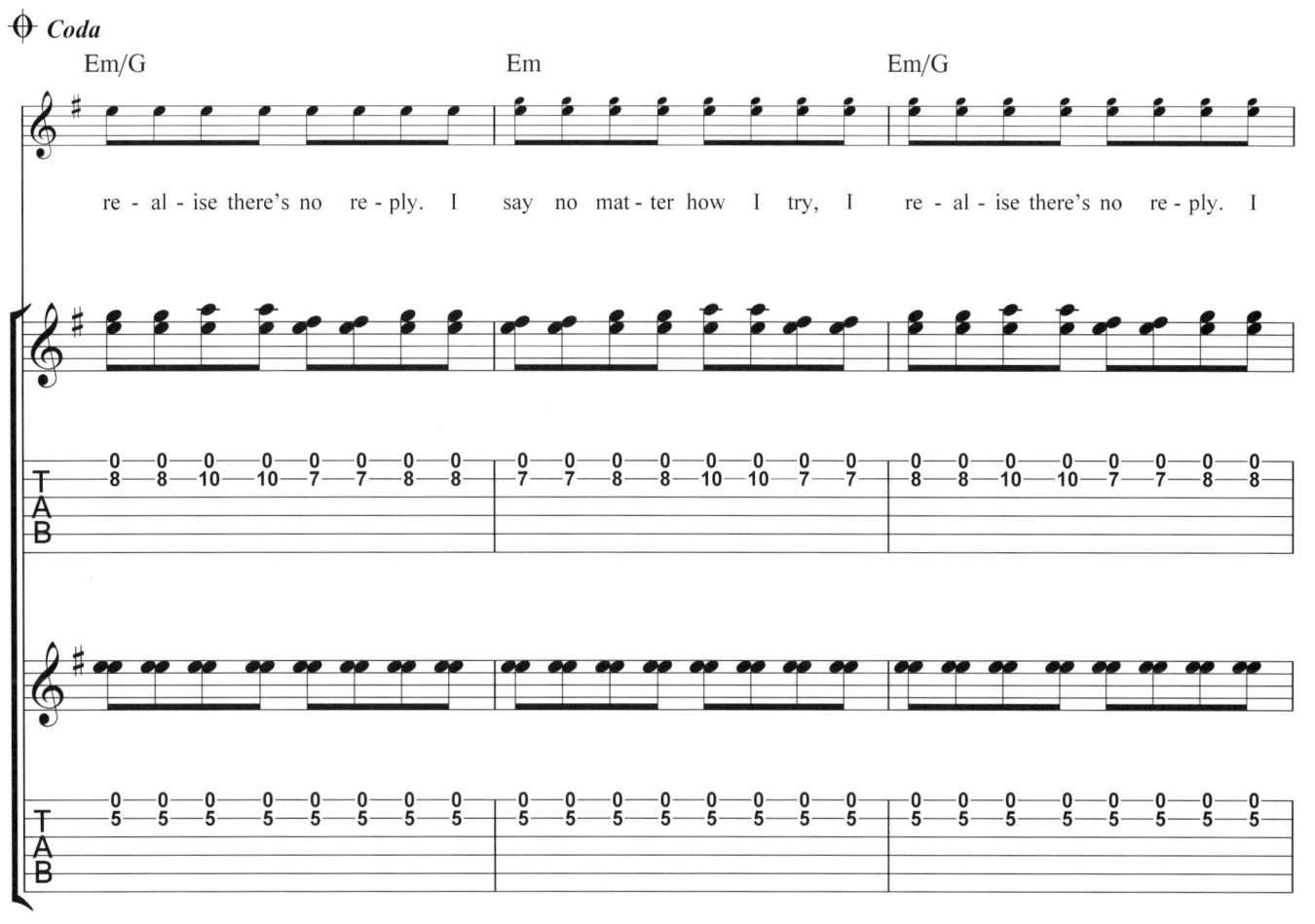

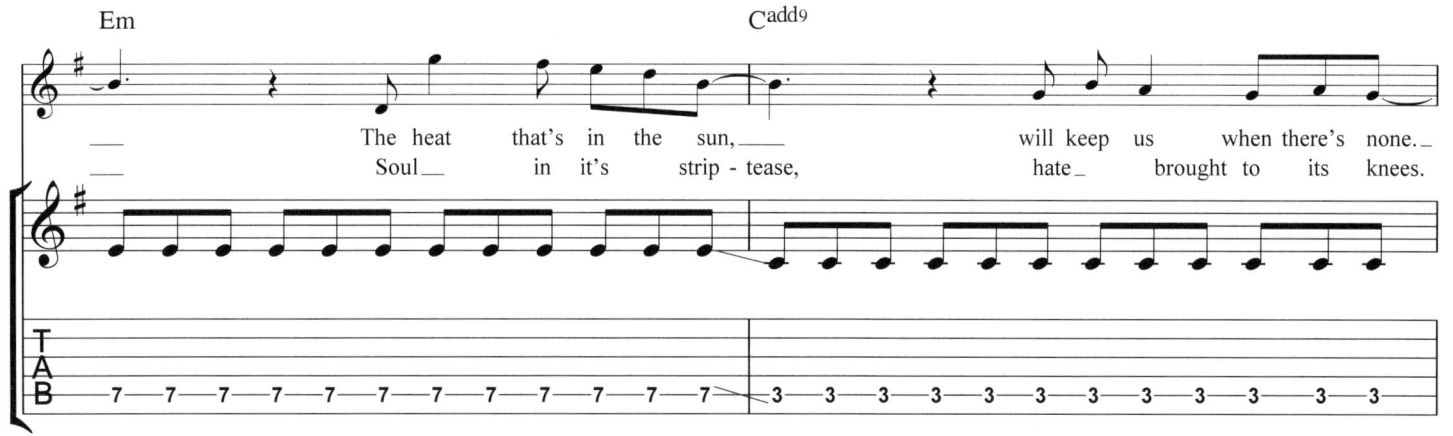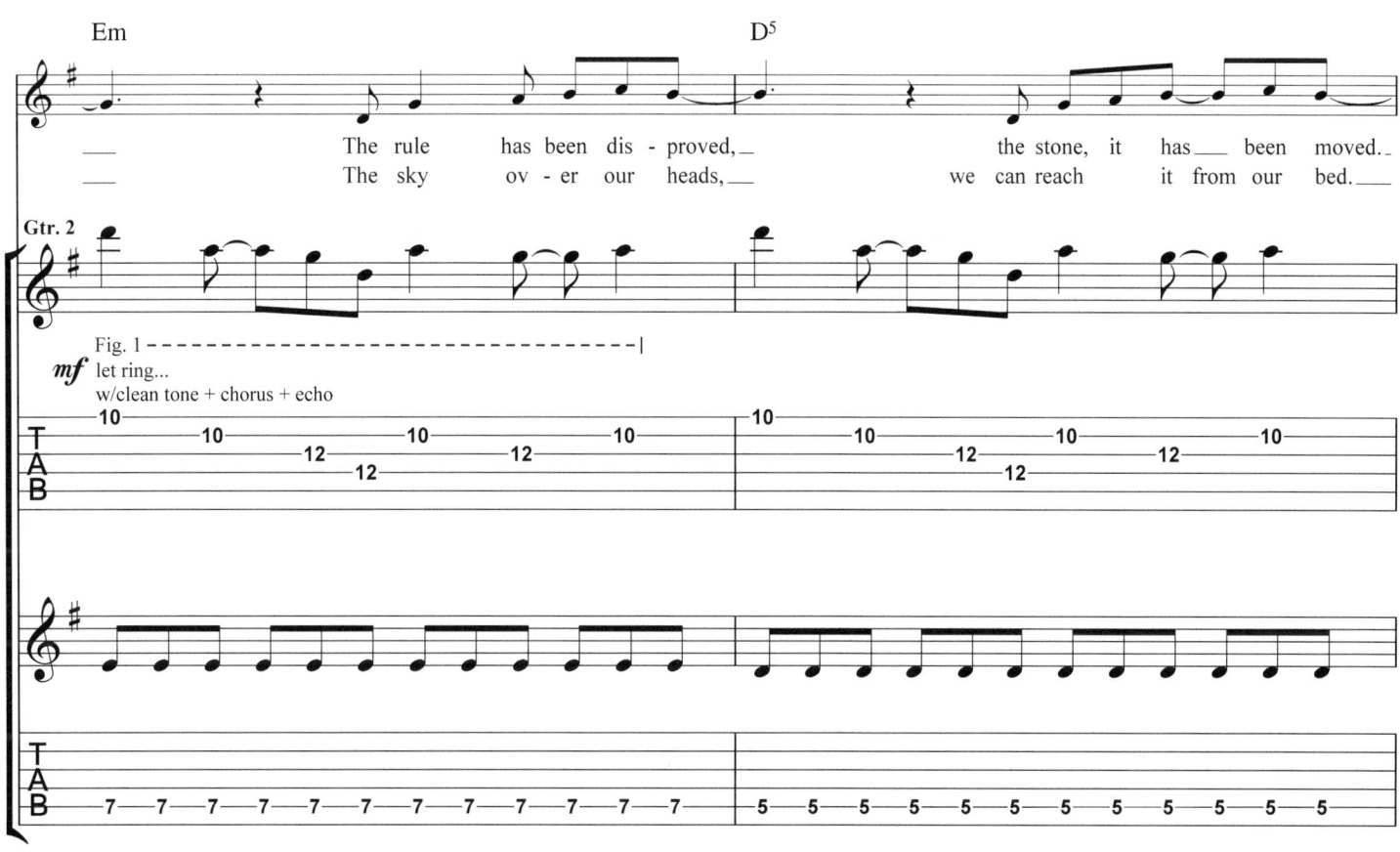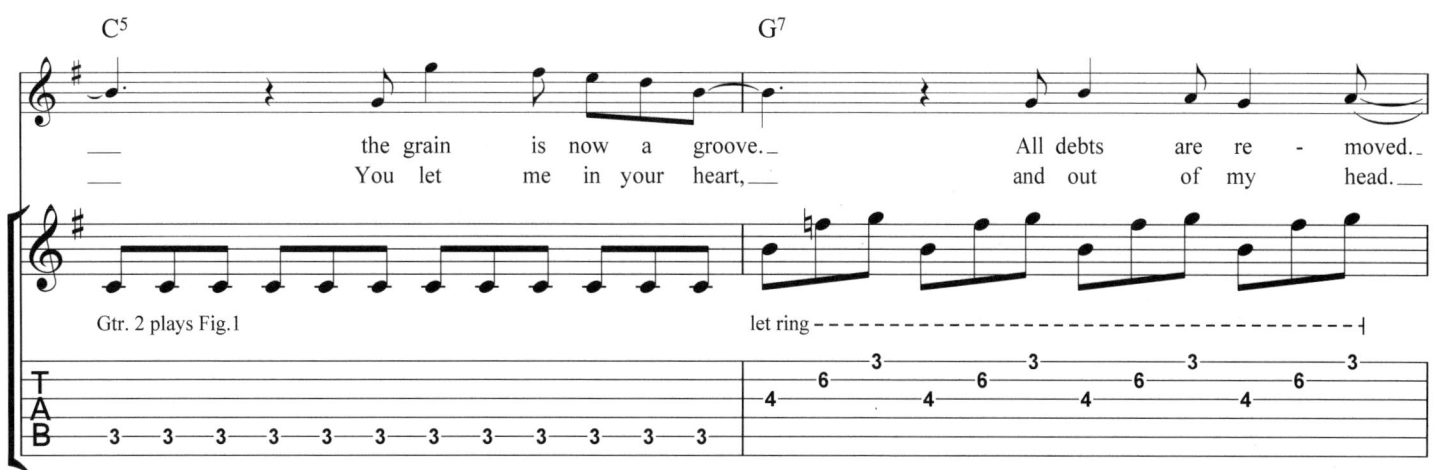

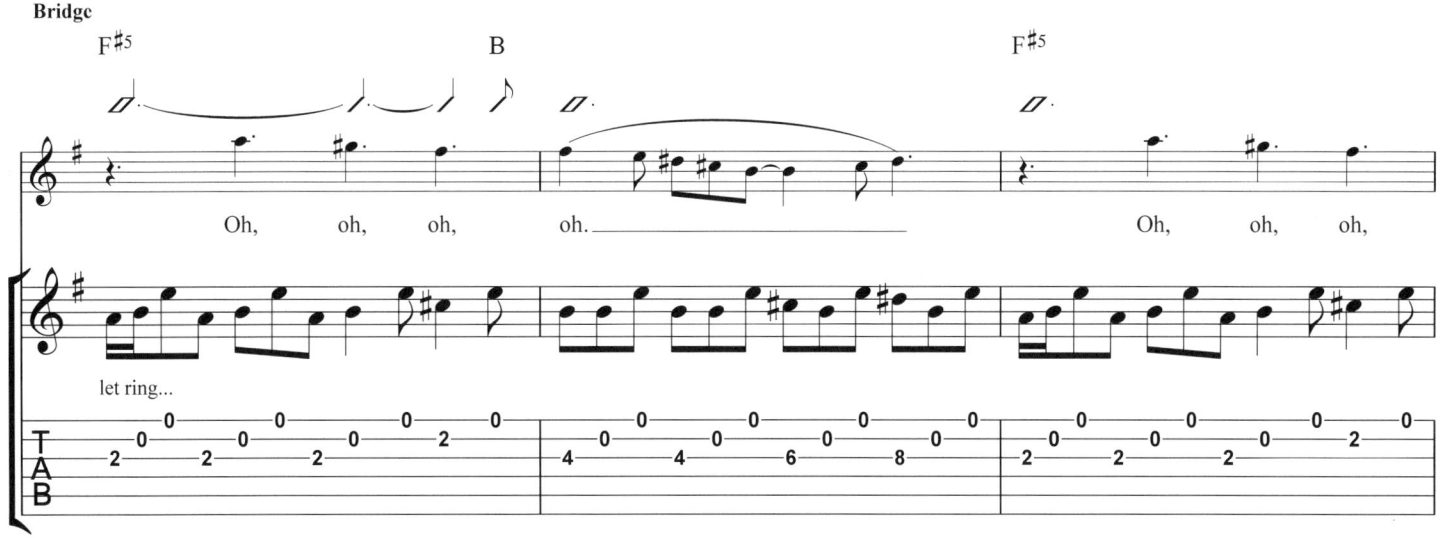
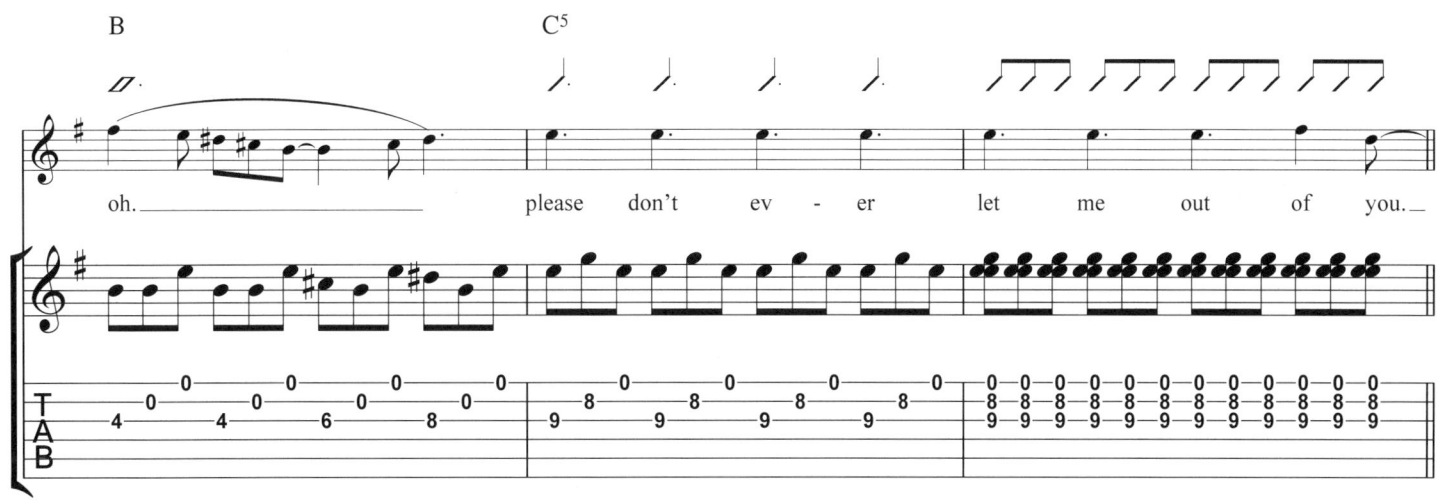

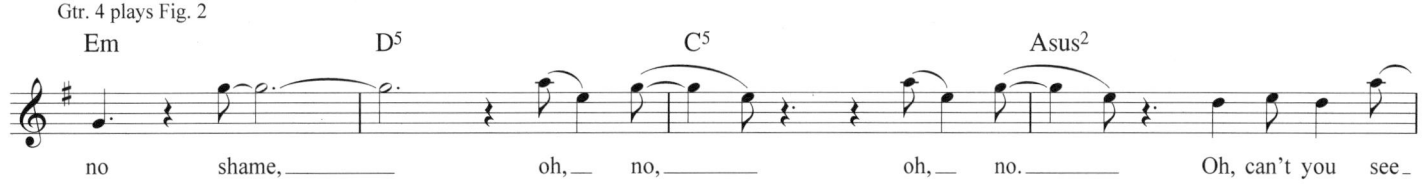

141

Guitar Tablature Explained

Guitar music can be notated in three different ways: on a musical stave, in tablature, and in rhythm slashes

RHYTHM SLASHES: are written above the stave. Strum chords in the rhythm indicated. Round noteheads indicate single notes.

THE MUSICAL STAVE: shows pitches and rhythms and is divided by lines into bars. Pitches are named after the first seven letters of the alphabet.

TABLATURE: graphically represents the guitar fingerboard. Each horizontal line represents a string, and each number represents a fret.

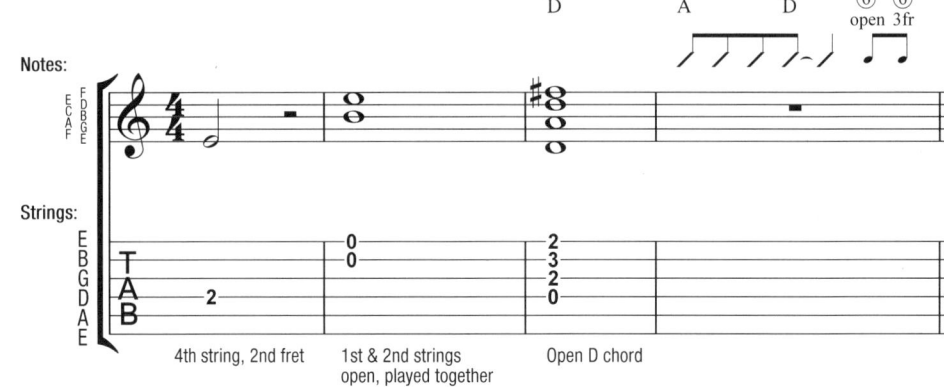

4th string, 2nd fret   1st & 2nd strings open, played together   Open D chord

Definitions for special guitar notation

SEMI-TONE BEND: Strike the note and bend up a semi-tone (½ step).

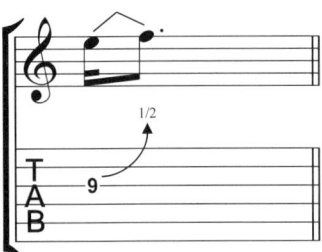

WHOLE-TONE BEND: Strike the note and bend up a whole-tone (full step).

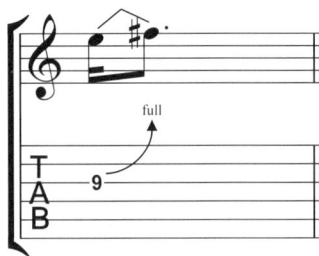

GRACE NOTE BEND: Strike the note and bend as indicated. Play the first note as quickly as possible.

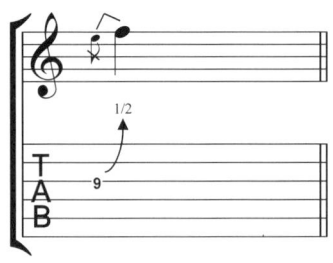

QUARTER-TONE BEND: Strike the note and bend up a ¼ step.

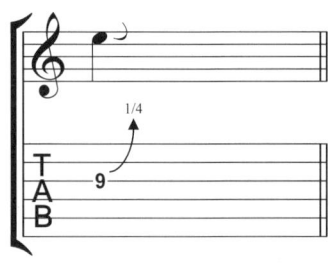

BEND & RELEASE: Strike the note and bend up as indicated, then release back to the original note.

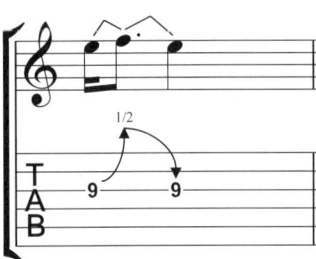

COMPOUND BEND & RELEASE: Strike the note and bend up and down in the rhythm indicated.

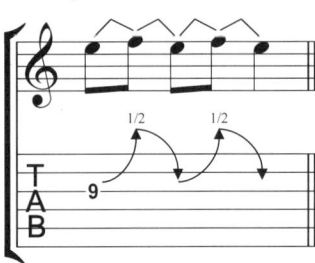

PRE-BEND: Bend the note as indicated, then strike it.

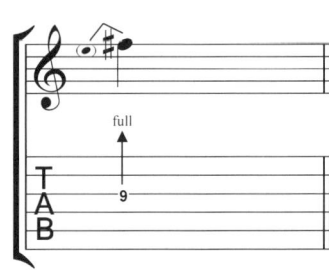

PRE-BEND & RELEASE: Bend the note as indicated. Strike it and release the note back to the original pitch.

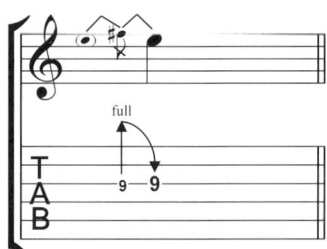

HAMMER-ON: Strike the first note with one finger, then sound the second note (on the same string) with another finger by fretting it without picking.

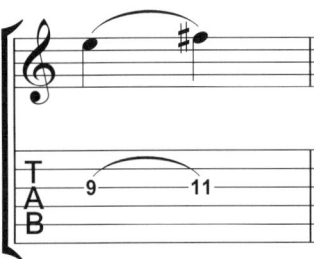

PULL-OFF: Place both fingers on the note to be sounded, strike the first note and without picking, pull the finger off to sound the second note.

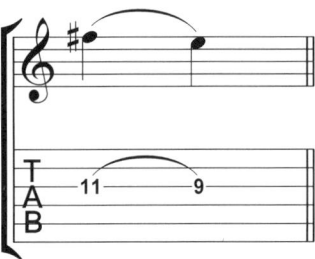

LEGATO SLIDE (GLISS): Strike the first note and then slide the same fret-hand finger up or down to the second note. The second note is not struck.

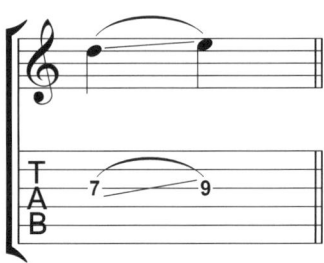

MUFFLED STRINGS: A percussive sound is produced by laying the first hand across the string(s) without depressing, and striking them with the pick hand.

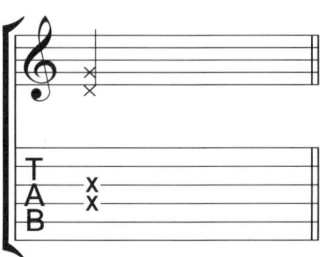

NATURAL HARMONIC: Strike the note while the fret-hand lightly touches the string directly over the fret indicated.

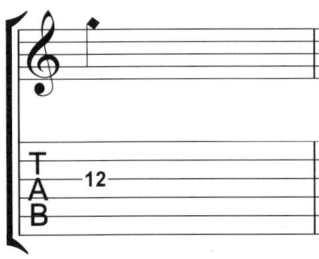

PICK SCRAPE: The edge of the pick is rubbed down (or up) the string, producing a scratchy sound.

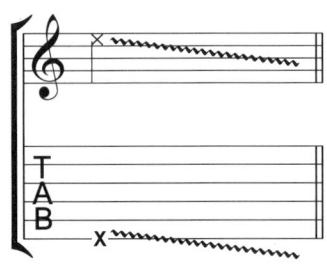

PALM MUTING: The note is partially muted by the pick hand lightly touching the string(s) just before the bridge.

SHIFT SLIDE (GLISS & RESTRIKE): Same as legato slide, except the second note is struck.

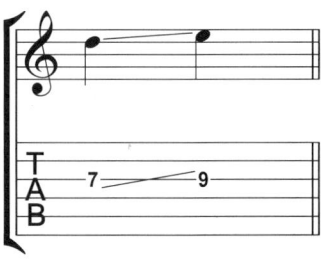